SOUTH AFRICA

SOUTH AFRICA

A SHORT HISTORY

Arthur Keppel-Jones

Professor of History
Queen's University, Kingston, Ontario

Generously Donated to
The Frederick Douglass Institute
By Professor Jesse Moore
Fall 2000

HUTCHINSON UNIVERSITY LIBRARY
LONDON

HUTCHINSON & CO (*Publishers*) LTD
3 Fitzroy Square, London W1

London Melbourne Sydney Auckland
Wellington Johannesburg Cape Town
and agencies throughout the world

First published 1949
Reprinted 1953, 1956
Second edition 1961
Third edition 1963
Reprinted 1965, 1966
Fourth edition 1968
Reprinted 1972
Fifth edition 1975

© for new material Arthur Keppel-Jones 1961, 1963, 1975

Printed in Great Britain by litho by The Anchor Press Ltd
and bound by Wm Brendon & Son Ltd
both of Tiptree, Essex

ISBN 0 09 123990 7 (cased)
0 09 123991 5 (paper)

CONTENTS

PREFACE TO FIFTH EDITION

The previous edition of this book took the story up to the declaration of the Republic in 1961. This one takes it up to 1974, when it went to press; what was the final chapter has been turned into three chapters, divided thematically. 1974 is not a satisfactory terminal date, because it is the year of General Spinola's *coup* in Portugal. For southern Africa that event obviously marks not an end but a beginning. Its consequences, at the time of this writing, lie in the future and cannot be told, but they will certainly be far-reaching.

The last edition included some changes in nomenclature. The black people were called Africans in accordance with the now accepted usage, not *natives* or *Kaffirs* except where these words seemed appropriate to convey the atmosphere of the time and the prejudices of those who used them.

It had been intended to introduce further changes of this kind into the present edition, but as considerations of cost have prevented this for the present, some explanations will be given here. The reader is asked to take the will for the deed.

Two kinds of change would have been involved. One is in spelling. For example, the tribal name formerly spelt Baca is now Bhaca, and there are many other changes of that kind. Secondly, it used to be the practice to include in tribal or national names the plural prefixes ba, ama, etc. It would still be correct to do this where the plural is meant. But as few readers understand these languages they are apt to commit such mistakes as 'a Basuto' or 'to speak Matabele'. It is therefore now the custom to use only the roots of these names. *Basotho* is plural; the singular is *Mosotho*; the language is *Sesotho*. To save the general public from these pitfalls it is now usual to write merely *Sotho* in all contexts.

To have made the changes throughout the book for this edition would have increased the cost unjustifiably. As a second best, here is a glossary of names as they will still be found in this book, followed by the forms which are now correct.

Glossary

Baca	Bhaca
Bakwena	Kwena
Bapedi	Pedi
Barolong	Rolong
Basuto	Sotho
Bataung	Taung
Batlokua	Tlokwa
Dingaan	Dingane
Fingo, Fingos	Mfengu
Gaika	Ngqika
Ketshwayo	Cetshwayo
Kreli	Sarili
Mankorwane	Mankurwane
Masau	Mosweu
Mashona	Shona
Matabele	Ndebele
Montsiwa	Montshiwa
Moshesh	Moshweshwe
Moshete	Moswete
Panda	Mpande
Pondo	Mpondo
Tembu, Tembus	Thembu
Umlanjeni	Mlanjeni
Umsilikazi	Mzilikazi

A. K–J.

INTRODUCTION

The history of South Africa, as of other countries, has been greatly influenced by geography. A few important features of South African geography must therefore be borne in mind by the reader.

The concentric lines of mountain ranges, roughly parallel to the southern and eastern coast, for long hindered access to the interior; and when these obstacles were overcome by the pioneer pastoralists, they in turn were cut off from the outside world. The main watershed of the Drakensberg runs up the eastern side of the country. The long rivers flowing westward from this to the Atlantic, the Orange and its tributaries, are shallow and sometimes reduced to little more than a succession of pools; the shorter streams running east are greater in volume, but broken by falls. All have sandbanks at their mouths. Thus no navigable river gave either entry to the country from the sea or a route to the interior from the coastal plain. The colonists had to move by ox-wagon over difficult country.

As the traveller goes north from the south coast, after crossing each mountain range he debouches on to a plateau higher than the last, till the great plateau of the interior is reached. In the eastern Transvaal a steep escarpment divides High Veld from Low Veld, while from the Witwatersrand (6000 feet above sea level) the drop to the Limpopo valley in the north is more gradual.

The interior plateau, whose altitude varies from 4000 to 6000 feet, is healthy; the winters are cold and the nights cool even in summer. But the pioneer trekking northwards, when he descended to the Low Veld of the eastern or northern Transvaal, encountered malaria and the tsetse fly. For most, therefore, the Transvaal High Veld was the furthest limit of the migration.

The direction of the trekking movement was influenced too by the rainfall. In the eastern part of the country, below the Drakensberg and for a little distance to the west of that great divide, this is from thirty to fifty inches, and similar figures are recorded in the mountainous country of the south-west coast. But inland from these regions, to the north and west, the precipitation decreases to fifteen, ten, five inches. Migration inland from Cape Town therefore tended to take a north-easterly direction, and was deflected into the drier north only by the resistance of the Bantu on the old Eastern Frontier.

In the neighbourhood of Cape Town and in a narrow belt up the west coast the rain falls almost exclusively in winter; elsewhere only in summer. The winter rainfall area, the earliest settled, was and is the country of wheat, wine and deciduous fruit. A different agriculture is suited to the area of heavy summer rainfall. But South Africa has, on the whole, a poor soil, and is better adapted to pastoral farming than to tillage. The great natural wealth of the country is in minerals —diamonds, gold, coal, iron and other base and precious metals. When these were discovered the political map had already been roughly drawn, and it was found that mineral wealth was distributed in a way likely to disturb the political arrangements. Much of South African history is the result of this circumstance.

North of the Limpopo, the high plateau of Southern Rhodesia (4000 to 5000 feet) is suited to European settlement. But this was not colonised till the end of the nineteenth century, and then was reached either by the old Missionaries' Road through Bechuanaland or from Beira on the east coast. The Transvaal Boers, therefore, unlike the French Canadians, had no Ontario beyond them which could be approached only through their country. But for the discovery of gold their isolation would have been complete.

In relation to the world South Africa was, till recently, more like an island than a continental country. The interior of Africa was barbarous and for a long time little known. All links with the outside world were by sea, and the voyages long. Southampton is some 6000 miles from Cape Town; Bombay and Perth nearly 5000. This remoteness accentuated the isolation of the country; and though its position on the ocean route from Europe to the East subjected Cape Town and the nearer districts to influences from both those parts of the world, the topography of the country prevented those influences from reaching the interior.

The discovery of diamonds and gold gave the first effective

impetus to the building of railways, various ports competing with one another for the trade of the mines. The Witwatersrand became the hub of the railway system, and the main lines spokes radiating from it to points on the coast. This development gave the Rand even greater political importance than it would have had on the merits of the mining industry. The building of these railways and the access they gave to various ports and internal markets helped, in turn, to determine the development of the rural areas.

South Africa 1902

Cape Eastern Frontier
.... 1775
—·—·— 1780–6
×××××× 1819–24
          1847
          1853–54
▨ 1847–66 British Kaffraria

Railways
++++++++

0   100   200 miles

I

THE HALF-WAY HOUSE

On a February day in 1488 a band of Hottentots was pasturing some cattle near the beach at Mossel Bay, on the southern coast of Africa. These Hottentots were a pastoral people who had no knowledge of cultivation. They lived in encampments made of portable huts which could be packed up when the grass was eaten or the water failed, and people, cattle, fat-tailed sheep, dogs and possessions would move to a new habitation. They were a light brown or yellow-skinned people, with little tufts on their heads to serve for hair; they would in the future be described by unfriendly critics as lying, stinking and thieving, speaking a tongue that sounded like the clucking of hens, and their name would be used as a proverbial synonym for a people destitute of civility.

Yet they were the conquerors of the land they lived in, and the bearers of the highest civilisation that it had yet seen. Two centuries earlier, perhaps, their ancestors had arrived on the west coast of tropical Africa, coming from the direction of the Great Lakes. Since then they had trekked steadily southwards, keeping to the coastal regions, and then eastwards when the southern extremity of the continent had been reached. The eastward advance was still continuing.

In that long trek one human enemy had been met and overcome— the pygmy race of Bushmen. The Bushmen, short of stature but otherwise so far resembling the Hottentots in appearance that the white men could not at first distinguish them, were not pastoralists but hunters. Every band of Bushmen had its hunting grounds on which no stranger might trespass. If the Hottentot invaders had the temerity to do so, how could they expect mercy? The poisoned arrow, cunningly shot by an unseen enemy, vindicated the rights of the true owner of the soil. And as for those helpless, slow-moving beasts that accompanied the Hottentots everywhere, bagging them was child's play to the expert hunters of the fleet and timid antelope. The Hottentots, on the other hand, were better organised and well able to punish these aggressions. The Bushmen themselves were not the oldest inhabitants of the country, but the successors of others known to us only by their bones and implements that have been discovered. Now the Bushmen in turn were dispossessed by the Hottentots.

Some retired to the dry and stony plains of the interior. Others remained in the Hottentot country nearer the coast, but sought the safety of the mountains. There, in the deep afforested kloofs where streams splashed over boulders and pebbles, or in the caves under the steep buttresses flanking the kloofs, the pygmies hid themselves. Like the leopards and baboons that shared their retreat, they sallied forth at night to prey on the flocks and herds of the Hottentots. No quarter was given on either side.

That was the political and economic background of the herdsmen who happened to be at Mossel Bay on the February day in 1488. Gazing thoughtlessly, perhaps, to seaward, they caught a sudden sight of something new, unheard-of, terrifying. Two large objects, the like of which had never been seen, floated on the surface and came to a stop at no great distance from the land. They were Portuguese caravels under the command of Bartolomeu Dias. Their arrival signified that Portuguese seamen had at last, after half a century of almost continuous effort, passed the southernmost point of the continent and reached the Indian Ocean by sea from the Atlantic. Dias had come down the west coast, keeping close to the land until a gale had blown him out of sight of it and far to the southward. Turning east again when the storm subsided, he saw no land, and dared to hope that he had found what so many had sought. The course of the ships was set to the north, they reached the coast again and came to anchor in Mossel Bay.

The Hottentots did not know that this event would lead to the extinction of their race, but they were frightened enough to flee at once into the interior with their cattle. Then, while the strangers filled their water-casks, the natives plucked up courage to pelt them with stones. The incensed Portuguese commander picked up a crossbow and shot one of the assailants. The sailors then continued on their way up the coast, found nothing of note and insisted on returning home. Dias gave way to the demand, set up a *padrão* on the promontory of Kwaaihoek to proclaim the authority of the King, and on his way back discovered and named the Cape of Good Hope which he had missed in the storm of the outward journey.

The mutual suspicion and hostility between Hottentots and Portuguese at Mossel Bay were renewed at many later meetings. In 1497 the voyage of Dias was followed by that of Vasco da Gama, who completed the work of his predecessor by reaching India. Da Gama's crew had a skirmish with the Hottentots at St Helena Bay. More voyages followed. Antonio da Saldanha discovered Table Bay, climbed Table Mountain, and had a fight with some Hottentots before departing. Francisco d'Almeida, the retiring Viceroy of the Indies, put into the same bay on his homeward voyage in 1510. There was a misunderstanding with the natives, a scuffle, and then a more serious engagement in which the ex-Viceroy and many others of high rank lost their lives. After that the Portuguese tended to steer clear of the dangerous neighbourhood.

This was not because they were afraid. The builders of the Portuguese Empire faced other and stronger enemies bravely. They would not have hesitated to deal with the Hottentots, if there had been anything to gain by doing so. Their lack of interest in the southern corner of the continent was due rather to their possession of other and more useful outposts.

Vasco da Gama had been the first to abandon the coastwise route in the Atlantic and to steer boldly south across the ocean from the Cape Verde Islands. The Portuguese soon established the best sailing routes: a wide westward sweep round the South Atlantic on the outward voyage, a straight run from the Cape of Good Hope to Cape Verde, touching at St Helena, on the return. The homeward-bound ships could therefore refresh at St Helena and gather the fruits and kill the animals that had been put there. The outward fleets, though unable to use St Helena, preferred not to stop anywhere west of the Cape of Good Hope because of the difficulty of rounding the Cape when sailing close to the shore. Giving the continent a wide berth, they struck northwards and made all haste to reach Mozambique and their other East African ports before the end of the monsoon on which they depended to cross the Indian Ocean. If they did not get to Mozambique before the end of September they would have to wait there a whole season. The East African harbours, supplemented by St Helena on the return voyage, therefore sufficed the Portuguese as victualling stations.

At the end of the sixteenth century the pioneers of the Indian Ocean trade lost their monopoly of it. The accession of Philip II to the throne of Portugal enabled him to exclude his rebellious Dutch subjects from the carrying trade of Lisbon, on which their lives depended. Some Dutchmen had been in the Portuguese service in the East, and were able to betray its secrets to their countrymen. The futile search for a north-east passage was abandoned, and a mania for fitting out fleets for the Cape route to the Indies seized the United Provinces. There was great risk in this venture, but the profit on a voyage might easily be two hundred per cent. The wealth thus acquired helped the Dutch to carry on their struggle with Spain, and there was the additional political advantage that Holland's gain was Spain's loss. The rebels would never make peace with their enemy except on terms which allowed them to continue the eastern trade; and the truce of 1609 allowed it.

The early Dutch voyages were attended by great dangers. But a worse disadvantage than the forces of Nature or of the Portuguese was the competition among themselves. Prices in the East rose, selling prices in Europe fell. Jan van Oldenbarneveldt understood that only amalgamation and monopoly would prevent this, as well as give efficient organisation for dealing with Eastern princes and protecting the fleets at sea. Overcoming strong resistance, he compelled the competing merchants in 1602 to form the United Chartered East India Company, the world's first joint stock company on the grand scale.

The first half of the seventeenth century saw the establishment of the Dutch company at many forts and factories in the East. Fleets in convoy made regularly the slow passage between the Texel and the Strait of Sunda, and from 1611 on the outward voyage they followed the route south and east of Madagascar, which the Portuguese had seldom used. Moreover, the Dutch never took possession of the Portuguese posts on the East African coast, though they did hold St. Helena for a time. Because they had no Mozambique, and because the Cape of Good Hope was the only landfall made by both outward and homeward fleets, the Dutch made a practice of calling at Table Bay for refreshment. The English for similar reasons did the same, and in 1620 two visiting captains hoisted the English flag; but nothing came of it.

Refreshment was badly needed. Six months was the average length of the voyage from Europe to the Indies in the seventeenth century. For most of that time the crews went without fresh meat, fruit and vegetables, and short of water. They had never heard of vitamins, but they knew well enough what it meant to be short of them. Van Riebeeck, on his voyage out in 1652, entered in his diary:

> 'March 12. Death of a child of the chief surgeon from scurvy—buried in the evening—all the rest are well—water supply getting low. Men placed on allowance.
> 'March 20th. Captain Turver coming on board, reports that there is no more than one month's supply of water and beer on board his ship.'

A month after his arrival two ships entered Table Bay from Holland, one having lost 45 men on the way and the other 85; and 'many still sick on board'. These circumstances had induced the Dutch and the English to call at the Cape both outward and homeward. At the Fresh River in Table Valley the water-casks were filled. If there were Hottentots in the neighbourhood cattle and sheep might be got by barter. Letters would be written and left, for the first fleet going in the opposite direction, under a stone on which might be written: 'The *London* arrived the 10 of M here from Surat bound for England and depar the 20 dicto 1622 Richard Blyth Captane. Heare under looke for letters.' Many such stones were inscribed and placed in suitable spots; some of them, by a happy coincidence, on the site of the future General Post Office in Cape Town.

The utility of the Cape as a calling-place gave rise to the idea of a permanent occupation. There was once a scheme for a joint occupation by the Dutch and English companies; but after the English interlopers at Amboina had been 'massacred' in 1623 no more was heard of it. The final impetus was given by the wreck of the East Indiaman *Haarlem* in Table Bay in 1647. There was no loss of life, and the cargo, including vegetable seeds and garden tools, was saved. The crew camped at Green Point, grew vegetables and bartered cattle and sheep from the Hottentots. They returned to Holland in the next homeward-bound fleet and a report on the advantages of a permanent post at the Cape was submitted to the Directors. That report led in due course to the despatch of the little expedition under Jan van Riebeeck which arrived in Table Bay on April 6, 1652.

Van Riebeeck's party consisted exclusively of employees of the Company. Its tasks were to build an earthen fort for defence against the Hottentots, to plant a vegetable garden, to obtain cattle and sheep by barter, to supply these commodities to the Company's ships and to care for the sick members of the crews who were left ashore to recover.

For more than two centuries from this time—until the opening of the Suez Canal in 1869—the settlement at the Cape existed mainly for purposes related to the trade of Europe with India. For much of that period the crews of the passing ships were the chief or even the only consumers of South African exports. In Van Riebeeck's time about twenty-five ships a year, on an average, touched at the Cape, and almost all were Dutch. By the 1780's the yearly average had risen to 164, and more than half were foreign.

Before 1869 the Cape had something of the strategic importance that has belonged to the Suez region since that time. International rivalry for trade and power in the East extended to the half-way house that could serve as a naval base for defending the route; or, what was more, for attacking any who used it. The power of Holland had reached its maximum, and was about to decline, at the moment when Van Riebeeck sailed for the Cape. That was 1651, the year in which the English Navigation Act struck the first serious blow at Dutch maritime supremacy. Thenceforward Table Bay, like a mirror, reflected every move in the international game of Eastern power-politics.

A stone castle begins to rise above its foundations on the flank of Cape Town: that is because their High Mightinesses the States-General are at war with the restored Charles II of England. The work proceeds feverishly, then is suddenly abandoned: peace has followed De Ruyter's audacity in the Medway. Again, the work is resumed, because Louis XIV with Charles II in his train has launched his long prepared attack on the Netherlands.

The seventeenth century was succeeded by the eighteenth, and Holland was no longer a great Power. The fate of the Cape depended on the part played by the Dutch in the world-wide conflict of Britain and France. When these Powers took opposite sides in the War of the Austrian Succession, in 1744, an elaborate extension of the fortifications at the Cape was begun. The Seven Years' War brought great prosperity to the Cape, as the ships of both countries came in great numbers and bid against each other for supplies. But Holland was neutral and her possession of the colony was not endangered.

In the next war, that of the American Revolution, Holland was ultimately involved. Britain immediately determined to seize the Cape, France to forestall her. Two squadrons raced southwards. They clashed at Porto Praya in the Cape Verde Islands; the French Admiral Suffren took some prizes and got away some hours ahead of his enemies. He landed troops at Simon's Bay in time to prevent a British attack, and the rival squadron did no more than capture a few ships in Saldanha Bay. From 1781 to 1784 the French garrison made Cape Town a 'little Paris' and then left it in the hands of its Dutch owners. The future Jacobin and Director, Barras, was one of the occupying troops.

It was thus only to be expected that when Britain, France and Holland again came to grips the seizure of the Cape would have a place in military plans. This time the execution of the plan could be covered by a show of legality. Pichegru invaded Holland, the Patriot Party was helped into power by its French friends and the Prince of Orange fled to England. The British force which came to Simon's Bay in 1795 was authorised by the Prince to take possession of the colony on his behalf and to hold it till he should be restored to power. Party divisions—Orange and Patriot—among the local officials and colonists weakened the defence and after the arrival of British reinforcements the place was soon surrendered. Though it was returned to Holland—not to the East India Company, now defunct—by the Treaty of Amiens, the outbreak of a new war was the occasion of a second and final conquest. The British troops that entered Cape Town early in 1806 had been in mid-Atlantic while Nelson was winning his last and decisive victory. Britain's dominion of the sea, of the route to India and of the Cape of Good Hope, was secure for a century. At the peace she insisted on retaining this possession, strategically so important as the gateway to India. The sum of £6 millions was credited to Holland on account of it in the post-war financial settlement.

When the Cape Colony, a century and a half old, came into British hands, its population had already undergone experiences, and been subjected to influences, that were to play a large part in shaping the history of the country to the present day.

First among the influences was the Company, mercenary, monopolistic, penny-wise, endowed with despotic power in its own theatre of operations. It would be difficult to exaggerate the effect on the colonial population of four or five generations of life under this counting-house régime. The Dutch East India Company was the first of the powerful monopolistic corporations, and has been succeeded by many others. What was peculiar about its position at the Cape was that it was not merely the only buyer and the only seller: it was also the government, executive, legislature and judicature. It was the judge in its own case.

Monopoly was the air breathed by the Company and its officials. The charter guaranteed it this monopoly, east of the Cape, against other Dutchmen; the sharp sword guaranteed it against foreigners. The Englishmen at Amboina were slain. Every year the *hongi* fleet sailed round the Moluccas to destroy surplus crops of cloves or nutmegs; the output must be kept down to a minimum, the price in Europe up to a maximum. Villages were burnt down, populations uprooted. With the parsimony of the pettiest tradesman the Company gave orders to save a guilder here, a stuiver there.

But for the oath of allegiance which bound the Directors to the States-General, the Company was a sovereign power in the East. It had its own army and navy, governed its own territory and made treaties with eastern princes. Its shares were very widely distributed among the Dutch people, but attempts by the shareholders to exercise some control, or even to compel the publication of the Company's accounts, were treated as impertinence and mutiny. From first to last the accounts were never published. The States-General should have stopped such abuses, but it did not: power was so organised that their High Mightinesses and the Company's seventeen directors were largely the same people.

In spite of oaths to the contrary, the whole personnel from the Seventeen downwards was less concerned with the Company's welfare than with private enrichment, largely at the Company's expense. Salaries were low, but were corruptly supplemented. An under-merchant in the service was paid £40 a year; but he cheerfully bribed the Directors £291 13s. 4d. (the standard rate) to get his appointment. Like England, Holland had her Nabobs; but when the Company's days were over there were still Dutch families proud of the fact that none of their members had ever entered its service.

For its first five years the settlement at the Cape was merely a Company post, a branch office, in which all the white inhabitants were employees. The post did not flourish much. As in Virginia and elsewhere it was discovered that the motive of private profit was needed for the success of a farming enterprise. After much delay the Directors agreed with Van Riebeeck that private settlers, 'Free Burghers', would serve the Company's purposes at the Cape more economically than a few platoons of soldiers on fatigue duty. In 1657, accordingly, the first handful of employees took their discharge and were given land, credit and instructions. They were settled along the Liesbeek River in what is now the Cape Town suburb of Mowbray.

Slowly, very slowly, other discharged servants of the Company
were added to the number. The Company's servants were not all
Dutchmen. In 1691 a fifth were foreigners; by 1778 two-thirds were
foreigners, mostly German. At the Cape this proportion had been
reached at the beginning of the eighteenth century; it was in the
military personnel that the preponderance of Germans was most
noticeable. Of the early settlers who left descendants about a half
were Dutch, more than a quarter German. The biggest element in
the remainder was French, but they will need some special attention.

Before the French came the life of a generation had passed since
the original settlement of 1657. The colonists had in that time learnt
the nature of the problems with which the Company's régime
presented them. The Company wanted them to grow wheat, which
it would buy from them at a 'fair price'. When the crops were ripe
the farmers wanted to know what this price would be. Van Riebeeck
dared not tell them, since the price of about 2s. 3d. a bushel, which
the Directors had fixed upon, was less than half of what the farmers
regarded as a necessary minimum. The price was raised, though
insufficiently. Tobacco was a paying crop, though the Hottentots
came by night to steal the growing plants. When the settlers took
steps to protect themselves from this danger, the government
forbade the growing of tobacco as it might lead to trouble with the
natives. Above all, cattle-trading with the Hottentots, which a
visiting Commissioner had allowed the farmers shortly after their
first establishment on the land, was forbidden a year later. The
Company wanted this lucrative trade for itself, and accused the
colonists of paying eight or ten times 'what the cattle were worth'—
that is, what the Company was prepared to pay. The prohibition
was not obeyed.

The conflict between the settlers and their monopolistic trading
government became sharper as the numbers of the former increased.
Dutch colonists arrived in small numbers, but in 1688 the French-
men came. They were Huguenots who had fled to Holland after—
a few of them before—the revocation of the Edict of Nantes. In
1688 and the following decade or two some two hundred of them,
men, women and children, accepted the Company's offer of settlement at the Cape. The Governor, Simon van der Stel, was careful
in allotting farms to them to intersperse them well with Dutch
colonists, and the Huguenots did not form more than one-eighth of
the white population of the colony. Most of them settled in the upper
valley of the Berg River, at Drakenstein and French Hoek. The
French names of the farms, many of which have remained in the

same Huguenot families till the present day, are a memorial to their
pioneering efforts.

Few as they were, they have left other and more important
memorials over the whole of South Africa. Being exiles for conscience'
sake they were no trimmers in religion, but Calvinists of the rigorous
sort. The earlier settlers were Calvinists in name, but being discharged sailors and soldiers of the Company's service, drawn from
every part of Protestant Europe, they were not fanatics. The new
element changed the religious tone of the colony and implanted in
its people an orthodoxy and ecclesiastical discipline that would
remain for centuries. The Huguenots contributed also a higher
cultural standard, a spirit of rebellion against oppression—the older
inhabitants were full of this too, and were glad to be reinforced—and
some of them had an expert knowledge of viticulture.

For years the Huguenots argued with the government about
a French schoolmaster, about a French-speaking clergyman and
French services in their church. Some of the original immigrants
never learned Dutch. But their children were bilingual and in the
third generation the knowledge of French died out. There had been
so much intermarriage that there was no longer a French section of
the population.

The amalgamation, complete as it was, might not have proceeded
so quickly if the two sections had not been drawn together by
common grievances. The earliest colonists had suffered from the
Company's monopoly both as buyer and as seller. The permission,
sometimes conceded and occasionally withdrawn, to trade freely with
passing ships after they had been three days in the Bay was a slight
mitigation of the hardship. The illegal trade with the Hottentots
was of greater importance. But at the end of the century a greater
menace than the Company itself was presented by the Company's
servants. A passing Commissioner-General had granted Simon
van der Stel a farm—Constantia, destined to be world-famous for
its wine and an architectural monument for tourists to admire. In
1699 he retired to live there and a grateful Company appointed his
son Willem Adriaan to succeed him.

The new Governor was no worse than his colleagues who made
illicit fortunes in the East. But the Cape offered little scope for such
ambitions. The most that could be attempted by the younger Van
der Stel was to get a Commissioner to make him a land-grant, then
himself to give more land to a man of straw and acquire it back
from him, so building up the princely estate of Vergelegen in Hottentots Holland. Thousands of vines were planted, thousands of sheep

and cattle pastured on runs hidden behind the Hottentot Holland mountains. Slaves and implements belonging to the Company were put to the Governor's private use; it was difficult to distinguish the Company's representative from the landlord of Vergelegen. A gang of fishermen at the secluded but windy harbour of Gordon's Bay provided food for the slaves, and unofficial fishermen were warned off the grounds. The monopolies of the sale of meat and wine were sold to the Governor's stooges. The Governor's father and brother and a few leading officials vied with him in large-scale agriculture.

Except for wheat, this official clique would soon produce enough of every commodity to supply the whole available market. In their private capacity they came to that market as sellers. In their official capacity they were the only buyers. The colonists might well ask themselves how they were supposed to make a living.

In face of this danger Dutch and French drew together. A list of complaints was secretly compiled and sent to Batavia, but no notice was taken of it. Then a memorial to the Directors was drawn up by Adam Tas of Stellenbosch and signed by sixty-three colonists. Thirty-one of the names were French. The Governor came to hear of these proceedings, arbitrarily arrested Tas and others, used wine and the threat of force to get signatures to a counter-petition. The original draft of the memorial was seized, but the fair copy was then safely on its way to Holland.

The Directors dared not overlook it. They had enemies at home who would welcome any chance of probing into the corruption of the Company, and a thorough enquiry would be most embarrassing to the *Heeren Majores* themselves. They hastened to recall the Governor, to redress some of the grievances and to forbid trading and farming by officials in the future.

The colony then settled down to the placid and regular development which continued through most of the eighteenth century. The Directors had had enough of colonists and gave no further encouragement to emigration. Most of the inhabitants at the time of the British occupation were descended from settlers who had come in the Van der Stel period or earlier.

2

THE AFRIKANERS

During the eighteenth century a new people evolved in South Africa, shaped out of the given human material by the peculiar geographical, economic and political forces of the country. The new people is described by travellers as divided, not horizontally, but vertically, into three classes.

The inhabitants of Cape Town were the first class encountered by the visitor. Before the end of the Company's rule Cape Town was said to contain more than twelve hundred houses. They charmed the beholder by their neatness and cleanliness, though this impression was sometimes modified by the smell of the oil applied by the slaves to their hair. Many of the houses had some claim to architectural beauty, a claim conceded by the taste of modern critics. They were double-storied, square-fronted, sash-windowed, square-shuttered, and the gables and pediments, fanlights and wrought-iron railings are much admired. Each had its flat *stoep* in front, and as these were of varying heights they gave the street an appearance of picturesque irregularity. The houses were whitewashed and accentuated the glaring brilliance of the summer sun.

All the trade of the colony was legally a Company monopoly, yet every inhabitant of Cape Town, official and unofficial, was in fact a trader. Rumour reported that Mijnheer This or Mevrouw That had got in a stock of some commodity, and the public collected in a casual way at the house indicated. The goods might have been smuggled from a passing ship, or brought in from the householder's farm in the country, or from another farm. Imported goods were sold to colonists, colonial produce to the visiting crews. With this

business most of the inhabitants combined that of taking in lodgers
and boarders. Every house was both shop and inn, and the townsmen had a bad reputation with local farmers and people from the
ships for cunning and extortion.

The Cape Town people had a good deal of social contact with
officialdom and with overseas visitors. The young ladies learned
French and English, went to balls, tried to follow the fashions of
Europe and were conscious of the distinctions of birth and official
rank. The townsmen invested much of their money in slaves, who
were not only used directly but hired out to others.

In the neighbourhood of Cape Town the second type of colonists
were settled, the wheat and vine growers. These were to be found
in the Cape peninsula, the valleys of the Eerste, the Louwrens and
the Berg Rivers and on the neighbouring hills. All this was the
Boland, the Overland, which was 'over' in relation to the high
interior only in the sense that London is 'up' from Snowdon or
Ben Nevis. The farmers of the Boland were a stable and fairly
civilised community. The great whitewashed gabled houses of the
eighteenth century, even more distinctive than the contemporary
town-houses, and still the centres of prosperous farms today, remain
as evidence of this civilisation. Dozens of such architectural treasures
lie within fifty miles of Cape Town. Their slave-bell-towers remind
the student of the 'peculiar institution' on which this kind of farming
was based.

The wealthier farmers of the Boland dispensed a lavish hospitality.
This was made possible by large-scale and diversified farming, and
a self-sufficiency which in some cases extended to the practice by the
farm slaves of a great many of the useful arts. The farmers catered
for a small market and were not rich in money.

Neither the town burghers nor the gentry of the Boland were as
distinctive a product of the colony, or as important in their influence
on its future development, as the third group—the pastoralists of
the interior. These *Veeboere*, no less than the other two classes,
were brought into being by the Company's policy.

In settling the first colonists on the land, the Directors aimed at
securing provisions for the fleets at little cost to the Company.
Cattle-barter, a lucrative trade, was at first denied to the farmers,
but the prohibition could not be enforced. A meat-trading monopoly
was then created and sold to the highest bidder, who could make his
own terms with the farmers and must sell to the Company at fixed
prices. By the end of the seventeenth century the colony was producing more agricultural supplies than were needed for the original

purpose, whereas the demand for meat was still unsatisfied. To hold the settlers to their prescribed task, the authorities at Batavia were compelled to import the surplus wheat of the Cape, but as the grain of India was cheaper this policy meant an unnecessary loss for the Company. It was bad business.

When the agitation against W. A. van der Stel and his official friends added insult to injury, it was obvious that there were too many colonists already. No further encouragement to immigration was given, though employees who were stationed at the Cape could and did take their discharge there. In 1717 the policy of restriction was carried a step further: no more farms in freehold were to be granted. By closing almost all the doors to the colonists, and leaving just one open, the Directors canalised the activities of the country in that one direction. Stock farming was allowed.

The earlier farmers held their lands in freehold, but it was open to them to use additional grazing land on another tenure. Beyond the outer limits of settlement the farmer could have his cattle-post on public land, protected in his occupation by a government licence. Before 1717 these posts belonged to men who were established on freehold land nearer to Cape Town. The cattle were looked after by the farmer's son, or perhaps a soldier given indefinite leave of absence to earn a living in some such way as this. Life on these cattle-posts had great attractions for young men; it was the life of adventure, of hunting, of brushes with Bushmen and Hottentots, of plunder perhaps, of release from the trammels of civilisation. This was the freedom in which many youths grew up. It developed in them a hankering that would drive some of their descendants beyond the Equator.

If a colonist grew wheat and vines in Stellenbosch or Drakenstein and kept cattle and sheep at a post in the Breede River valley, he soon discovered that the pastoral side of the business was the profitable side. Stock could walk to market and would fetch a reasonable price; apart from the natural increase, more could be got cheaply from the Hottentots. Wheat and wine hardly paid, the market was precarious, the transport to Cape Town difficult. Wagons had to cross the sandy and roadless waste of the Cape Flats, not yet bound down by the sour fig and the Port Jackson wattle.

When, therefore, no more freehold farms were to be got from the government, the colonists were quite satisfied with grazing licences as a substitute. The cattle post or *leeningsplaats* (loan place) was no longer a mere appendage of a wheat and wine farm. The newer settlers, who were to a large extent the old farmers' sons and ticket-of-leave soldiers who were accustomed to the frontier life, had no other farms than their loan places. The pioneer chose his abode, obtained his licence or *ordonnantie* in Cape Town, and soon established the custom that this entitled him to a circular area with a radius measured by walking a horse for half an hour in each direction, or to an equivalent area of a different shape. In theory, then, a farmhouse was one hour's walking pace from any of its neighbours. The authorities saw to this, or the neighbours did so for them. The average size of these estates was over 6000 acres.

At first no charge was made for the grant. Later a fee of £2 8s., ultimately raised to £4 16s. a year for each loan place was imposed. These fees became one of the biggest items in the revenue of the Cape government. They were called 'recognition money', recognition of the Company's ownership of the land. The grants had to be renewed annually. The renewal could be refused. Yet in spite of the fact that many farmers were years in arrear with their payments hardly any was ever disturbed in his possession. The colonists came to regard these loan places as their property in all but name. They sold them for prices which could not possibly be justified by the value of the *opstal* (farm buildings) alone. But the buyers would often be expansive neighbours, rather than young men starting in life. These would go beyond the limits of settlement and stake claims to new farms, at no cost beyond the annual payment of recognition money. This was their birthright.

There was one significant limitation on the farmer's power over his loan place: he could not subdivide it. Here was a sharp distinction between the new tenure and the old freehold of the more civilised districts. Roman-Dutch law, unlike English law, divided landed property equally among the sons of an intestate owner. Custom enforced the same practice when wills were made. But the loan place was not the farmer's property. It could not be divided among his sons. When he died, the next generation would very likely have already taken up new grants on the furthest borders of the colony. The place would then be sold as a unit, and the proceeds divided. As these people were prolific, childbirth easy, infant mortality low, the borders of the colony were advanced outward with corresponding speed.

By 1730 the migration had reached the Olifants River to the north, the Great Brak in the east. Then it flowed over the passes of the coastal mountains into the Bokkeveld and the Little Karoo. Leaping the barren Great Karoo, the northern movement had led by 1770 to the settlement of the Roggeveld and Nieuwveld mountains and

the high plains immediately beyond. From the Nieuwveld an advance
had been made eastward to the Camdebo, the present Aberdeen
district. By the same date, 1770, the other stream of migration had
flowed from the Little Karoo down the Long Kloof to the mouth of
the Gamtoos. In the 'seventies the eastern frontier was moved
onward, all along its line, to reach the Great Fish and Bushman's
Rivers. There the advance stopped. The Bantu migration had
reached the same line from the other direction.

The cattle and sheep farmers lived a life of the utmost simplicity.
They built houses that travellers likened rather to barns or hovels,
made of earth in some districts, of the loose flaked stones that were
plentiful in others. Two rooms might suffice for a whole family;
one room in the remotest and most primitive places. Meat was the
staple food, bread a rare luxury for which some families had lost the
taste. The diet varied, of course, from one district to another. Some
stock farmers grew a little fruit and wheat. Some had cattle, but in
other parts only sheep would thrive. Some were energetic and had
many products to take to market; others were lazy and lived merely
by the natural increase of their flocks. Clothes were unpretentious.
Children were taught the elements by peripatetic schoolmasters,
commonly discharged soldiers or sailors, who moved on from farm
to farm as their pupils had received a sufficient smattering or their
own repertoire was exhausted. The Bible was commonly the only
book in the household.

It was a homogeneous society. There were differences of wealth,
but they did not produce great differences in the manner of living.
One farmer had more cattle and sheep, and could proudly display
a herd all of the same colour—an enviable possession which his
neighbours might not be able to rival. But there were not great
differences, except as between the nearer and the remoter districts,
in housing, clothing, furniture, diet or education. Since the frontier
was open and anyone could have a loan place, social distinctions
were not hereditary and were no bar to marriage. This equality,
which did not exist in the urban society of Cape Town, was natural
on the *platteland* because every farmer was economically independent.
There the strongest prejudices prevented the young man from earning a living, however remunerative, as the paid employee of another.

As if in reflection of his loan tenure and his dependence upon
the grazing flocks and herds, the pastoralist was not tied by feeling
or habit to one spot. Families living on the snow-covered Roggeveld
or Nieuwveld mountains trekked down in winter and spring to the
Karoo plains, a vast commonage with no permanent possessors,

and returned to the higher altitudes before the heat and drought of summer. Children who had been rocked to sleep by the jolting of the wagon grew up with the thought of migrating far to the north or east to find homes for themselves.

Some families made an annual journey to Cape Town, some went once in three or four years, some once in a lifetime. At least once in a lifetime it must needs be, to appear before the Matrimonial Court which had to certify that there were no legal impediments before a marriage could take place. An important lawsuit would necessarily take the farmer to the capital; the recognition money ought to be paid there annually, and the bills of the butchers' agents needed to be cashed. The agents travelled about the interior to buy stock, for which they gave bills payable in Cape Town. These sums were increased by the sale of a few commodities such as butter and soap; soap was made with sheep-tail fat and the *ganna* bush, whose presence or absence in the veld had therefore some effect on migration and settlement.

The country visitor collected his cash and spent it on gunpowder, cloth, coffee, a few simple implements and articles of furniture, some brandy perhaps, and left the wicked city with all despatch. There was no desire to see the sights or share the pleasures of a society in which the simple countryman felt himself to be despised, and knew that he would be cheated. The return or 'down' journey (involving perhaps an ascent of 3000 feet), like the 'up' journey, might last weeks or even a couple of months. The wagon might be dismantled, and its parts and the contents taken over a pass on the backs of the oxen. Such a journey would exhaust the patience of a city man; the *Veeboer* had adapted himself to the pace of the ox.

At least once a year there was another journey to be made, a shorter one: to church. By the middle of the eighteenth century the frontiersmen had two churches that were more accessible than the old ones of the Boland. They were at Roodezand, the modern Tulbagh, and Swellendam. Even to these places the trek was a long one for many, but few would fail to appear at the communion service, *Nachtmaal*, once a year. The nearer inhabitants came four times. Some, however, would not come till there were another two or three children to be baptised.

On all the other Sundays and weekdays family prayers and Bible-reading took the place of the service. Whether the devotions were domestic or ecclesiastical, the Dutch Reformed Church kept a firm hold of the people and was their main link with civilisation. While their lives and thoughts were shaped largely by their geographical environment and the economic policy of the Company, there can be no doubt that the Calvinist religion was a primary factor in making them what they were. They went to church and revered the *dominie*, but there was little of the priest about him. They looked for salvation rather to the stern decrees of pre-destination. When this idea was associated with the Old Testament concept of a Chosen People, it was not difficult to see themselves as the objects of divine protection. Biblical stories of patriarchs and their sons and daughters, flocks and herds, maidservants and man-servants, of deserts and mountains and trekking through the wilderness, had a familiar ring to the *Veeboer*. He, too, could smite the Philistines hip and thigh.

The farmer's interest in the outside world, even in the nearer world of the Cape peninsula and the Boland, was slight. As the traveller Lichtenstein, a friendly observer who saw the colony during the Batavian occupation, remarked: 'In an almost unconscious inactivity of mind, without any attractions towards the great circle of mankind, knowing nothing beyond the little circle which his own family forms around him, the colonist of those parts passes his solitary days, and by his mode of life is made such as we see him.'

In the course of the eighteenth century, while three or four successive generations grew up under these conditions, the colonists developed their own distinctive language. That its formation owed very much to the Malay-Portuguese of the oriental slaves or to the broken speech of foreign settlers and Hottentots is hotly denied by modern philologists, who regard it as a development from seventeenth-century Dutch diverging from the development of the language in the Netherlands by the force of its own character. Some of its features reflect the influence of particular dialects spoken by early colonists; but it is an important fact that this isolated and apparently unchanging people did not maintain its old language in an archaic form as happened in Iceland or French Canada. Unnecessary inflections, grammatical gender and the old complexities of weak and strong verbs went by the board. New principles came into use. Where the attributive adjective had been inflected—or not—according to its gender and the nature of the word preceding it, its behaviour came to be determined by principles of euphony only. Difficult combinations of consonants were ruthlessly hacked apart; the first of the pair was retained, the second dropped, only to reappear when the word was inflected. The double negative, common in medieval Dutch but no longer used in Holland, established itself; he would be a bold philologist who denied that this usage was especially natural to the Huguenot. The meanings of words changed, and the vocabulary drew freely from the native tongues of Africa and the East.

The new idiom, later to be called Cape Dutch or the *Taal* (i.e. the language), and finally Afrikaans (which means African), was spoken for many generations before it was reduced to writing. The wandering pastoralist of the eighteenth century read the Bible, whose language was sufficiently archaic to allow his own spoken tongue to develop quite independently of it. The educated people of Cape Town and its neighbourhood, who were in regular contact with Dutch officialdom, and used the official language for reading and writing, must have modelled their speech much more closely upon it. It was not these people but the rustic semi-nomads of the interior that formed the nucleus of the future nation.

As their language came to be called Afrikaans, the people themselves assumed the name of Africans, *Afrikaners*. The colonist, from the beginning of the eighteenth century, also adopted as a badge of nationality the name of *Boer*, or farmer. This word was a contribution not of the stock farmers but of the tillers of the soil who overthrew W. A. van der Stel. Farmers, Africans—the names meant a turning of the back on Europe and the ways of living that connected one with Europe. The Company might, perhaps, have engendered a different spirit, though poor soil and lack of markets would in any case have made intensive colonisation difficult. But its policy had produced this exaggerated isolationism.

Europe in the eighteenth century experienced Enlightenment, Reason and Revolution; all these passed the African Farmer by. He carried his seventeenth-century inheritance forward into the nineteenth. When the influences of the new age thrust themselves right into his local politics he reacted promptly and violently against them. That reaction fills many pages of South African history. To understand it one must bear in mind, first, the circumstances which had formed the character of the Boer; second, the constitution and politics of the colony; third, the new frontier problem which caused Enlightenment, Reason and Revolution to reach Graaff-Reinet.

To say that the government of the colony was a bureaucracy would be technically correct but would give a false picture of the liberties of the *Veeboer* on his loan place. The Company had its servants at the Cape, graded in rank like the employees of any big firm, and the official world was a businesslike community of upper-merchants and merchants, under-merchants and book-keepers. A Commander was of higher rank than these, a Governor still higher. After 1691, when Simon van der Stel was promoted from Commander to Governor, the head of the colonial government was a man of that rank.

The Governor was assisted by a Council of Policy consisting of a number of senior officials, including two military officers. The members held their positions *ex officio*, and the Council contained no representative element. One of the Councillors was the Independent Fiscal, whose position was unique in that he took no orders from the Governor but was responsible immediately to the Directors. He had a large independent authority in financial and judicial matters, acted as prosecutor in the Court, and was supposed to be a check on the corrupt behaviour of the Governor. Yet the underpaid Fiscal was as much exposed to temptation as anyone else.

The Council of Policy, the highest executive and legislative authority, was the only organ of government in which the people had no share. It was obvious that such a body was unlikely to administer impartial justice in a community where the economic interests of the governors conflicted so sharply with those of the governed. So, while the Court of Justice consisted mainly of the same persons as the Council, three 'burgher councillors' sat with the others when cases involving colonists were tried. Similarly, two burghers shared with two officials the work of the Matrimonial Court, before which all couples had to appear before marriage to prove that there were no legal impediments. For some of the remotest settlers this regulation was, as we have seen, the occasion of the only journey to Cape Town in a lifetime. Again, two burghers and two officials and a President constituted the Orphan Chamber, which protected the interests of the children of a widow or widower who remarried, and sometimes acted as trustee.

In the earliest stages of the colony's development these burgher representatives were selected by the government from lists drawn up at meetings of the handful of colonists then in the country. As soon as the settlement had expanded beyond parochial limits this method was abandoned. The burgher councillors retired in rotation, and before any did so they drew up a list of names, double the number of the places to be filled. From this list the government made its choice. It was a system of co-option tempered by selection.

To the people beyond the Cape Flats the institutions of local government were more important and interesting than those that functioned in Cape Town. After the foundation of Stellenbosch it was necessary to station some official there to represent the central authorities. Further dispersion in the eighteenth century caused a repetition of this arrangement further and further afield. By the time of the first British conquest the colony was divided into four districts, the Cape, Stellenbosch, Swellendam and Graaff-Reinet. In each except the Cape there was a Landdrost, a paid magistrate who presided over the local court and attended to all the interests of Government.

The Landdrost was assisted in his judicial and local government functions by six Heemraden, ordinary citizens serving without pay in much the same spirit and manner as the English Justices of the Peace. Unlike the latter, the Heemraden could not act singly or on their own initiative. Their court dealt with petty civil cases and handled such administrative matters as local trading, the maintenance of roads and passes and pontoons on the principal rivers. A revenue was derived from these sources and from a tax on stock. Like a feudal lord, the Stellenbosch court had a milling monopoly, and all the local authorities could requisition the labour, wagons and oxen of the inhabitants. In the Cape district there was no Landdrost, but a Court of Commissioners, complete with burgher councillors, which dealt with petty cases.

At a still lower level, and closer to the individual farmer, stood the *Veldwachtmeester* who was changed under the Batavian régime into the Field-Cornet. He served a ward or field-cornetcy that was to be not more than thirty-six miles in diameter. He had some judicial authority, notably over the punishment of slaves and in settling boundary disputes, and it was noted that he seldom failed to have close ties of blood or friendship with one of the disputing parties, so that his judgment was not always regarded as impartial. He knew all the farmers in his ward personally, did regular tours of inspection, made the laws and decrees of the government known to all. The Field-Cornet received no pay, but was exempt from the ordinary charges and taxes on his land.

The system of local government had also its military side, and of all the institutions this was the one that concerned the inhabitants most intimately. In the earliest days of the settlement the men had been formed into a militia, controlled in each district by a *Krygsraad* which made appointments and promotions subject to the approval of the government. Twice a year the militia turned out for drill and inspection, and once annually in each district the force paraded before the Governor. There were both foot and mounted units.

Before the end of the seventeenth century the colony waged a full-dress war against the Hottentots and had to defend itself against the plundering raids of Bushmen. In 1715 bands of the pygmies came down from their mountains, murdered herdsmen and drove off hundreds of cattle and sheep. As the farmers pushed further inland the Bushmen, from their last mountainous retreats, struck back with desperate boldness. This presented the militiamen with a problem of defence that interested them vastly more than the parade ground evolutions at the Drostdy each October. Indeed, their absence from home for this ceremony was accepted by the Bushmen as the best occasion for attack. Special means of defence were devised to meet it.

The unit appropriate for the purpose was the commando, destined to be used successively against Bushmen, Bantu and Englishmen. Its name and spirit have spread even more widely in recent times, when Commandos have gone into action in Europe against the most dangerous enemies in the world. The most modern commandos have more than a fanciful or romantic continuity with the most ancient. And in South African history this organisation has had a development that obscures its origin as a means of defence against the most primitive and incoherent people of the country.

Between the claims of the Bushmen and those of any other people, whether Hottentots, Bantu or Europeans, no compromise was possible. The Bushmen's lands were his hunting-grounds. He could not tolerate the appearance of a settled, an agricultural or even a pastoral people upon them. Year after year, as he realised that his last remaining possessions were being encroached upon, he descended upon the farms, killed white people and Hottentots, burned houses and drove off the stock. Questioned by a Hottentot messenger in 1738, they explained 'that they did it to drive the white men out of their country; that they were living in the Bushmen's country; that this was only a beginning and they would do the same to all the people living thereabouts. That if that did not help, and the people did not depart thence, they would burn all the corn that was now standing in the fields, when it was ripe, so that they would be forced to leave the Bushmen's country.'

The farmers could not wait for the slow response of Cape Town and its garrison. In every neighbourhood one of them held the rank of Field Corporal, later to be called *Veldwachtmeester*. This leader summoned his neighbours for commando service; a mounted troop turned out, each man bringing his own arms, horse and scanty supplies, with ammunition provided by the government. The trail was followed, the enemy pursued into the mountains, as many shot as were seen and would not surrender, and the booty recaptured if possible. After a week or two of this the party might return empty-handed, or it might have recovered most of what had been lost.

By 1774 the depredations were so serious that the government took a step towards co-ordinating the isolated reprisals. A Field Commandant was appointed for the whole of the northern frontier—that is, the Bushman frontier—and under his command the burghers fought a regular campaign to subdue the irrepressible enemy. Only six years later Adriaan van Jaarsveld was appointed Field Commandant of the *eastern* frontier, a very different matter. The commando system was to be turned against the Bantu, a people many ages ahead of the Bushmen in culture and organisation.

A generation later, as has been shown, the *Veldwachtmeester* became the Field-Cornet, with judicial and administrative functions. But his military responsibility remained.

When the colony passed into British hands, its Boer or Afrikaner people had developed a distinct philosophy and practice of government. When the savage threatened, the farmer was called on commando by the Field-Cornet, on the responsibility of the Commandant. The government supplied the ammunition. The same Field-Cornet, and other representative farmers called Heemraden, settled the little disputes among the farmers themselves. The Landdrost was expected to see things from the same point of view as 'the public'. As for the distant authorities that appointed him, they sent the powder and they sanctioned the farmer's tenure of his loan place. It would be difficult to think of any other useful purpose that they served.

3

SLAVES AND HOTTENTOTS

The recorded history of South Africa begins with a hostile encounter between Portuguese and Hottentots at Mossel Bay. But the natives of the country were not to be seriously threatened in their possession of it or in their manner of life till the Dutch made a permanent settlement in Table Valley.

Van Riebeeck had no sooner landed than a band of people whom the Europeans called Beachrangers made their appearance and established themselves as hangers-on of the white community. They were an impoverished and disorganised set of Hottentots who had supported a bare existence on shellfish and other natural products of the peninsula. Now they made their kraal on the lower slopes of Signal Hill, began to tender their services as herdsmen and to allow their children to collect firewood and go into domestic service, and for the rest—according to the white men—begged and stole. There were not more than a few dozen of them altogether.

The Beachrangers were not representative of the Hottentot race. Better organised clans, possessing large flocks and herds, travelled slowly round a grazing area which included the Cape peninsula. Their fires were seen far to the north; messengers heralded their arrival; then thousands of cattle were seen behind Table Mountain and the nomads pitched their camp. A brisk barter, cattle for trinkets, was begun. Many times this process was repeated. It might happen that the tribesmen had no beasts to spare for sale, but their thrift and caution usually broke down under the temptation of tobacco, brandy and arrack.

After a time some of them showed resentment at the permanent intrusion of the settlers upon their lands. They murdered a few and drove off their cattle. Twice the white men waged war upon them. After that they settled down to a quiet acceptance of the situation. As the stock of the nearer clans was bartered away the traders went further afield, and tobacco and strong drink spread to the more distant peoples. Some suffered from diseases introduced from Europe and Asia; a foretaste of what was to come. In 1713 smallpox came. The white settlers suffered, and the slaves more severely. The Hottentots, as an organised and self-conscious nationality, were wiped out. Tribal names were forgotten, except in the remotest parts. This catastrophe happened just four years before the stopping of freehold grants, and about that time the rapid expansion of the colony into the interior began. The Hottentots had bartered away too many of their animals; their race itself was largely destroyed by smallpox; and after this the migrant farmers moved in to occupy their land.

Beyond the northern borders the tribal system stood the shock, and in those parts a few pure Hottentots are still found today. But the historical importance of their relations with the white invaders does not lie in this unimportant survival. It lies rather in the precedents that were set for the white man's relations with the Bantu, and in their effect on the people living today who are partly, but not purely, descended from the Hottentots.

The older race, even when its cattle and land had gone, could not satisfy the demands of the colonists for labour. And in the early days it lacked the stimulus of destitution. Before the colony, therefore, lay the alternatives of white immigrant labour and of slavery. The future character of the country depended more upon the choice made between these than upon any other decision that it fell to the Directors to make. Historians have remarked that, if free white labourers had been preferred, South Africa would have developed into a true European colony like any of those north of the Mason and Dixon line.

But it may be doubted whether, in the earliest stages, this alternative was practical politics. Van Riebeeck was begging the Seventeen for slaves, and the Batavian authorities for industrious Chinese, before the first white settler had put his plough to the soil. Ships were sent out to capture Portuguese slavers off the West African coast, and a regular East Indiaman landed a captured cargo at the Cape in March, 1658. The free burghers had already complained that they could do nothing without slaves. The few white labourers that were tried were too expensive. Given the difficulty

of finding Europeans, Dutch or foreign, willing to become landowners in the new colony, one may suspect that the search for free
labourers in any numbers would have been fruitless. The slaves were
landed, some sold to the burghers and some retained by the
Company. Did this transaction, on so tiny a scale, irrevocably
determine the fate of the sub-continent?

In 1691 the white colonists numbered about 1000 and their
slaves 386. Among these the men outnumbered the women by five
to one, so that the continuance of slavery as a basis of the country's
economy would depend on continued importations. As late as 1717
the future social character of the colony was still regarded as an
open question. The members of the Council of Policy had been
asked by the Directors to answer a number of questions, of which
one concerned the relative advantages to the Cape of white settlers
and of slaves. The commander of the garrison, Captain D. P.
de Chavonnes, pleaded for white settlers, as helping to defend the
colony and increase its revenue, and because of the danger to society
of rebellious and criminal slaves. Every other member of the
Council, including the Governor, took the opposite view. Slaves
were cheap and they were docile. This view prevailed, and no
further encouragement was given to emigrants from Holland. It
has been seen that the grants of land in freehold were stopped at the
same time. Professor Eric Walker regards the decision of 1717 as the
principal turning-point in the whole history of South Africa.

The decision was questioned more than once in subsequent years.
In 1743 the Baron van Imhoff, a Commissioner who visited the
Cape, regretted that 'most agriculturalists in this colony are not so
much farmers as lords of plantations, and many of them would
think it a shame to work with their own hands'. He tried to discourage the further dispersion of the population on loan places, and
to bind the distant frontiers more closely to the capital. In 1768
J. W. Cloppenburg, the *Secunde* or Vice-Governor, drew up a
report in the same spirit, recommending that no more loan places
be granted and no more slaves imported, so that the poorer colonists
should be forced to work for others and a more closely knit society
enabled to develop. These proposals were not adopted, and the
social system of the colony continued to grow along the lines already
marked out.

The landowners of the older settled districts were, therefore,
slave-owning planters. The citizens of Cape Town used slaves not
only as domestic servants but as artisans whose labour was hired out.
Slaves were also employed on the distant loan places of the interior,

but there they were greatly outnumbered by Hottentot servants. The presence of Hottentots indicated the care of stock, and some desultory domestic service, while the thorough cultivation of the soil called for slaves.

During the eighteenth century, contact with slaves, Hottentots and Bushmen developed in the minds of the Europeans a set of attitudes and prejudices concerning race and colour. The first settlers had made distinctions of religion only, Christian and heathen. The baptised black was socially equal to a white Christian. But this principle was soon abandoned. As almost all black people were slaves, and almost all white people masters, skin-colour became a fairly accurate index of status. The Hottentots were regarded with contempt and the Bushmen with pitiless hostility. Even the instruction of slaves in Christianity was abandoned, since a baptised slave was in the earliest period thought to have a right to manumission. 'Christian' became in practice equivalent to 'white'.

There is some difference of opinion whether the eighteenth-century colonists despised manual work or not. Some observers reported that they would not do a hand's turn on the farm or in the warehouse. ' 'Tis slaves' work! What are slaves for?' Other evidence suggests that a farmer had no rooted objection to manual labour in his own concerns, but regarded labour of any kind in another man's employment as the characteristic of the slave. Along both of these lines the prejudice was destined to grow after the eighteenth century was over.

Before the end of the Company's rule burgher militiamen are found refusing to drill when a dark-skinned man was promoted to corporal, though they had not objected to having him in the ranks. A frontier farmer, reports the traveller Barrow, had riveted a pair or iron rings to the legs of a Hottentot boy, who was said to have hobbled about with them for ten years. General Vandeleur brought boy and master to his headquarters, had the rings removed from the Hottentot and fastened to the farmer's legs. 'For the whole of the first night his lamentations were incessant; with a stentorian voice a thousand times he vociferated, *"Myn God! Is dat een maniere om Christian mensch to handelen?"* ("My God! Is this a way to treat Christians?") His, however, were not the agonies of bodily pain, but the bursts of rage and resentment on being put on a level with one, as the boors call them, of the *Zwarte natie*, between whom and the *Christian mensch* they conceive the difference to be fully as great as between themselves and their cattle, and whom, indeed, they most commonly honor with the appellation of *Zwarte Vee*, black cattle.'

George Thompson, another traveller, was surprised by the complacent manner in which a frontier Commandant described his service on thirty-two commandos by which 200 Bushmen were massacred. The same Commandant, on hearing of the killing and spoliation of some Bushmen by a party of Kaffirs, 'spoke with detestation of the conduct of these intruders, and applauded the punishment inflicted upon them without seeming to be aware how close a resemblance existed between their own conduct and that of the Caffers'.

These illustrations would have to be multiplied many dozens of times to give an adequate impression of the ideology of the 'boor'. The mastership of the white man, the obedient and respectful service of Hottentot and slave, were the axioms on which his social and political systems were based. Any tampering with that relationship meant the dissolution of the world to which he belonged. Given slavery, the cultural gulf between European and Hottentot, and the growth of an isolated colonial society out of touch with Europe, such an outlook was perhaps inevitable. But it was to have a pernicious development when slavery had been abolished, the cultural gulf narrowed, and the isolation broken in upon.

In the meantime the slave and Hottentot populations were undergoing a change that would add a new element to the future racial complexity of the country. The slaves were of very various origins. The greater number is believed to have come from East Africa and Madagascar. There were other Africans from West Africa, chiefly Angola, and lastly, in smaller numbers, prisoners from the Eastern possessions of the Company. The males were far more numerous than the females, a disparity which naturally led to the cohabitation of men slaves with Hottentot women. There were also many offspring of slave women by white fathers.

From these beginnings miscegenation continued, in ever-increasing complexity, to produce a mixed race in which Hottentot, Bantu, Malagasy, Malay and European elements were confused. These people, proud of their superiority to the pure Hottentots, called themselves Bastards, a name afterwards abandoned in favour of the *Cape Coloured*. One section of them, the progeny of Europeans and of Hottentots of the Grigriqua or Chariguriqua tribe, passed beyond the north-western border of the colony during the eighteenth century and settled in the valley of the Orange River. Under missionary influence this tribe adopted the name of Griquas. Another fragment of them, descended mainly though not entirely from the East Indian slaves, was held together by its profession of the Moslem

religion. Many slaves of other origins, whose religious instruction
was neglected by their masters, became Moslems and were therefore
absorbed by this community. Today they are called, not altogether
accurately, the Malays and are an important and distinctive element
in the population of Cape Town and its neighbourhood.

Many racial differences were thus becoming blurred in the Cape's
formative period. The distinction between slavery and freedom
remained, but hardly connoted any practical advantages to the 'free'
Hottentots. They were thought of from the first as being in the
colony but not of it. While tribes decayed, the Company maintained
an out-of-date fiction by recognising, even appointing, chiefs. A
Hottentot captain even beyond the colonial borders thought his
authority insecure till he had received a gift of a copper-headed cane
bearing the Company's monogram. The captains were expected to
settle disputes among their own followers, whom the colonial courts
disregarded unless they were involved in disputes with white men.
The Hottentots paid no taxes, but they had no land and few cattle.
Unless they entered the service of the farmers, they were condemned
to wander over the country or withdraw themselves to its most
neglected and unnoticed by-ways. Our own age has invented a term
which approximately describes their condition: they were Displaced
Persons.

The age of the French Revolution, Napoleon and Wilberforce
was, for the Cape Colony, the period in which the condition of the
Hottentots ceased to be universally accepted as inevitable. They
acquired friends ready to speak on their behalf in high places, though
not very influentially at first. Difference of opinion, where before
there had been unanimity, turned the despised outcasts into a
'problem'.

The new opinion was held by missionaries and a few officials.
Mission work in South Africa may almost be said to have begun in
1799. The Moravian Georg Schmidt, who founded Genadendal in
1737, was so restricted by official pressure that he gave up his
attempt after a few years. The Moravian Brethren re-founded the
same station in 1792. When, however, Dr Vanderkemp arrived in
1799 the explosive force of the London Missionary Society was
injected into colonial politics, where it was to continue to play a vital
part directly for more than a generation and indirectly to the present
day.

The developments of the seventeenth and eighteenth centuries
have been permanently important for their influence on institutions,
attitudes of mind and the structure of South African society. But

after the arrival of the missionaries—and very largely because of it—
the country entered a period in which the events themselves became
historic memories powerful in their effects on national development.
In retrospect, it was as if this date divided the forgotten influences
of the people's infancy from the bitter memories of its later childhood.

Dr Vanderkemp, after some discouraging experiences among the
Bantu beyond the frontier, decided to devote himself to the Hottentots. The Batavian Governor, General Janssens, in 1803 granted him
and the Rev. James Read a farm near Algoa Bay on which to found
an 'Institution'. It was called Bethelsdorp. To the Hottentots it
offered an alternative to service with the farmers, and many took
advantage of this. The L.M.S., moreover, within a few decades
founded a number of new stations both in and outside the colony.
Like Bethelsdorp, they were refuges for those who wished to escape
farm labour.

Conventional opinion then and since has drawn a sharp distinction
between the Moravian (and a few other) missions, where 'habits of
industry' were inculcated, and those of the London Missionary
Society, which confined itself to the principles of religion and
incidentally taught a dirty and ragged population to become independent and disrespectful. The distinction has certainly been
overdrawn. The London missions were mostly in the eastern districts
and beyond the northern border, and it was largely because of their
location that they differed from the stations in the older and more
settled west as well as from those among the Bantu.

When the British slave trade was abolished in 1807 the slaves of
the colony acquired a scarcity value, and the farmers looked with
increasing interest to the wandering Hottentots as a source of labour.
The 'Institutions' which withdrew these from the market, as well as
unsettling those already in service, therefore became doubly
obnoxious. The farmers' complaints were heard with some sympathy
by English Tory Governors, and led to the Earl of Caledon's
Hottentot Ordinance of 1809. The objects of this were to stop
vagrancy and to secure a labour force to the farmers. The shadowy
jurisdiction of the 'Captains' was abolished and their subjects fully
subordinated to the colonial laws. Every Hottentot was required to
have a fixed abode, which was registered with the Landdrost.
Contracts of service for a month or longer were to be in writing and
similarly registered. The Hottentot could not leave the farm without
a pass from his employer, the ward without one from the Field-
Cornet, or the district without one from the Landdrost. If unable to
show a pass to any European who demanded it he could be arrested

as a vagrant and dealt with—in practice assigned under contract to a farmer—by the Landdrost.

The complaint that Hottentots' children were fed by their fathers' employers without being under any obligation in return led to a further ordinance in 1812, providing that any child in these circumstances could be apprenticed to the farmer from the age of eight to that of eighteen. This arrangement tended in fact to bind the child's father too, since he would not be willing to leave the farm without his son. And when one son's contract had expired, others would in the meantime have been entered into. Further, servants were commonly in debt to their employers and were tied to them by that circumstance. That wages should have been paid largely in kind, including brandy and tobacco, was inevitable in a community that had few dealings in money.

The year in which this second ordinance was passed, so far from witnessing an exhibition of gratitude to the government, found the frontier seething with anger and indignation. The farmers of the remoter districts had grown accustomed, in the previous century, to an official neglect which allowed them to discipline their dependants with little fear of interference from Cape Town. In 1811 this freedom was ended by the institution of a Circuit Court which brought the Cape Town judges on annual visitations to the drostdies. Since the missionaries, especially those of Bethelsdorp, had been listening eagerly to tales of the ill-treatment of servants by masters, they took advantage of the opportunity to lay a number of charges before the Circuit Court at Uitenhage and George in 1812.

The missionary Read, an injudicious man, had spoken wildly of 'upward of 100 cases of recent murders in Uitenhage'; twenty-two cases of all kinds were actually brought before the court. That eight or more charges of violence to servants, and others of withholding wages, were substantiated, shows that the protection which the new court offered to the servant class was not unnecessary. To the frontiersmen and their descendants the number of acquittals has appeared more significant. The 'Black Circuit' has come to connote the bringing of frivolous charges against respectable burghers on the evidence of lying Hottentots; the tarnishing of decent reputations by the action of a band of fanatical and irresponsible missionaries. Yet it may well be believed that the passions were aroused not so much by the sense of injustice as by the very equality of the races before the law which the proceedings exhibited. 'My God! Is this a way to treat Christians?'

The extent of the shock to conventional opinion may be gauged by some evidences of that opinion in the preceding decade. In 1797 the Heemraden of Stellenbosch had refused to listen to a Hottentot's charge against his mistress for the withholding of wages. They doubted 'whether a Hottentot had the right to sue a Citizen in their Court; and if this were allowed, would it not encourage the Hottentots to think that they were of the same standing as a citizen?' A few years later, under the Batavian régime, the Landdrost of Uitenhage wrote to the Governor that 'it is difficult and often impossible to get the colonists to understand that the Hottentots ought to be protected by the laws no less than themselves, and that the judge may make no distinction between them and the Hottentots'. Against this background the blackness of the Black Circuit stands out more clearly.

Shortly after this event a frontier farmer named F. C. Bezuidenhout was summoned to appear at Graaff-Reinet on a charge of ill-treating a Hottentot servant. The summons was repeated a number of times, but the accused declined to obey it. When in October, 1815, a party which included some Hottentot soldiers was sent to arrest him, he retired to a cave, fired upon his assailants and was then shot. His death provoked some of his relations and friends to plot rebellion and revenge. They tried unsuccessfully to get help from the Xhosa chief Gaika, and the small party of rebels eventually dispersed when opposed by troops and a commando of burghers. The ringleaders were captured and, on the sentence of a special commission of the High Court, five of them were publicly hanged at Slagter's Nek, near Somerset East, in 1816. Lord Charles Somerset refused to mitigate the sentence, in spite of public opinion on the frontier. The loyal burghers who had assisted the troops thus found themselves partly responsible for the deaths of their friends, a responsibility they would never have incurred if they had foreseen it. Slagter's Nek became a potent cause of anti-British feeling among the Afrikaners, and has remained so to the present day.

In the meantime Vanderkemp had died, and Read was a poor advocate. The London missions, offspring of the Congregational Church, tended to fall into the anarchy which is the weak side of Independency. To counteract this the Directors of the society in 1819 sent Dr John Philip to superintend its affairs in the colony. Within three years he had become the regular spokesman and avowed champion of the interests of the Hottentots. His connections with the Evangelical party in Britain, and its representatives at Westminster, enabled him to bring to their side stronger influences than even those of the colonial government. The weak position of the

Tories in England made their ministers unwilling to let the affairs of the Cape develop into material for Opposition attack. The Governor, Lord Charles Somerset, left the colony for good in 1826, in spite of the supposed power of the Beaufort connection. In 1828 it was the colonial government itself that devised the fiftieth ordinance, the most important single result of all the missionary propaganda.

The fiftieth ordinance abolished the pass system and allowed the Hottentots freedom of movement; it removed some abuses in the apprenticing of servants' children, though not abolishing the system; it limited the duration of oral contracts to one month and of written ones to a year; specifically guaranteed the right of Hottentots, which had been doubtful, to purchase and possess land in the colony; forbade payment of wages in liquor or tobacco; forbade the summary 'domestic' correction of Hottentots, their arrest for vagrancy and their forced allocation to farmers. In most respects, though not all, it gave free persons of colour an equal legal status with Europeans. Philip, who was in England at the time, procured there an addition to the ordinance forbidding its amendment or repeal without the sanction of the British government.

It was to be expected that this legal revolution would be followed by a wave of vagrancy and crime; but the extent of these consequences was greatly exaggerated in the colony. Like the 'bandits' of 1789 in France, the lawless Hottentots were believed to be everywhere, expected to arrive everywhere, but never seen in the flesh.

The alarm of the farmers was increased when an Act of the British Parliament emancipated their slaves in 1834. Having lost their firm hold over one half of the labour supply, they were now to lose it over the other. The ex-slaves, when their period of apprenticeship expired in 1838, would be as uncontrollable as the Hottentots. In 1834 a complaisant Acting Governor introduced an ordinance, which the new Legislative Council passed, to revive the principles which had just been abolished. Every humble official was required to apprehend all such persons found within his jurisdiction as 'he may reasonably suspect of having no honest means of subsistence— or who cannot give a satisfactory account of themselves'. In short, a supply of farm labour was to be guaranteed by the old means. The missionaries worked hard in opposition to the proposal, and Philip's prevision in having the fiftieth ordinance entrenched was rewarded. This measure was in effect a repeal of that ordinance, and required the assent of London; that assent was refused. Thus the new status of the free persons of colour as the equals, in most legal respects, of the Europeans was maintained against colonial hostility by the firmness of the British Government. After 1838 that equality was to be enjoyed by every inhabitant of the colony.

During the period of these agitations there was a class, the slaves, that was not directly affected by them. The trade was abolished, and the slaves became more valuable. They were, in general, better treated than free servants precisely because they were property whose value must be maintained. It may well be believed that the slaves were not made to work as hard at the Cape as in countries producing cotton or sugar for export. The farms of this colony produced less for sale, and more for direct consumption, than the West Indian plantations. The slave-owners belonged to families permanently resident in the country, and attached in successive generations to the same slave property; in the older districts to the same landed property also. They were not birds of passage with their eyes on rotten boroughs.

A consciousness that this was so combined with the deeper feeling that slavery necessarily meant the absolute power of the master to produce resentment at government interference with the institution. Regulations, framed in London on the basis of West Indian experience, were applied to the Cape. First came registration, to prevent the re-enslavement of those who had been emancipated and the illegal importation of new slaves. A Protector of Slaves was appointed. Then came regulations concerning punishments and hours of work, forbidding the separate sale of members of a family, admitting the evidence of baptised slaves in the courts, allowing slaves to hold property. Then the slave was to have the right to his freedom by tendering his appraised price. Finally, a Punishment Record Book was to be kept by every master and the Protector was given access to slave quarters.

These steps, taken between 1816 and 1831, were regarded by slave-owners as seriously encroaching on powers which were essential to the institution. But the institution itself was presently abolished. The Reform Act removed the 'West India interest' from Westminster, and made it easier for the very first reformed Parliament to pass the measure for which Wilberforce and his friends had long striven. Unlike the recently despoiled borough-owners, the slave-owners were compensated for their loss. But the compensation allotted to the Cape Colony amounted to little more than a third of the sum at which slave property had been valued locally. It was payable only in London; agents in the colony charged a heavy discount when they bought the claims for cash. The loss was felt more acutely and immediately than it would otherwise have been because of the extent to which slave property had been mortgaged.

When the period of apprenticeship came to an end in 1838 most of the old farm slaves remained in their places as wage labourers, and the distinction between slaves and Hottentots, already blurred in the racial sense, disappeared from the legal, social and economic points of view. The colony knew now only the Europeans and the Coloured People, and these very nearly equal in the eyes of the law.

4

THE BANTU FRONTIER

The obstacle that stopped the eastward expansion of the Boers during the 1770's was a people with whom close contact was then made for the first time, the Bantu. The name, first applied to them by the philologist Dr Bleek, described not a race but a group of languages, and is taken from the word which, with slight variations in the many Bantu tongues, means *people*. The speakers of these languages are the dark-skinned natives of the continent living south of a line running roughly from the Cameroon mountains to Mombasa. At the end of the eighteenth century the southern limit of their territory was marked by the Kalahari desert and an uncertain line which reached the south-east coast in the neighbourhood of the Great Fish River. In this region the land of the Bantu had, before the arrival of the white men, marched with that of the Hottentots.

It is the members of this darker race—to use the term loosely—who alone are called *Natives* or *Africans* in South Africa today. Yet over a large part of the country they are immigrants of no longer standing than the Europeans. They have moved down slowly from the north, and the stages of their migration in the eastern coastlands can be measured by the reports of travellers, Arab in the Middle Ages and European from the time of da Gama. When the boundary of the Cape Colony was officially advanced in 1775 to the Fish River in its upper reaches and the Bushman's River nearer the coast, the Bantu had reached roughly the same line from the other side.

The Arabs had called the African people *Kaffirs*, infidels, and this name was similarly applied to them by the Europeans. A good deal was known about them even before the two streams of migration had met, as hunters and shipwrecked crews had made their acquaintance. It was understood that the Kaffirs were a people radically different from the Hottentots. Unlike the latter, they were agriculturists who tilled the soil. Their social and political organisation was much more highly developed. The future would show that their powers of resistance and survival were of a high order.

They were ruled by hereditary chiefs. Polygyny was practised, but led to no uncertainties about the right of succession. Among the many wives of a chief, one, usually married late in life and for political reasons, held the rank of great wife, and her eldest son had the undisputed right to succeed his father. Next in rank came the wives of the right-hand and of the left-hand house respectively. Their eldest sons were commonly provided with subordinate chieftainships and tribal followings, but recognised the paramountcy of their chief of the great house. The followers of a chief constituted a tribe. Membership of it was normally hereditary, but the subjects of an unpopular chief often threw off their allegiance and attached themselves to another. Inter-tribal disputes about land and cattle were frequent, and often led the defeated party to migrate further south and west, where the feeble Hottentots could be driven out or absorbed. 'Man,' they said, 'begets, but land does not beget.'

Among the Bantu, cattle played a peculiar part in social, economic and even religious life. All agricultural and domestic work was the province of the women; the handling of cattle was a man's work. Social status depended largely on wealth in cattle, and this could be built up rapidly by those who were successful in raids upon neighbouring tribes. The essential feature of marriage was the payment by the bridegroom to his father-in-law of a number of cattle, the *lobola*. Without this, there was no marriage tie and no children were legitimate. A father, receiving *lobola* cattle for his daughter, could use them to procure a wife for his son. If the son wanted more wives, he must first acquire more cattle. Cattle were sacrificed to the ancestors. More than that, their possession entered in a special way into the Kaffir's emotions. Like money to a capitalist, land to an aristocrat, books and *objets d'art* to a collector, they were the basis of his self-respect.

These points must be mentioned, however briefly, if we are to understand the conflict that now began on the border-line where Boer and Kaffir met. The class of frontier farmers had begun its career by bartering cattle from the Hottentots, in defiance of prohibitions. Kaffir raids upon the eastern Hottentots for the same purpose were not unusual. When the gap filled by this race was at last closed, strong-armed cattle-rustlers on each side of the border at last met their match.

For three-quarters of a century from this date the relations of the colony with the Kaffirs constituted a problem of foreign, not domestic, politics: border warfare, frontier demarcation, trading across the border, treaties, forts—these were the subject-matter. Like the Crusades, the Kaffir Wars have been given serial numbers for the assistance of schoolboys and others; but the classification is a little artificial, as there were periods of serious friction which have gone down to history unnumbered, and the beginning and end of a 'Kaffir War' are not always easy to determine.

No less than the conflict over the treatment of servants, the handling of the frontier problems by successive governments produced resentment among the Boer pioneers. A legend was built up, and enshrined in the pages of the classic historian Theal, that hordes of barbarians were continually breaking over the border, murdering, burning and looting; that the frontiersmen, anxious to defend their homes, were for ever being thwarted by a government determined to see no good in them, and no evil in the 'noble savages'. In recent times this opinion has been effectively attacked by Professor J. S. Marais for the earlier period and by Professor W. M. Macmillan for the later. Every contribution to a true and unbiassed account of the frontier conflicts is of great value, not only in itself but in its bearing on the race relations of later times.

Who, it may be asked of each of these wars, started the trouble? As robbery and murder were being committed intermittently by both sides, it is hard to give a categorical answer to that question. But certain important relevant facts are known. Much of the old interpretation depended on the assumption that the Zuurveld, the coastlands between the Bushman's and Fish Rivers, was colonial territory which the Kaffirs repeatedly 'invaded'. It is now clear that this area was occupied (and probably bought from the local Hottentots) by Kaffir tribesmen before the first white pioneers reached it. It follows that every attempt to 'clear the Kaffirs out of the Zuurveld' was an aggression, though not necessarily unprovoked, by the Europeans. This object was said to have been successfully achieved in the first of the wars, though it is known that the Zuurveld was again full of Kaffirs shortly afterwards. While the frontier farmers complained in 1779 of Kaffir raids on their cattle, which forced them to abandon their farms and led to hostilities, it is at least very probable that these raids were only reprisals for others made by the

Boers. One consequence of this outbreak was the appointment, already mentioned, of Adriaan van Jaarsveld as Commandant of the eastern frontier in 1780. The following year he began operations by a 'trick', namely the shooting of a number of Kaffirs while they were picking up pieces of tobacco that had been thrown to them. In those operations many of the enemy were shot and many of their cattle captured. Thus ended war number one.

The second war, in 1793, was quite certainly initiated by a farmer called Barend Lindeque, who had recently taken up a farm near the mouth of the Fish River. This was in country which the Bantu had occupied before the Europeans. Lindeque organised an unofficial commando, called in the help of Kaffirs hostile to those of the Zuurveld, and launched an attack. The desertion of one section of the Boers caused the defeat of the others, and this was succeeded by a Kaffir campaign of plunder extending far to the west. There followed a pacification which left the natives in the disputed area. The farmers had made many complaints, before this war, of losses of cattle and the murder of Hottentot servants. On analysis the losses are found not to be great, and most of them occurred in the Zuurveld; that is to say in the area to which the Kaffirs had a prior claim. Enormous losses were reported during the war itself: as the Landdrost of Graaff-Reinet pointed out, the losses claimed were eight times as large as the same farmers' total wealth in cattle as returned for purposes of taxation.

This Landdrost, H. C. D. Maynier, was very unpopular with the border farmers. Their hatred, vented on him, was in reality directed against certain fundamentals of policy which were common to the old company, the British and the Batavian régime. There were frequent complaints that the Boers were not allowed to pasture their stock beyond the Fish River in Kaffirland; that they were not allowed when on commando to capture some 'little Kaffirs'; that the Kaffirs were not driven out of the Zuurveld; and, of course, that all these governments preferred the interests of Hottentots to those of the farmers. The disaffection led, early in 1795, to a little revolution in Graaff-Reinet. The Landdrost was driven out and a republic proclaimed, with much effusion of French Revolutionary jargon. The British, on taking over the colony, had this insurrection on their hands.

The pacification of Graaff-Reinet which followed was only temporary. A new rising was provoked by the arrest of Adriaan van Jaarsveld for forging the date on a receipt. As this rebellion was being put down by troops from the Cape, the Kaffirs of the Zuurveld became alarmed for their safety, and it was they who started the conflict of 1799. The danger to the colonists was very greatly increased by the support which rebellious Hottentots, using firearms, gave to their enemies. The government made peace without victory; the British occupation was temporary and a large expenditure not justified.

Such were the first three Kaffir Wars, which illustrate clearly enough the turbulence of the eastern border. They were fought in the eighteenth century, before the influence of the London Missionary Society was felt in the colony. Something of the missionary spirit, however—or rather of the spirit of enlightened eighteenth-century Europe—inspired such officials as Maynier, and it was this that provoked the hostility and indignation of the frontier malcontents.

The border wars that began after the final conquest of the Cape by Great Britain filled the greater part of the nineteenth century. The endless chronicle of border forays, cattle-lifting, murder of white men and Hottentots, shooting down of Kaffirs and driving off their stock, and in the background the treaties, the 'policies' and the conflict between frontiersmen and Whitehall, is not easily intelligible to the casual reader of Theal or Cory. It can be made more so by concentrating on certain general features of the struggle.

The first feature to note is the constriction of the Bantu territory. A steady expansion to the south had been a condition on which the preservation of the old Bantu society had depended, just as expansion to the north and east had been necessary to a people with the social and economic traditions of the Boers. The Boers found means to continue their trekking, but in doing so they put a stop to Bantu expansion and, indeed, turned the foremost Kaffir ranks about and drove them back upon the others following behind. The congestion which resulted could lead only to war or to a revolution in the Kaffir mode of life. Both these consequences followed in turn.

Both were inevitable. The mere halting of the Bantu advance, not to speak of its reversal, produced a tension of which raids on the colonists' cattle and attempts to drive them 'into the sea' were symptoms. If these deeds were successfully punished, the colonial government could not always resist the demand for annexation of territory and its opening to white settlement. The governments of the trekker Republics made no attempt to resist it. This conceded, the tension in Kaffirland increased and led to fiercer conflict than before.

In the early decades of the century the importance of this tension was difficult to appreciate because the white men experienced Kaffir pressure on one side only, the Fish River frontier. Beyond lay the whole immensity of Africa—surely large enough for any number of savages? But when the Trekkers moved out of the colony in a body in the 'thirties, and new states were set up in the north, it was possible to watch the effect of any outside impact on all the tribes from the Fish to the Limpopo.

This is the second feature of the struggle to be observed. When South Africa was divided into several colonies and republics, the dealings of any of them with the tribes on its borders produced repercussions all over the sub-continent. This became an argument for uniting or federating them and devising a 'common native policy'; but it led also to unpopular moves by the British government, and further complicated the relations of British and Afrikaner colonists.

Thirdly, the long frontier struggles produced in the white people an attitude of mind that was out of date almost from its first appearance, yet has survived with great vitality to the present day. Even in the eighteenth century a few of the Bantu had entered the service of colonial farmers. Thereafter the break-up of tribes in native quarrels and the increasing congestion of Kaffirland led more and more to do so, even in the old colony. In Natal and the Republics they were the regular labour force. Yet the Europeans who employed them thought of the Bantu not as an element of their own society but as an enemy on the other side of a border-line. All, it was thought, with the exception of those whose labour was needed, should be driven over that line. These habits of thought, with the contradictions they involve, persist in the twentieth century under conditions which will be described later.

The fourth Kaffir War of 1811–12 served to drive the Bantu out of the territory west of the Fish River, an object long desired but never before attained. It should be remembered that this achievement came in the same year as the Black Circuit and the second (Cradock's) Hottentot ordinance; from the colonists' point of view a rather mixed bag of blessings. For the first time the westward movement of the Bantu was actually reversed. The result was significant. The Fish River had served to divide the followers of Gaika from those of Ndlambe. Gaika was a paramount chief, Ndlambe an uncle who had been regent during his minority. The regent had captured the loyalty of many of the tribesmen, and when the hereditary chief asserted his rights the tribe was split. Ndlambe crossed the Fish River to the west, but now the white men drove him back. In 1818 the two chiefs fought it out in the great battle of

Amalinde, a complete victory for Ndlambe. Gaika called on the colony for help, on the strength of a friendly agreement recently made with the Governor. The call was answered by the war of 1819.

The settlement of 1812 had excluded the Kaffirs from the land west of the Fish; that of 1819 removed them, in theory, from the 'Neutral Territory' between the Fish and the Keiskamma, intended as a buffer between the races; after the war of 1835 British rule was extended to the Kei, but this was the Governor's own policy and was disavowed by the Colonial Office. The empty 'Neutral' belt was, almost immediately, being described as the 'Ceded' Territory, and in a short time Kaffirs drifted back into it from one side and colonists were brought into it from the other. That the British government permitted the settlement of English and Hottentots there, but not at first Boers, was naturally a sore point with the latter. They had great hopes of farms beyond the Keiskamma in 1835, but these were dashed when Glenelg, then at the Colonial Office, insisted on the abandonment of the annexed territory.

The pressure on both sides was so great as to make a farce of the policy which the British Governors had taken over from their Dutch predecessors, the policy of strict separation of the races. In the seventeenth century the colonists had been forbidden to trade with Hottentots, even to admit them into their houses. Now there were similar attempts to forbid intercourse with the Bantu. At a fort in the neutral zone a fair was established at which trade was conducted. It was lucrative, and in due course the restriction to this one controlled mart was abandoned. Kaffirs crossed the border to work on the farms. The farmers, too, crossed the border—on patrols pursuing stolen cattle.

This pursuit of stolen cattle was one of the thorniest of the frontier difficulties. Could the spoor be followed to the first native kraal, and that kraal made responsible for the loss? Or was it innocent if the tracks could be shown to lead further? Could only the animals actually stolen be taken back? As to the number stolen, could the farmer's word be believed without supporting evidence? If there were to be a proper check on the frontiersman's rough and ready methods of justice, it might be better to allow pursuit only while the stolen cattle were still in sight; or perhaps to entrust the work to the regular troops and forbid it to the aggrieved civilians.

On all these points official policy was frequently changed. Complaints poured in from the colonists, that the restrictions prevented them from recovering their property; from the Kaffirs, that the lack of restrictions exposed innocent kraals to summary spoliation at all times.

This argument proceeded, and these changes of policy occurred, at a time when the natives on the eastern border of the colony were being subjected to exceptionally severe pressure from behind. It was occasioned by the rise of the 'Black Napoleon', Shaka. The illegitimate son of a petty chief, he had been brought up at the kraal of Dingiswayo, the paramount chief of a number of tribes in what is now Zululand. At his father's death Shaka was able with Dingiswayo's help to succeed him as chief of the insignificant Zulu tribe. When Dingiswayo was killed, in 1818, Shaka began his career of despotism and conquest. Friendly tribes were absorbed into the Zulu nation; enemies in all directions were exterminated.

It will be remembered that this year 1818 was one of inter-tribal war on the Cape frontier, followed by hostilities with the colony itself. These had been caused mainly by the pressure on the Kaffirs from the west. But from that moment the border tribes found themselves between two fires. Remnants of the broken people of Natal, fleeing before the Zulus, attacked others further to the south. This movement was the ground-swell behind the waves that constantly beat on the colonial frontier. In Natal, south of the Tugela, the only remaining inhabitants hid in inaccessible places. Some became cannibals.

The sharp point of the Zulu stabbing-spear was felt not only to the south, but to the north and west of Zululand as well. Tribes fleeing from the wrath of Shaka, if they were blessed with competent leadership, became in their turn a terror to those still further afield. In this way the Bantu of the inland plains were decimated, their tribes broken up, and the lucky ones found refuge among the natural defences of the Drakensberg. Here they were organised into a new people, the Basuto, by the self-made chief Moshesh. Others preferred aggression to security. Three bands of these swept across the High Veld like Huns, looting, absorbing and destroying, only to meet their Châlons at a place called Dithakong; there they were broken up by a party of the half-breed Griquas, who had guns and horses.

This battle was fought in 1823. At the same time the High Veld submitted to the even greater scourge of the Matabele, the followers of a Zulu general, Umsilikazi (or Moselekatse, as the Basuto called him) escaping from the anger of his master. The Matabele settled in what is now the western Transvaal, and like their kinsmen in Zululand made a wide belt of 'scorched earth' all round them.

The extent of all this slaughter has never been exactly measured, though wild guesses have been made. But the migrations of tribes have been observed. There is no doubt that the Tembus pressed upon the Cape frontier north of the Amatolas because they were propelled forward by the disturbances in Natal; nor that the disorganised refugees called Fingos, and ultimately given asylum in the colony, were the remains of tribes broken up in the same process. When the Voortrekkers entered what are now the northern Free State, southern Transvaal and Natal, they found these areas very thinly peopled by Bantu. To what extent the emptiness of the country was due to Shaka's wars is another of the unsolved riddles.

In Shaka's lifetime—he was murdered and succeeded by his brother Dingaan in 1828—there were at least empty spaces to take the shock of the Zulu explosion. But then the reconnaissance patrols of the Great Trek discovered these deserted lands, and beckoned to the main body of the trekkers to come on and take them. The story of the Trek will be told in the next chapter, but it will be necessary to anticipate it a little in order to follow the history of the frontier to its conclusion. It must be borne in mind, then, that emigrants from the Cape Colony set up in the interior various unstable republics with ill-defined boundaries. One area, Natal, was ultimately annexed by Britain. In another, which later became the Orange Free State, British sovereignty was maintained for a time. Britain's withdrawal from it was due mainly to the difficulty and expense of defending its frontier against the Basuto.

The Trekkers entered this area in some force in 1836. The 'Boer with his roer'—his old muzzle-loader—meant security from the old attacks, so the Basuto came down from their cramped quarters in the mountains to sow and reap their crops on the plains. Timid fugitives came out of their hiding-places in Natal, others poured across the boundary rivers to the safety of the white man's land. The Boers were glad enough to have a labouring population for their farms, but the expansion of tribal territories into the land claimed by the republics was another matter.

The republicans in Natal decided to allow five native families on every white man's farm, and to keep all other Africans at arm's length. On the frontiers the old colonial story of cattle-lifting and infiltration was repeated, and in 1840 a commando went forth to punish the Baca tribe on the southern border of Natal. The Bacas were defeated and a number of 'orphans' brought back as 'apprentices'. The attack on a tribe in that locality was an almost direct threat to the security of the Cape frontier, and the taking of apprentices touched the Colonial Office on one of its few raw spots. These events, then, led a reluctant British government to annex Natal to the Empire, as will be seen in the next chapter. They led also to the final development of a Cape policy which had been devised ten years earlier.

Even before the Trek the disturbances caused by Europeans as well as Africans beyond the colonial border were a ticklish problem for a government that was almost irrevocably determined not to push that border any further forward. At the end of 1834, therefore, a treaty was signed with the Griqua chief Waterboer (ruling the country north of the Orange near its junction with the Vaal), by which he agreed to keep order in his territory, to protect that sector of the colonial frontier, to assist the colony in the pursuit of criminals and bandits taking refuge in his country. In return he was given a salary and promised a supply of arms and ammunition. After the war of 1835 other treaties were made with many of the chiefs on the eastern frontier. After the expedition of the Natal Boers against their southern neighbours the Cape made a treaty with the Pondo chief Faku, recognising his authority over lands in which his writ had never run. And to another treaty Moshesh the Basuto chief put his mark.

The Basuto, however, were neighbours of the Trekkers in what became the Free State. On that border the old story of the Cape frontier was re-enacted, with the additional complication that the disturbances of the Cape and those of the Free State now had mutual repercussions. The Bantu of the old eastern frontier, the AmaXhosa, were in an explosive condition after being checked in the west by the colony. A trivial incident was enough to produce the war of 1846–7 (the Seventh), which broke out at a time when the British authorities were having difficulties with the Trekkers north of the Orange, and when those of Natal were leaving that colony because the Union Jack now flew there.

The peace of 1847 involved the annexation of the old neutral territory to the colony, and that of the country between Keiskamma and Kei to the Empire as the province of British Kaffraria. Apart from troops, officials and a handful of other Europeans this territory was inhabited entirely by Africans, who had undertaken in 1847 to obey such rules as Sir Harry Smith imposed on them. Among other barbarities that they were expected to abandon were the punishment of people guilty of witchcraft and 'the sin of buying wives'. Bantu society was not ready for such revolutionary changes.

The restive chiefs of British Kaffraria, backed by a witch-doctor

called Umlanjeni, prepared to strike once again at the white man.
When they did so the repercussions were felt over the whole of
South Africa. The frontier colonists expected trouble, and induced
Sir Harry Smith to come east and see for himself. The Governor
summoned the chiefs of the new province to meet him at Kingwilliamstown in October, 1850. Most of the important ones failed
to appear, so Sandile, the principal offender, was deposed and a
well-qualified European appointed in his place. A small military
force which was sent in December to seek out the deposed chiefs was
ambushed at the Boomah Pass; on Christmas Eve the frontier
villages of military settlers were overwhelmed, the colony invaded
and the Eighth Kaffir War begun.

The war was complicated by the desertion of an important
section of the Hottentots to the enemy. As usual, the operations of
the British forces were inconclusive because of the crudeness of the
Kaffir economic and political organisation. There was no capital,
no nerve-centre or depot whose capture would paralyse the enemy.
Forests, kloofs and mountain fastnesses were scoured, few Kaffirs
seen, yet when the troops had passed the barbarians returned to their
old haunts and continued as before. When Sir George Cathcart
succeeded Sir Harry Smith in 1852 he introduced new methods
which soon proved effective. Small and cheap defensive works were
built in large numbers to hold the country that had been cleared.
The colonists were told that if they did not turn out on commando
in full force the regular troops might be withdrawn. Early in 1853
the last of the rebel chiefs submitted. More land, to the north of
British Kaffraria, was annexed to the colony, and much in both
territories was in due course opened up to white settlement.

The operations against the Kaffirs had extended as far as the
Orange River, so that the Basuto chief Moshesh was brought into
contact with the disturbance. He had, in any case, regular feuds with
many of his neighbours, and these were now conducted more fiercely
than before. The early successes of the Kaffirs against the colony
in 1851 stimulated the restless ambition of chiefs from the Keiskamma to the Limpopo. Cattle-lifting and border disputes between
Moshesh and his northern and western neighbours were intensified.

The British Resident in Bloemfontein assumed the responsibility
of keeping order among these quarrelling tribes. A small force, with
native auxiliaries, was sent to the assistance of one chief against
another. Moshesh intervened and won a complete victory at Viervoet
in June, 1851. The British Resident had to retire from the contest,
and the news of the famous victory spread southwards to Kaffraria

and northwards to the Transvaal. In that turbulent land, whose independence had just been recognised by the British, two little campaigns were fought in August, 1852. One was against the Bapedi of Sekhukhuneland, who were besieged on a hill fortress and reduced by thirst. The other was directed against the Bakwena on the western border. The republican pretext—an afterthought—was that the Bakwena had given shelter to a fugitive chief whose followers had since the news of the Basuto success become troublesome cattle-lifters, and who had fled when summoned to appear before the nearest court. Actually the desire for land and labour inspired the attack. The Bakwena were defeated and the vacant house of their missionary, Dr Livingstone, found to have been broken open and pillaged. Livingstone believed, possibly with some justification, that the Boers had done this, and through him the little expedition received wide and one-sided publicity in England.

The peace of 1853 was therefore a precarious one. At every point where the white man's land marched with the black man's there was tension and fear. How much longer would this dreary story continue? By a strange chance which could not be foreseen, it had already ended for the Cape Colony. The AmaXhosa, not yet effectively subdued by their enemies, became the victims of their own superstition.

During 1856 the natives of British Kaffraria and their kinsmen beyond the Kei were seized with an almost unaccountable madness. The story circulated that a young girl called Nongqause, when drawing water from a stream, had spoken with the spirits of the dead. Her uncle, who claimed to be something of an expert in such matters, then went to the stream and established contact with the ghostly visitors himself. Through him they gave their orders to the chiefs and people at large. The people were to kill and eat their cattle, consume all their crops; in short, to eat or destroy everything edible in their possession. Then, on a certain day—finally fixed at February 18, 1857—the miracle would occur. Two blood-red suns would rise—or alternatively one sun which would circle in the sky and then set in the east. A great hurricane would drive the white men and the unbelieving black men into the sea. Fields of ripe grain, herds of beautiful cattle, would miraculously appear. The deluded people actually made skin bags to receive the abundance of milk that was expected, and strengthened the props of their huts against the violence of the storm.

The colonial government tried in vain to stop the destruction. Defensive measures were therefore taken on the frontier, and stores of food collected. When the great day came, and no miracle, the spirit of the AmaXhosa was broken. The depth of the disillusionment was in proportion to the extravagance of the hope and excitement. Many made no effort at all, but sat down in groups to die. Some became cannibals. Others, emaciated and submissive, poured into the colony to beg for food and work.

British Kaffraria lost about two-thirds of its population. Some clans ceased to exist as effective units. Though one more Kaffir War was to come, twenty years later, the border disturbances of the old kind were over and race relations entered a new phase.

What lay behind this hallucination? It was generally believed that the whole thing was a device of the Paramount Chief Kreli, perhaps instigated by Moshesh, to goad his people to a desperate onslaught upon the colony. If so it was badly mismanaged; it is known in history as 'the suicide of the AmaXhosa'.

5

THE GREAT TREK

Long before the seventh and eighth Kaffir Wars the aspect of South African affairs had been profoundly changed by the Great Trek, 'the central event in the history of European man in southern Africa'.

The story of the Trek has been so thickly overlaid with the interpretations which later generations have given it in the light of their own experiences that there is some difficulty in seeing it as it appeared to contemporaries. On the one hand it has been regarded as the birth-struggle of a nation; on the other, by a natural reaction, as a mere continuation, on a larger scale, of the old frontier trekking in search of more and better land.

Neither of these explanations is adequate. As appeared later in the lands immediately north of the Orange River, there was a sharp distinction between the Voortrekkers and the older type of border expansionists who had for generations been moving further and further out and dragging the colonial frontier after them. The Voortrekkers deliberately left the frontier behind. Their motives were political, social, ideological if you like; and of course economic motives were inextricably interwoven with these. But from the short term point of view the trek meant, for many, economic loss and not gain. On the other hand the picture of an oppressed nationality struggling to be free has been overdrawn. The factors that go to the making of a nation were present, but they had to operate for a long time yet before producing a recognisable result.

The farmers of the eastern frontier had a sense of grievance and of frustration. Their position may be summed up by saying that, during the eighteenth century, they had evolved a pattern of life

in which their ideas, tastes, economic needs and practical abilities
were integrated and harmonised; and that in the nineteenth century
the survival of this way of life was endangered by the impact of the
outside world. By far the most important shock was that administered
to the old ideas on how to deal with Hottentots, Slaves and Kaffirs.
The Black Circuit and the Slagter's Nek episode had been dramatic
illustrations of the passing of the old order; the fiftieth ordinance of
1828 completed the process. Hottentots could no longer be kept in
their places. In 1834 slavery was abolished and the owners insufficiently compensated. The frontiersmen were not slave-owners
to any great extent, and were not much affected materially by the
emancipation. They objected to it as a sign of the times and as a part
of the whole social revolution which was destroying their world.
They complained also that the government would not protect them
against the depredations of the Kaffirs.

These complaints were not all the reflection of political principles.
Many people were conscious of practical grievances without concerning themselves overmuch with politics. If a man were summoned to a distant court to defend himself on a frivolous charge,
he might have to leave his wife and small children unprotected on a
dangerous frontier. His natural reaction was to demand that the
government should keep the Kaffirs at bay and not listen to Hottentots, but he might well be open to political conviction if only he were
given security.

To most of the Voortrekkers, however, it was a matter of principle.
Anna Steenkamp, in giving reasons for the emigration, said that it
was not so much 'their freedom that drove us to such lengths, as
their being placed on an equal footing with Christians, contrary to
the laws of God and the natural distinction of race and religion, so
that it was intolerable for any decent Christian to bow down beneath
such a yoke; wherefore we rather withdrew in order to preserve our
doctrines in purity'. Piet Retief, in a manifesto published in
Grahamstown, asserted that 'whilst we will take care that no one is
brought by us into a condition of slavery, we will establish such
regulations as may suppress crime and preserve proper relations
between master and servant'. Another of Retief's points reflected a
widely felt grievance: 'We complain of the unjustifiable odium which
has been cast upon us by interested and dishonest persons, under the
name of religion, whose testimony is believed in England to the
exclusion of all evidence in our favour.'

In addition to these there was another set of causes that increased
the discontent, but would hardly by themselves have provoked the

Trek. The colony was being anglicised in various ways. Between 1823 and 1828 English completely ousted Dutch as the official language. In 1828 the old courts were abolished, and although the new ones were technically an improvement they had no popular element like the old heemraden. In 1813 came a change in the land system. No more loan places were to be granted, but farms on perpetual quit-rent tenure, the rent varying with the value of the land and being much higher than the old recognition money. Some pressure was applied to the existing landholders to convert their tenures to the new system, and to pay the cost of a survey. It was hoped that farms that could be divided among heirs, together with the abolition of the old free access to land, might discourage the *Wanderlust* and cause families to strike roots in the soil.

Instead, the reform became a grievance—a birthright of the people had been taken away. In 1832 there was something worse. The shadow of Gibbon Wakefield fell across the colony: no more land to be granted except by auction sale after upset price and quit-rent had been fixed. Though this instruction seems not to have been carried out, the threat was alarming.

It is difficult to assess the relative importance of these factors. It may well be that, taken together, they gave the frontiersman a vague feeling that he no longer 'belonged'; that he was being surrounded by an alien environment and could not freely be himself. This feeling was not expressed by the trekkers who left accounts of their motives; they dealt with specific grievances, but their position at the time and their later history suggest that the general one may have been important.

By 1834 the idea of departing from the colony and severing their connection with it had been formulated and was widely supported by the eastern farmers. The matter was discussed in one farmhouse after another as visitors gathered for social occasions. Nothing was said in public, as it was feared the government might put obstacles in the way. One obstacle could certainly be foreseen—a prohibition of the export of powder and lead, and large quantities of these would be needed if the venture was to be a success. Supplies were therefore accumulated and hidden, and the large amounts so collected give some indication of how long the plan had been maturing.

The last straw, or rather straws, were provided by the British government's veto of the vagrancy law of 1834 and its reversal in 1836 of D'Urban's annexation of the province between Keiskamma and Kei. That annexation had given rise to hopes of land, and with other aspects of D'Urban's policy had suggested that a firm way with

Kaffirs might be expected of the government. When those hopes were dashed the emigration began to assume large proportions, but the first parties of trekkers had already departed by then. While the War of 1835 was being fought, some scouting parties, *commissie treks*, were spying out the land in various directions. Shaka had laid it waste, Dingaan had succeeded him, and Natal and the inland plains were found to be nearly empty of people.

In the same year the first important parties of emigrants, those of Louis Trichardt and 'Lang Hans' van Rensburg, crossed the Orange River. In the course of the next three years they were followed by many others, some in large parties under recognised leaders, others going as individual families—in the patriarchal sense of the word. The emigration from the old colony did not end in 1838 or at any other time, but only the pioneers are counted as Voortrekkers. They may have numbered about 12,000. They came in great majority from the eastern frontier districts such as Graaff-Reinet and Uitenhage.

Over the plains beyond the Orange the processions of tented ox-wagons moved slowly northward. The men and boys rode on horseback. Sometimes Hottentot or Kaffir servants drove the flocks and herds along with the party; commonly the white children had to do this, for few servants trekked with their masters. The plains were full of game, which were hunted and shot for food. Every now and then the company would stop at a place where the grazing was good and camp for days or weeks to rest the animals. There the children played with their toy wagons and clay oxen, which trekked and outspanned after the manner of the big ones. Clothes were washed, wagons mended, game brought in by the hunters, the children taught, religious services held; and then the trek was resumed.

Between the Orange and Modder rivers lay territory occupied, though sparsely, by a branch of the Griquas which was shortly to recognise Adam Kok III as its chief. In the same area were farmers from the northern districts of the colony—not Voortrekkers but migrants of the old type who had no quarrel with their government. The trekkers therefore passed over these lands, crossed the Modder, and foregathered at an isolated mountain beyond it called Thaba 'Nchu. This became the rendezvous at which large numbers collected in the course of 1836.

The parties of Trichardt and Van Rensburg were not there. They had crossed the Vaal, given the Matabele a wide berth, and advanced over highveld and bushveld to the distant Zoutpansberg. The Van Rensburg party pushed on to the Limpopo, where all were murdered by Africans. Trichardt remained a long time in the Zoutpansberg, hoping to renew contact with his friends from the south. A. H. Potgieter had visited him and promised to return. For good reasons, to be mentioned presently, Potgieter and others failed to appear. Trichardt then decided that communication with the Portuguese at Delagoa Bay was essential to the survival of his party. A letter was sent to the Governor, who could not read it; but he invited the trekkers to come down to him.

The journey was one that taxed the strength even of those tough pioneers to the limit. Over the mountains where the Olifants River breaks through to the lowveld the wagons had to be tobogganed with their wheels removed. Cattle died. Lions had to be warded off. In the lowveld the people were stricken by malaria. At Delagoa Bay Trichardt's wife, then the leader himself and many others died of it. A small remnant of the party took ship for Natal and there joined their friends.

As Trichardt had been moving northwards to the Zoutpansberg he was followed by the party under Potgieter, a leader who was destined ultimately to be more successful in the region which Trichardt abandoned. Makwana, a Bataung chief, welcomed these newcomers as likely to give him protection against the Matabele. In return for that protection and a gift of cattle he ceded to Potgieter the whole of the land between the Vet and Vaal rivers, reserving only a small area for his tribe. The main body of the party remained in this tract while their leader and a few others went northward to visit Trichardt. On his return, after promising to make contact with the latter again, Potgieter found that some small bands of his followers had been killed by the Matabele.

The trekkers now (in October, 1836) used what were to become their standard methods of defence against the Africans. Their wagons were drawn up in a circle or *laager* on a hill afterwards called Vegkop. Three thousand Matabele attacked this camp, which was defended successfully by forty men and boys. They had firearms, but it has been reasonably suggested that the difference in effect between an assegai and one of those muzzle-loading *roers* was less than between the latter and a modern rifle. The camp was saved, but all the cattle were driven off by the enemy and the defenders became immobile. Their friends at Thaba 'Nchu were informed, cattle were sent to Vegkop and the party was brought back to the rendezvous.

Another important band of trekkers had then reached Thaba 'Nchu, led by the prosperous—almost dandy—wagon-maker of Graaff-Reinet, Gert Maritz. When the whole population of the

C

camps assembled at the end of 1836 to adopt a form of government
and to choose leaders, the offices of Chairman of the Volksraad
(people's council) and Landdrost of the court were given to Maritz,
while Potgieter became Commandant and Chairman of the Council
of War. Potgieter and his followers regarded this as a snub. The seeds
of dissension had been sown.

The seeds were watered when, four months later, a further
political development at Thaba 'Nchu followed the arrival of the
greatest of the trekkers, Piet Retief. Retief was chosen 'Governor',
Maritz Landdrost, and Potgieter nothing at all. From that time
Potgieter went his own way. Early in 1837 he had led an expedition
against the Matabele of the western Transvaal—their headquarters
were in the present district of Marico—had punished them severely
and had captured many cattle. In October he repeated this exploit,
defeating the enemy so effectively in a nine days' battle that the
Matabele left the country, wandered in the wilderness for a few years
and then settled beyond the Limpopo in what is now Matabeleland,
Potgieter, who had purchased the land between the Vet and Vaal
rivers from Makwana, could now claim to hold by right of conquest
the whole area which Umsilikazi had dominated by terror. He settled
down in it with his followers and founded the town of Potchefstroom.
Some of his party remained at Winburg, a village they had built in
the Vet-Vaal territory in 1837.

The main body of the emigrants, who had elected Retief and
Maritz, had no taste for Potgieter's kingdom. Their hearts were set
on Natal, the future Garden Colony, the land described by scouting
parties as flowing with milk and honey and, by grace of Shaka and
Dingaan, empty of people. Moving slowly towards the Drakensberg
passes they camped near the edge of the plateau at Blyde Vooruitzicht
—Happy Prospect. Retief took a small party down to the coast and
up to Zululand, where Dingaan received them and undertook to
grant Natal to them if they would first recover some cattle taken
from him by the Batlokua chief Sikonyela. It had been said that white
men had taken the cattle, and they must prove their innocence and
good faith by bringing them back. In due course Retief returned
with the cattle to Dingaan's kraal and received the land grant in
writing, while the bulk of his followers descended the mountain
passes into Natal. Retief and his company numbered sixty-seven
Europeans and about thirty Hottentots. On February 6, 1838, they
were entertained in the royal kraal before taking their leave. At a
command from Dingaan his warriors seized them all, dragged them
to a neighbouring hillock and clubbed them to death.

Many reasons can be given for this massacre. The chief had complained that though the cattle taken from Sikonyela had been returned to him, the guns and horses had not. When it was pointed out that these had been the white men's and not Zulu property in the first instance, he let this pass. More important were two factors of a superstitious kind. When Dingaan had murdered his brother Shaka, the latter had taunted him with a prophecy: it will not be you, he said, but the white men who will rule over the land. This had weighed on the assassin's mind. And after Potgieter's victory over the Matabele, Retief had pointed the moral to Dingaan: 'thus God punishes wicked tyrants'. Zulu tradition adds another and very curious factor. About two years before Retief first visited Dingaan the latter's kraal had been reached by Piet Uys of the *commissie trek* to Natal. Asked his name, he gave it as Piet. Retief, in answer to a similar question, said *his* name was Piet. Was he the only Piet in command of the Voortrekkers? He was. On the first occasion he was a tall man with a rough voice and a large black beard. Now he was a short man with a soft voice and a brownish beard. Verily, these men were magicians! It may be that the witch-doctors developed such thoughts in the chief's mind. On the fatal day the command he gave to his warriors was 'Kill the wizards!'

No sooner was this deed done than the *impis* set out to destroy the rest of the emigrants, who were scattered along various rivers in the neighbourhood of the present Estcourt, Weenen and Colenso. The most advanced parties were surprised and overwhelmed at night. Those further back formed *laagers* in time and warded off the attack. The Zulus retired, but the outlook for the trekkers was bleak.

Help came from their friends beyond the Drakensberg, but an expedition which Uys and Potgieter led against the Zulus was a failure. Uys was killed, Potgieter returned home over the mountains, and the remaining leader in Natal, Maritz, died. Then the *deus ex machina* appeared—Andries Pretorius, the last great trekker leader to leave the old colony. He put heart into the people, made careful plans and led a strong force into Zululand. It formed a *laager* beside a river, soon to become the Blood River, and was attacked by the whole might of the Zulus on December 16, 1838. The enemy was beaten off with disastrous losses. Dingaan was not destroyed, but this event was the culmination of the Trek. The Zulu military power was broken for a generation. It was on December 16, 1938, that the centenary celebrations reached their climax.[1]

There were more expeditions against Dingaan; many of his own

[1] See p. 169.

people turned against him, he was driven out as a fugitive and finally done to death in Swaziland. The Voortrekkers could at last settle down in Natal and establish a republic. Pietermaritzburg was founded. In accordance with a vow made before Blood River, the Church of the Vow was built at that place, and December 16 was ordered to be solemnly commemorated every year. Then the trekkers ran into another obstacle—their old enemies the British.

The British had in fact reached Natal before the trekkers. A handful of adventurers had settled at Port Natal in 1824 and, thanks to some effective medical attention to Shaka, had received from him a part of the same land that Dingaan was afterwards to grant to Retief. There were no white women in this party. Some of the Englishmen 'went native' and gathered under their sway clans of refugees from the Zulu despotism. From time to time they requested that the territory should be annexed by Great Britain. In 1835 they planned a town which they called D'Urban after the Cape Governor, and the missionary ex-naval officer Allen Gardiner was appointed magistrate there by the Cape authorities. Still the British government refused to annex Natal; it was firmly resolved not to extend its commitments in that part of the world.

When Retief came down on his first visit to Dingaan he went to D'Urban and was well received by the inhabitants, who welcomed the prospect of reinforcements to defend them against the Zulus.

The British government, however, gathered from missionary reports coming in after Blood River that a harmless African population was threatened with extermination or enslavement by aggressive Boers. When these Boers established their headquarters at Pietermaritzburg and set up their Republic of Natalia, their contact with the outside world through Port Natal and the facility with which they could import arms and ammunition began to look sinister in Whitehall. Possessing a port, they might admit foreign Powers to South Africa. A hostile naval base would directly threaten the Cape and the Indian Ocean. The merchants of the Cape, moreover, had counted on monopolising the trade with the trekkers, and the government of the colony on monopolising the customs duties. So the situation in Natal gave rise to protests.

From the end of 1838 to the end of 1839 a small British force was stationed at Durban—to use the modern spelling—for the purpose of closing the harbour except to trade under licence from the Cape government. As there was still no intention to annex the country, this force was then withdrawn. Not long afterwards the Republic made the serious blunder, already referred to, of attacking the Baca tribe to the south and carrying off 'apprentices'. The direct consequence of this action was the arrival of British troops at Durban in May, 1842. The Republic was to be discouraged from further adventures that might disturb the tribes on the colonial border. The Boers regarded this as an invasion of their country. The British authorities took the view that the trekkers were still what they had always been, British subjects, and could not change their status by migrating into the wilds: *nemo potest exuere patriam*. Hostility to the British troops would, on this view, be rebellion.

However that might be, hostilities broke out. The British troops, in a camp protected by simple earthworks, were besieged by the Boers for a month. When the siege began a local resident, Dick King, was ferried with his horse and African servant across the bay, and then rode the 600 miles to Grahamstown in ten days to call for help. The romantic exploit of this Paul Revere of South African history barely succeeded in its object. When the besieged force was very near the end of its resources, the firing of rockets and the booming of guns at sea heralded the arrival of two ships with reinforcements. The bar was forced, troops landed and the Boers driven away.

Great Britain thus found herself more deeply committed to operations in Natal than she had intended or foreseen. Negotiations at Pietermaritzburg revealed divisions among the trekkers. The agent of the Cape government was cornered by a crowd of angry women and for two hours given a piece of their mind. Some of the Boers from beyond the Drakensberg came down to defend their rights. But when they found that the Commissioner was not interested in their part of the country they went home, and the men in authority at Pietermaritzburg finally but reluctantly accepted the British terms. Natal thus became a British possession in 1843 and two years later was organised as a dependency of the Cape.

A few of the Boers were content with this arrangement, and settled down on their farms, mostly in the northern parts of the new colony. The majority was of a different opinion. The British authorities, they complained, were allowing tens of thousands of natives to pour into the colony and squat on land, much of which the Boers claimed as their farms. Full-sized claims were not recognised unless there had been *bona fide* occupation for twelve months. How could farms have been occupied at that time, when the men had been fighting and the countryside was unsafe? The new régime, moreover, insisted on making no distinction between black and white in the eyes of the law. It was to establish just such distinctions that the pioneers had trekked. So there was nothing to do but go back

over the Drakensberg, to join their friends in the Winburg–
Potchefstroom area. And this after the martyrdom of Retief, the
massacre of Weenen and the victory of Blood River!

Early in 1848 Sir Harry Smith, the new Governor of the Cape,
who had just brought the seventh Kaffir War to an end, arrived in the
country below the Drakensberg where some of the trekkers were
tarrying on their way out of Natal. In addition to the governorship
he held the new office of High Commissioner for South Africa,
which enabled him to represent the British government outside the
colony itself. He visited this band of trekkers with the object of
persuading them to stay where they were. He had known these
Boers when he and they had fought together against the Kaffirs
thirteen years earlier. He had got on well with them and they had
trusted him. But even his personal influence could not now persuade
them to remain in Natal. As they went their way, Sir Harry issued a
proclamation annexing the territory between the Orange and the
Vaal—the Orange River Sovereignty—to the Crown.

Many of the trekkers received this news very bitterly. After all
their sufferings and hard-won victories they found Britain coming
after them to snatch the rewards out of their hands. First Natal,
now the Sovereignty—and this included the land which Potgieter
had fairly bought from Makwana. Sir Harry Smith was an impulsive
and over-confident man. He believed the majority of the Boers
trusted him and would support his action. From the legal point of
view they were all British subjects; if they owed allegiance to the
Crown it was better that they should get some protection and
effective government in return for that allegiance. And the Cape
Colony could not afford to have its frontiers perpetually endangered
by the native wars in which the trekkers got themselves involved.
The British government reluctantly consented to the annexation
of the Sovereignty on the understanding that it was necessary to
prevent disorder and bloodshed, that the people of the territory
wanted it, and that it would reduce the burden on the Treasury.

Sir Harry had been hasty, but it was not his fault that he was not
justified by the sequel. True, to judge by the signatures to petitions,
some three-quarters of the Boers in the Sovereignty were opposed
to the annexation, but this opposition could be expected to diminish.
A substantial minority welcomed a government which promised
greater efficiency and better amenities than could, as yet, be provided
by themselves. And the ranks of the majority began to thin when
malcontents in the Winburg district began a new trek over the Vaal.
Those abandoning Natal moved in the same direction. All that were

most irreconcilably anti-British were gathered into the cave of Adullam that was to be the Transvaal.

Pretorius, who was now in that country, could not accept the loss of the Sovereignty as final. He had a grudge against the Cape Governor for annexing the territory, since Sir Harry had asked him to ascertain the views of the people, and, as he understood the arrangement, there was to be no annexation until their views were known. From the meetings held in various places by Pretorius, as well as from the petitions presented, it was evident that the Boers were hostile. Yet the annexation had been proclaimed without waiting for the results of this investigation.

Pretorius therefore brought a commando across the Vaal, gathered support as he advanced through the Sovereignty, chased the British Resident from Bloemfontein and meant to establish the independence of all the Boers north of the Orange River. This scheme was frustrated by Sir Harry Smith at the 'severe skirmish' of Boomplaats. Pretorius left the Sovereignty with a price on his head, followed by large numbers of the die-hards. Their places were taken by new immigrants, of the opposite political persuasion, from the Cape Colony.

The difference in political character between the lands north and south of the Vaal was further accentuated at the beginning of 1852 by the action of two special Commissioners sent to the Sovereignty by the British government. It was obvious that the Transvalers would not willingly submit to British rule, and likely that they would repeat their former attempt to expel the British from the Sovereignty. If an agreement could be made with them, there might be a chance of consolidating the régime south of the Vaal. By the Sand River Convention, therefore, the independence of the Transvalers was recognised. Sixteen years after the beginning of the Trek Great Britain abandoned her claim to the allegiance of these trekkers at least. Some 20,000 of them were now free to realise in the far interior the aims which they had pursued for so long in the wilderness.

This concession may perhaps be regarded as inevitable, or at least as wise and statesmanlike. The step which followed was of a different character, one of a series of blunders and vacillations which the British government committed either through ignorance of South African affairs or indifference to them or through lack of foresight. One example of this had already occurred in Natal. After repeatedly declining to annex that territory Britain suddenly did so, but only after the trekkers had established themselves there with great difficulty and loss. From the Whitehall point of view this was a step taken reluctantly for the sake of strategic security and under pressure from Cape interests and missionary influences. From the trekker point of view it was a dog-in-the-manger attitude and became for generations a bitter memory to complicate South African affairs.

Now the annexation of the Sovereignty, the battle of Boomplaats, the concession of independence to the Transvaal, the migration of republicans across the Vaal and of loyalists across the Orange had collected there, among about 10,000 settlers, a majority loyal to the Crown. The original nucleus of this party had been the emigrants from the northern districts of the Cape who had come before the Great Trek and did not feel the political impulses of that movement. The natural destiny of the Sovereignty, in the eyes of many on both sides of the Orange, was annexation to the Cape Colony. Had this occurred the old Colony would have dominated the sub-continent sufficiently, perhaps, to avert many of the disasters that were to come. Her liberal institutions and traditions would have reached the Vaal and, perhaps, withstood the pressure of the opposite traditions from beyond that river. There would have been no dispute over the diamond fields. Some of the obstacles that stood in the way of federation in the 'seventies would never have been erected.

The price Britain would have to pay for these benefits was an expenditure of money on defence which, though trivial in comparison with the sums that had ultimately to be spent because the opposite policy was adopted, were more than the British treasury and public were then prepared to pay. Moshesh in 1851 had discomfited the British Resident at Viervoet. The Cape Governor Cathcart in 1852 tried to teach the Basuto a lesson, but withdrew after the indecisive engagement at Berea. Thus the settlers in the Sovereignty lost confidence in the government's determination or ability to defend them, and those who supported the Resident in his operations against Moshesh were selected by that chief for spoliation and destruction. The burghers therefore would not turn out on commando. A fair-sized army would have overawed the Basuto and rallied the white inhabitants, but the government in Britain was unwilling to provide one and its agents on the spot would not take the responsibility of badgering it into doing so. The tide of opinion in England was flowing strongly against the possession of colonies. Disraeli had just been calling them 'millstones round our necks'. The corn laws and the navigation acts had been repealed. Free Trade, 'Little Englandism' and economy combined forces with the colonial reform and self-government party to attack expansion and Colonial Office rule. The decision was therefore made to abandon the Sovereignty.

Representatives elected by the people protested. They were

then dismissed as 'obstructionists' and a body of republicans consulted instead. Their party, hitherto weak, increased in strength as news arrived of petitions against abandonment which had been drawn up in the Cape Colony and cast the same sort of aspersions on the Sovereignty people as the missionaries had often done on the Boers in general—'unjustifiable odium'. One of these odious petitions came from the Swellendam presbytery of the Dutch Reformed Church, which now spoke the same language as the London Missionary Society.

The contemplated step was taken in 1854. The Orange River Sovereignty became the Orange Free State. As has been hinted above, the change was ultimately to strengthen the Transvaal influence throughout South Africa. It even formed a precedent against the later retention of the Transvaal by Great Britain. When a deputation from that territory interviewed Sir Michael Hicks Beach in 1879 to demand independence, and he asked them to name any country over which the British Crown had voluntarily renounced its sovereignty, Kruger immediately named the Free State. Yet the policy of 1854 was initiated not by the Transvaal but by Great Britain, and the historian must judge policies by their effectiveness in serving the ends they were meant to serve. This one was therefore a blunder.

The burghers of the Free State drew up a constitution and elected a president. Two years later the people of the South African Republic, as the Transvaal was now called, took the same step. But whereas the Free State people were united in a common loyalty, their northern neighbours were deeply affected by the anarchic conditions of their long trek. During all those years the primary loyalty of the trekker had been to the leader of his own little company. As all the more determined bands arrived in the country beyond the Vaal the rivalry of their leaders produced political dissension that sometimes ended in violence.

Potgieter in 1845 moved from Potchefstroom to the far north-east and founded Andries-Ohrigstad in an unhealthy locality indeed, but far from British influence and within reach of Delagoa Bay. This settlement was soon moved to the neighbouring but healthy site of Lydenburg. The emigrants who abandoned Natal and the Sovereignty moved into the vacated district of Potchefstroom; but some of these, too, preferred Lydenburg. At the latter place therefore Potgieter and his supporters were no longer in undisputed control; so they trekked again, this time to the remote Zoutpansberg where the leader had visited Trichardt in the first days of the trek. Four

Commandants-General now divided the allegiance of the burghers. In Potchefstroom and Rustenburg, its northern neighbour, each could choose either Pretorius or Potgieter for his lord—a curious and baneful example of non-territorial sovereignty. Lydenburg and Zoutpansberg refused to acknowledge the constitution adopted by the other districts.

Though nominal unity was achieved by 1860, the anarchical principal had bitten deeply into the people. In later generations, under vastly different conditions, the tendency to resolve differences of opinion by secession and *non possumus* was still strong. That tendency was apparent in the very first year of the trek—it was implicit in the trek itself—it appeared in the republic of Natalia and again in the South African Republic, but not in the Free State.

The original constitutions of the two surviving republics are of interest both for their differences and for their similarities; as illustrations of the reaction against the latter-day liberalism of the Cape and of the experience gained in the course of the trek. The Free State constitution was modelled to some extent on that of the second French Republic, recently defunct. It was a concise statement of fundamental law and owed its stability partly to the circumstances of the country, partly to the provision that it could be altered only by three-quarters majorities in the Volksraad in two successive sessions. The 'fundamental law' of the South African Republic, on the other hand, was a diffuse document in which constitutional matters are mixed up with the 'wishes' of the people on various subjects, the minute regulation of the proceedings of clerks and poundmasters, and the hours at which the public offices shall be open: '10 a.m. to 3 p.m., Saturdays, Sundays and holidays excepted'. As a further encouragement to civil servants 'all services required for the public shall be rewarded by the public'. This constitution was, on paper, even more rigid than that of the Free State, since Article 42 provided that 'any matter discussed shall be decided by three-fourths of the votes recorded.' One of the interesting things about the constitutional history of the South African Republic is that Article 42 was a dead letter from the beginning, and that no one seems ever to have drawn attention to its existence; except, in 1889, to alter 'three-fourths' to 'a decided majority'. In practice the constitution was so flexible that it could be altered by mere resolution of the Volksraad.

Both countries had the usual organs of central government: an elected Volksraad of one chamber, a popularly elected President and, to assist him, an Executive Council partly of office-holders and partly of members chosen by the Volksraad; a compromise, therefore, between responsible government and the separation of powers. Both had Landdrosts and Heemraden on the old Cape model in each district. The only central court was a bench of several Land-drosts, and this made an annual circuit. The President, too, was required to visit every district town once a year.

The military system was based on the frontier methods of the old colony. Every burgher between sixteen and sixty was liable for service. The burghers of a ward elected their Field-Cornet, and (in the Transvaal) Assistant-Field-Cornets; the burghers of the whole district elected their Commandant. These officers, in the Free State, chose a Commandant-General in time of war to command them, but the office did not exist in peace-time. In the northern republic there was always a Commandant-General, chosen by popular vote. The army, therefore, consisted of units and sub-units of irregular size, divided geographically and without any fixed numerical strength, and commanded by elected officers. The Field-Cornets were officials with civil as well as military duties. There was no military uniform.

In the South African Republic the *vox populi* was listened to with great respect. Every proposed law, except such as 'brooked no delay', was to be published in the *Government Gazette* three months before its introduction in the legislature, so that 'the public' might make its views heard in time. It had been usual in the early evanescent trekker republics for the Sovereign People to attend the sessions of its representatives and to make its own contributions to their discussion. The Transvaal constitution would not infringe this liberty further than to say that 'no person present, who is not a member of the Volksraad, may speak, except when he has to reply to a question from the Chairman'.

As the two republics were founded by trekkers it was natural that they should admit newcomers to citizenship on easy terms. A landowner acquired the right immediately in the Transvaal, after a year in the Free State; even without land, one year's residence in the Transvaal, three in the Free State, sufficed. An oath of allegiance was required, but all these arrangements seemed, in the 'fifties, to be straightforward and uncontroversial. In the next generation the survival of the South African Republic was thought to depend on their revision.

There was another, an indispensable, qualification for citizenship —a white skin. 'The people' of the South African Republic 'desire to permit no equality between coloured people and the white inhabitants, either in Church or State'.

6

DIAMONDS AND ENGLISHMEN

The Cape Colony, before 1820, contained no more than a handful of people of British origin. Apart from official and military personnel there were a few merchants in the Cape peninsula and an insignificant number of farmers. This situation was slightly modified in 1817, when a few hundred settlers arrived; but not seriously till 1820. The '1820 Settlers' were the first considerable body of British colonists to make their homes in South Africa.

They came for three reasons. The aftermath of war produced depression in Britain, unemployment and a rise in the poor rates. The government was anxious to divert the flow of emigration from the United States to the British colonies. And Lord Charles Somerset wanted a dense white population on the Cape's eastern border as a barrier against invasion. This need was felt all the more urgently after the Kaffir War of 1819.

On certain conditions free passages to the Cape were provided, and small land grants were to be made in the Zuurveld area between the Bushman's River and the Fish. The land and the passages were not to be granted to individuals but to the heads of parties, each of whom was to bring not fewer than nine other men with him. The leader would receive a hundred acres for each man in his party. Most of the parties, however, did not actually consist of a master and his dependants as envisaged by Lord Charles, but of independent emigrants who chose a head as their intermediary; the latter agreed to divide the land among the party on arrival. They came from all parts of the United Kingdom and from all classes of society, but with a great preponderance of artisans, tradesmen and labourers.

Rather more than half were agriculturalists by origin and experience, but that of course would not help them much in South African farming. At the same time as the organised parties, many came at their own expense. Altogether nearly 5000 settlers arrived in 1820 and 1821.

The shores of Algoa Bay were crowded with tents. As more ships unloaded their passengers the earlier arrivals departed in wagons hired from the Dutch farmers. At last all were deposited on the locations between Grahamstown and the coast. There, with a hundred acres to a man, they must fend for themselves. A closely packed agricultural population must create a smiling countryside out of the wilderness and build up a human wall against the Kaffirs. The settlers were to have no slaves, and there could be no question of the traditional 6000-acre farms.

This scheme was misconceived. It could not be known in advance that disease and flood would destroy three successive crops of wheat. On the other hand the high wages of artisans and labourers in the villages of the colony would be an insuperable menace to the policy of keeping the settlers on the land, and the large farms granted to the older population would provide grounds for the argument that the grants in the Zuurveld were too small to work. These things at least might have been foreseen.

The canvas camp at Algoa Bay grew into a town. Sir Rufane Donkin, acting Governor while Lord Charles was on leave, named it Port Elizabeth after the wife he had lost, 'one of the most perfect of human beings'. A few of the settlers of 1820, fishermen from Deal, refused to budge from it when they had landed, and plied their old trade in the bay. Others deserted their locations in Albany, as the new frontier district had been named, and made their way to Grahamstown or back to Port Elizabeth, to trades and crafts, to a competence or even more. Some went to towns further afield, others took to trading with the Kaffirs and hunting in the interior. Two years after their arrival three-quarters of the settlers had abandoned the land for other occupations.

This perversion of the 1820 scheme from its original intention was to have such far-reaching effects that it is worth while to consider the influences bearing upon it then and later. The agrarian conditions in the colony did not favour intensive agriculture. As the settlers who remained on the land in Albany enlarged their farms they developed into a prosperous community, but largely because they turned to sheep-farming. It was thus shown that an English-speaking rural population could be established in the country, provided that it worked the land extensively, almost in the manner of the Dutch farmers. The numbers that could be settled on the land were therefore severely limited by the amount available in possession of the Crown. Within the existing limits of the colony this hardly extended beyond Albany itself, deserted by the Boers because of Kaffir irruptions. Thus a British farming community established itself along the frontier, from the Winterberg and the valleys of the Baviaans, the Koonap and the Kat, through Albany and along the coast to Port Elizabeth and Uitenhage. In this area, too, there were towns; but elsewhere the British element was purely urban, except where occasional farms were bought by the more prosperous. This happened in the neighbourhood of Cape Town and in a few isolated pockets elsewhere. Some notable families settled in the wild coastlands of Knysna.

As the frontier was pushed further eastward, British colonists settled on the new lands of Queenstown, Cathcart and British Kaffraria. The great empty interior was occupied by the trekking Boers. When these abandoned the greater part of Natal, that colony was the sole remaining area available for British rural settlement. In a very short time even this was seriously diminished by the rapid influx of Africans across the borders. Attempts were made to settle British immigrants on what remained. The enterprise of J. C. Byrne brought out about 4500 settlers between 1849 and 1851, but the land grants were too small to be remunerative. Exactly as had happened in Albany, the majority left the land for the towns, while some abandoned the colony altogether. The freedom of sale which had prevailed caused large areas to be bought by speculators. These usually found that charging a rent to African tenants was the most profitable way of using the land, and 'Kaffir farming' thus became an obstacle to the settlement of European immigrants.

The conditions exhibited, and even created, by these early schemes determined the fate of later settlers. A few more batches of organised and assisted immigrants came from Britain before 1870, notably in 1858–62 when nearly 10,000 were brought to the Cape. Many of these left the colony during the prolonged depression of the 'sixties. Most of the others settled in the towns. Then diamonds were discovered, Kimberley sprang into existence and immigration no longer needed official encouragement.

Here is the net result: in 1891, as far as can be gauged from the inadequate census returns of that year, about 35 per cent of the white population of the Cape Colony was of British origin. Of that element nearly three-quarters lived in urban areas. Of the whole British section between 25 and 30 per cent were concentrated in the Cape peninsula, a similar proportion in the towns of the Eastern Province, and perhaps 12 per cent in Kimberley. The rural areas of the old eastern frontier region accounted for most of the rest.

Of the Afrikaans-speaking people, on the other hand, almost 80 per cent were country-dwellers. The distinction between town and country, the conflict between urban and rural interests and ideas, almost coincided with the difference in national origins and the deeper difference between the seventeenth and nineteenth centuries. The coincidence was in fact greater even than the figures suggest, because the Afrikaners in the towns tended to be anglicised; the British element in the Dutch countryside tended to a less extent, and much more slowly, to be assimilated to the people among whom it lived.

The anglicising process was advanced both by the arrival and concentration of the British colonists and by the deliberate policy of the government. In 1822 six schoolmasters were brought from Scotland to open, in the principal towns and villages, schools of a more advanced kind than had yet been seen in the colony. The medium of instruction was English, and many of the older inhabitants regarded the schools with hostility on that account. But the opposition was gradually broken down by the educational advantages offered. The influence of the schools was felt much more in the towns where they were situated than in the countryside which had no such easy access to them. As they began to train up a new generation a further step followed. On the initiative of people of both white nationalities the South African College was founded in Cape Town in 1829; of a status intermediate between high school and university college, it was the beginning of higher education in the country, and the parent of a school and a university in the fullness of time.

Other steps were taken to the same end. English was made the sole official language of the colony, by stages beginning in 1823 and culminating in 1828. At the same time as the schoolmasters, clergymen were recruited in Scotland, taken to Holland for a quick course in the language, and appointed to Dutch Reformed livings in the colony. The ultimate result was to turn the descendants of these Murrays and Frasers, Robertsons and Sutherlands, into Afrikaners; but in the meantime the English language was heard in consistory, presbytery and synod. Dutch Reformed churches came, as the process went on, to hold some services in English. It looked to some people as if the anglicisation of the colony would be complete.

These were the measures of Lord Charles Somerset. There were other aspects of anglicisation for which the Tory Governor had not bargained when he brought out the Settlers. They came from an England hot with political passion over Cobbett and Hunt and the suspension of Habeas Corpus, over Sidmouth, Peterloo and the Six Acts. When the affairs of the Albany settlement went awry, the new colonists turned to thoughts of organisation, public meeting and petition. They discovered that all these could be, and were, prohibited by the word of an autocratic Governor. The birthrights of Englishmen were taken away from them. Other measures, as we have seen, appeared to be taking away the birthrights of the *trekboer*. The two nationalities reacted differently, each in its characteristic way, to threats which they regarded in much the same light. The Boer trekked. The Englishman founded a newspaper, sent protests to England, got the Whig M.P.s on to their feet to attack the house of Beaufort, to expose the tyranny of its scion the Governor of the Cape, to belabour the shaky Tory ministry with every complaint that arrived from Cape Town or Port Elizabeth.

The Liverpool Government had not so secure a hold on office that it could safely expose itself to this attack. These were times in which the liberty of the subject and of the press could no longer be tampered with as in the heyday of the anti-Jacobin reaction. It became known at Westminster that South Africa's first newspaper, launched in 1824, had been suppressed by Lord Charles for refusing to be silent about a libel case in which he was concerned, and the publisher expelled from the colony. The first magazine, started in the same year, collapsed after airing the grievances of the Albany settlers and incurring the Governor's displeasure. These journalistic ventures, and the petition which went to England after the Governor's suppression of them, were largely the work of the new British settlers. Lord Charles was given 'leave' to repair to London with his explanations, after which he was not sent back to the colony. The freedom of the press, with the usual limitations concerning libel, was established in the colony on instructions from the Secretary of State. A nominated Executive Council placed slight restrictions on the hitherto despotic power of the Governor. The Charter of Justice of 1827 brought regularity and, indeed, legality into the judicial system. These were some of the first results of the agitations that had been set afoot by the new colonists.

More were to follow. Englishmen naturally regarded an elected legislature as their best protection against the abuses from which they had been suffering in their new home. In the very year of the Charter of Justice they petitioned the Crown for this boon. In 1830 they did so again. The Dutch of the settled West, in this as in many other matters, shared the English view and supported the petitions. When the Mother of Parliaments was reformed the resistance to colonial demands could no longer be so vigorous, but the racial division at the Cape still seemed an insuperable obstacle to real popular government. Nevertheless a step was taken in that direction in 1834, when a legislative council of nominated members was added to the old executive council as a check on the Governor's powers.

For twenty years this council was the legislating body of the colony. Half of its members were officials holding their seats in virtue of their offices, and voting as instructed by the Governor (except, sometimes, when he was away on the frontier!). The other half were colonists, nominated by the Governor but not removable during his tenure of office. As the Governor's vote would be decisive when the members were equally divided, officialdom always had its way, and the colonists regarded the system as little better than a farce.

All the time popular pressure was exerted to obtain more political freedom. One of the consequences of parliamentary reform in Britain was the reform of municipal government, and within a year of that development elected municipal boards were granted to the Cape. The franchise depended on a small property qualification—identical with the borough franchise of 1832 in England—and without distinction of race.

Slowly the colonists acquired the experience that was thought to fit them for greater responsibility. As part of a scheme for the development of roads, Road Boards were elected in the divisions. Commercial, cultural and religious organisations accustomed people to the technique of self-government. The Synod of the Dutch Reformed Church was freed from official supervision and given full control of its affairs.

The principle of the equality of all races was so well established in the laws and habits of the colony that the greatest objection to granting an elected Parliament was now thought to have been removed. There remained the danger of conflict between Dutch and British. This obstacle was overcome in a dramatic fashion. As the Australian colonies resisted the continued transportation of convicts to their continent, the thought of sending them to the Cape occurred to Whitehall. A shipload of them reached Simon's Bay in 1849. This was a danger perfectly fitted to unite the colonists of all races, however divided on other questions. The Anti-Convict Association rallied all to resist the pollution of the colony by such immigrants. The Governor, Sir Harry Smith, agreed to prevent their landing until he should have received further instructions, but the people

boycotted thẹ government and the commissariat and pledged them-
selves never to receive or succour the convicts. Anyone having
dealings with the unwelcome ship was ostracised, Councillors and
Field-Cornets resigned their positions. Under this pressure the
Colonial Office gave way and the convict ship sailed for Van Diemen's
Land.

Many of the people thus rejected by the proud colony were
political rather than criminal offenders. One of them, the Irishman
John Mitchell, afterwards expressed his admiration of the colonists'
patriotism on this occasion. But they must have included their share
of potential 'sundowners', bushrangers and robbery-under-arms
men. The struggle was not unimportant in itself, for South Africa
was then a law-abiding country and was destined long to remain so.
The indirect consequences were still more important. The leading
colonial journalist, John Fairbairn, was not exaggerating when he
claimed that 'the people of the Cape of Good Hope have shown to
the world what it is that constitutes a state'. And indeed it was
difficult to withhold further political liberties from people who had
thus proved themselves. Discussion of constitutional details, begun
before the anti-convict agitation, continued. In 1854 the new
constitution took effect.

Other British colonies possessed representative institutions, some
already of old standing. Yet in some respects the Cape system was a
new departure. In a community where the coloured races were twice
as numerous as the white, the franchise knew no distinction of race.
The occupation of immovable property of a capital value—not
annual rent—of £25 was sufficient to qualify. This would exclude
the occupant of the Kaffir hut, of the *pondok* of sacking or cor-
rugated iron, and (on the Attorney-General's ruling) farm labourers;
but few others. Voting was by word of mouth, not by ballot papers,
so there was no literacy test. For many years a large proportion of
the qualified coloured people failed to make use of their privilege;
but it could not be denied to them.

There were two houses of Parliament. In most colonies the upper
house, the Legislative Council, was nominated; at the Cape it was
elected by the same voters as the House of Assembly. The Legislative
Council was a conservative body because its members had to possess
a high property qualification, but they and their house enjoyed the
prestige conferred by popular election.

Apart from the franchise, the most significant thing about these
parliamentarians was their division on geographical lines. In 1836,
after the Sixth Kaffir War, the colony had been divided into a

Western and an Eastern province by a line which ultimately extended from a point on the coast east of Plettenberg Bay to the Orange River east of Prieska. During the next eleven years various men held the office of Lieutenant-Governor of the Eastern Province, with the special duty of dealing with the problems and dangers of the frontier. As most of the British settlers were concentrated in that province they soon adopted as their aim its separation from the west as a distinct colony or a federated province, or alternatively the removal of the capital to the east. They claimed that as the main function of government was to defend the frontier they could have no confidence in rulers whose view extended no further than the shadow of Table Mountain. The new settlers had thus, by a curious geographical determinism, stepped into the vacated shoes of the old Graaff-Reinet republicans and others who were now handling frontier problems further north.

Under these circumstances the 1854 constitution consecrated the division into provinces. Though there were far more voters in the Western Province, it possessed only two more seats in the Lower House than the east. The Legislative Council was elected quite frankly by the provinces, each of which formed one constituency: the west chose eight members in one block, the east seven. There were to be occasions when each of these factions voted solidly, west against east.

The conflict was modified by the circumstance that this Parliament had no control over the executive. It existed only to legislate. The Governor governed, assisted by men who were not ministers depending on a parliamentary majority, but pure bureaucrats, permanent heads of departments. As in seventeenth-century England, this Governor and his faithful Commons were permanently at loggerheads. The 'sixties were a time of severe depression. 'Retrench,' said Parliament. 'Increase taxation and the powers of the executive,' suggested the Governor. In the background were the Easterners with their refrain of 'separation or the removal of the capital'. Once, in 1864, Parliament was summoned to meet at Grahamstown, causing such an upheaval in the civil service that the experiment was not repeated. Such upheavals were to be an annual event in the twentieth century, but the bureaucrats of the eighteen-sixties could not take it.

There might have been a way out of this deadlock if the legislators had been united, but they were not. The 'Easterners' had before their eyes the separation of Upper from Lower Canada in 1791, and of Victoria from New South Wales in 1851. The Eastern Province was to be the Ontario of South Africa, the British province on the frontier. Unfortunately their analogies were not applicable. It was not the whole Eastern Province, but only its south-eastern triangle, that was British. The rest, the 'Midlands', was Dutch. The Midlanders had no taste for a Settler government ruling them from Grahamstown. The British section in the Cape peninsula and other western districts would be weakened by the detachment of the east. Thus it came about that the separation of the provinces was opposed by the British of the west as well as the whole of the Afrikaner population.

In 1866 the Westerners got some new recruits. The old crown colony of British Kaffraria was annexed to the Cape by a British act of Parliament which hung *in terrorem* over the Cape legislature. The latter then passed an annexing act, but with a bad grace. The white people of the new territory were mainly British, though including a large German element of ex-legionaries of the Crimean War. They did not, however, fall easily into line with their neighbours the Easterners. These were essentially the party of a Grahamstown and Port Elizabeth clique, which to some extent repelled the Kingwilliamstown and East London people.

Though there were no organised parties, this picture gives the rough preliminary sketch of a future party system. Still, there were cross-currents. The obvious solution to the political deadlock was to follow the example of Canada and most of Australasia and introduce a responsible cabinet in place of the old executive. This idea was naturally opposed by the Easterners because they were a minority. It was opposed by others for other reasons. Responsible government might mean full responsibility for colonial defence: no more imperial troops. This touched the British Kaffrarians in their need for security, and touched everybody in his pocket. Some were afraid of the coloured vote, some were just conservative by temperament. So no majority could be found for responsible government, nor for strengthening the executive, nor for separation of the provinces.

This favourite eastern idea had other weaknesses besides the large opposition in the Eastern Province itself. The whole colony felt that imperial troops were needed on the frontier. The expense of that service, too great for the whole, would be unbearable for the part. Even if the provinces were federated, it was precisely defence that would be the chief federal concern. The Easterners wanted to control frontier policy without being in a position to pay for it. There was a discrepancy between their autonomist sentiments and their human and economic resources.

This inability of a British community to establish itself as a separate entity in South Africa was significant and prophetic. The fundamental reason for it may be expressed in a few words. When the British came the only areas left for them to occupy were either on the dangerous frontiers or already largely inhabited by Africans. Such areas were the costliest to administer but the cost had to be borne mainly by the other regions. There was no escape from this dependence.

At the end of the 'sixties a new era began in South Africa, the British element in the population increased and the distinctive character it had already acquired was sharply accentuated. Over the depression of that time hung a threat that intensified the gloom: the Suez Canal was being dug and would shortly push South Africa off the great trade route into a sluggish backwater. But two years before the canal was opened a diamond was found on the banks of the Orange River.

It was just one of a number of stones used as playthings by a farmer's children. It attracted the notice of a visiting farmer, was instantly presented to him, then tested by an expert and the news was out. In the course of 1868 and 1869 more were found, mainly along the banks of the lower Vaal River, well beyond the borders of the colony. Fortune-seekers rushed to the scene from all parts of South Africa and from overseas. In 1870 attention was diverted from the river diggings by the discovery of the far richer deposit—the richest in the world—where Kimberley now stands.

In whose territory were these diggings? The answer to that question was as complex as the unravelling of the titles to Schleswig-Holstein which had recently troubled the diplomatic world. Rival claims to the disputed territory had been put forward well before the first diamond was picked up. The land thereabouts was so barren that one may wonder why anyone troubled to claim it. A Colesberg law agent named David Arnot was one of the class of imperial expansionists represented afterwards by Southey and Rhodes. He was one of the first to see the possibilities for Britain in the as yet wild lands west and north of the Transvaal. Hunters, traders and missionaries had been entering the lands of the Griquas and the Bechuana, passing to the west of the country settled by the Trekkers. If the Republics should expand westward far enough to control that road, there could be no British advance into the interior. M. W. Pretorius, President of the South African Republic, knew the importance of the road as well as Arnot. For that stake Arnot played an exciting game against Pretorius and others. He afterwards said that he had won the game without a single trump card in his hand.

Arnot became legal adviser to the Griqua chief Nicholas Waterboer, and set about establishing the latter's claim to a wide territory.
Waterboer's sovereignty had to be defended against other Griqua
and Bantu chieftains, but primarily against the Free State. Briefly,
Waterboer's case was based on a series of treaties among the chiefs
and with the Free State and the British. If the treaties were recognised, the case was good. The Free State replied by pointing out
that the Orange River Sovereignty had included the land bounded
by the Orange, the Vaal and the Drakensberg, and that the Free
State had succeeded to all of it. This claim was untenable, as the
Free State itself recognised the independence of various African
tribes within those bounds. What was more to the point was the
fact that the Free State had for many years actually governed
the disputed land south of the Vaal, which included Kimberley
and was the chief bone of contention. The Free State claim rested
on occupation and prescription, Waterboer's claim on treaties; and
it might be said that some of the treaty-makers disposed of lands
which were not theirs in the first instance.

Further north various Bantu chiefs disputed the boundary with
the South African Republic. In that region it was the Transvaal that
depended on treaties, and even verbal agreements imperfectly
remembered, whereas the Africans could show actual occupation.
Their case was analogous to that of the Free State, whereas the
Transvaal claims were on the same basis as Waterboer's. Yet such
were the passions involved that all later commentators have tried
either to defend or to reject the claims of the two republics in one
and the same breath.

It was the practice of the South African Republic to grant farms
to its burghers and to put them on the map while their occupation
by Africans made it physically impossible for the grantees to take
possession of them. Then the nominal owners would claim that
natives were squatting illegally on their farms. Much of the
expansion of the Republic had taken place on this basis. When
diamonds were found on the north bank of the lower Vaal in 1868,
Pretorius acted in the spirit of this policy: he annexed by proclamation the whole country westward to the longitude of Lake
Ngami, and on the east a narrow strip to the sea. It was hoped that
actual occupation would follow the paper claims. But the Cape
Governor, the missionaries and the Portuguese all protested, and
Pretorius tacitly dropped his measure.

He then approached the matter from other angles. A monopoly
of diamond digging on the lower Vaal was granted to a syndicate;

and the diggers on the spot immediately set up their own republic. A treaty was made with the Portuguese, and Pretorius claimed to inherit from them the whole interior. By shifting his ground so often he weakened his case. But the diggings could not continue in anarchy, and when the new High Commissioner, Sir Henry Barkly, arrived on the scene in 1871 he persuaded the Transvaal, though not the Free State, to submit its claims to arbitration. Keate, Lieutenant-Governor of Natal, was the final arbiter. His award went against the Transvaal, placing its western boundary at the Maquassi spruit.

The anger of the Transvalers was turned against Pretorius for his bad handling of their case. He was forced to resign the presidency. But the principal diggings were no longer in the lands which Pretorius had claimed and lost. They were south of the Vaal. Keate was not concerned with that area, but in fixing Waterboer's north-eastern beacon he accepted, by implication, the whole of Arnot's argument. Waterboer in the meantime had asked for British protection. Barkly therefore, without loss of time, annexed the whole of Griqualand West, as shown on modern maps, to the British Crown.

While the Transvaal had little reason for righteous indignation, the dismay of the Free State was shared by a great body of opinion throughout South Africa, including many of the British colonists. The Free State had been deprived of territory over which it had been actually exercising sovereign authority for many years. This had happened after diamonds had been discovered in the territory, and, although Waterboer was the rival claimant, it was Great Britain that had acquired the country. In spite of its plausible basis in law, the whole proceeding had an ugly look. The historian Theal, who lived through this experience, thought a generation later that this annexation had done more to embitter relations between the two white communities than any other single event.

7

THE IMPERIAL FACTOR

The annexation of Griqualand West was one of a series of events that mark a major change in British colonial policy. The vacillations of the Colonial Office were not due to the alternations of the parties in power. They were caused by the slow operation of forces in the background of politics, old pressure-groups losing their strength, new interests rising to predominance. These changes take their place naturally and easily in a history of Britain; but in their impact on South Africa they appear merely as inconsistency and breach of faith. The South African situation remains essentially unchanged, but the British attitude to that situation is reversed and reversed again. Much bitterness and misunderstanding have been the result. Agar-Hamilton accuses the Colonial Office of a 'century-long failure to decide on the purpose of its being in South Africa'. Having no clearly conceived purpose, it was buffeted about by the force of circumstances.

In the early part of the nineteenth century the memory of the American and French Revolutions hung over colonial policy. Colonies were destined to fall like ripe fruit from the tree; democratic institutions would hasten the fall. Some Englishmen regretted this necessity, others welcomed it, but all felt that the parting, if unavoidable, should be friendly. Self-government was therefore conceded when it was loudly enough demanded. But in the case of South Africa there was a force working in a contrary direction, causing Whitehall to keep a firm hold on the Cape. This was the humanitarian movement of which the abolition of the slave trade, then of slavery, then the Protection of Aborigines, were aspects.

Missionary societies, responding to reports from their men in the field, wielded great influence at Westminster, and Colonial Secretaries were very sensitive to it.

By the 'forties this influence, though still considerable, was losing ground. Economy was becoming a stronger motive, the British taxpayer a more powerful influence than the missionary. The introduction of the income-tax made it possible to dispense with the revenue from protective duties, and the Irish potato famine gave the final impetus to the movement towards free trade. A rise or fall in the rate of income-tax affects the interests of the taxpayer very directly and obviously, and Chancellors of the Exchequer now showed more tenderness to these interests than ever before. Moreover, free trade destroyed what was supposed to be the basis of the Empire itself, the complementary economic rôles of mother country and colonies and their mutual interdependence.

Under these circumstances imperial expansion appeared an absurd and mischievous process, and British expenditure on colonies as bad business. Bad business, to the Manchester school, was something not far removed from sin. Yet it was not clear that expansion would always and inevitably mean greater expenditure. An annexation here or there might bring a secure natural frontier, cheaper to defend than the old one. When a South African High Commissioner could show that this would follow, he might, though with misgivings, be given permission to push the border further out. Thus the persuasive Sir Harry Smith had no sooner reached the Cape than he annexed British Kaffraria and the Orange River Sovereignty. Natal had been taken five years earlier under pressure of various special circumstances.

This expansion was the last for twenty years. The Colonial Office soon got the impression that it had been fooled by its trusted 'man on the spot'. So little were these measures a guarantee of economy that Britain was almost immediately involved in the most expensive of all the wars on the Cape frontier—that of 1850-3—and the Resident in the Sovereignty was sharply defeated by the Basuto.

The angry Whitehall men responded to this disillusionment by a policy of 'scuttle'. The independence of the Transvaal was recognised, the Sovereignty abandoned and the Cape given a Parliament, all in the space of two years. Shortly afterwards Natal was disconnected from the Cape Colony and given a legislature in which officials and an elected majority sat in the same house.

The Crimean War and the Indian Mutiny intensified the reluctance to spend money on South Africa. The economising motive was, nevertheless, a dangerous factor. Penny-wise might turn out to be pound-foolish. In that case the need to spare the British taxpayer would lead to a reversal of policy that would involve the breach of engagements and even the tearing up of treaties. One Colonial Secretary would firmly veto a scheme propounded by an enthusiastic Governor, and even recall him for his disobedience; another would involve South Africa in years of strife by attempting to force on the country the very scheme that his predecessor had taken so much trouble to scotch.

When the scuttling operation had been carried out Sir George Grey arrived at the Cape. Under the influence of his experiences in New Zealand and his observations in South Africa he came to the conclusion that the best, as well as the cheapest, policy for the latter country was one of greater unification and the reversal of the tendency to disruption. It was obvious that the native wars conducted by the republics would have repercussions on the colonial frontiers; that the weakness of the republics in men and money was a cause of their perpetual frontier disturbances; and obvious too, Grey thought, that a united white community could maintain peace and order where many weak states could not.

These considerations acquired a new urgency when the Free State declared war on its Basuto neighbours in 1858. Though boundary lines had often been laid down on maps, there was no real frontier between Free Staters and Basuto. The Boer pastoralists, to maintain their way of life, needed more and more land and tended to spread over it as quickly and inexorably as their ancestors had been doing since the days of Simon van der Stel. The Basuto, a new nation composed of fragments dispersed by the Zulus and Matabele, were fast increasing. They had taken shelter in the mountains, but when the danger had passed could no longer survive without spreading rapidly over the fertile plains below. Their huts and gardens sprang up on those plains, where their stock and that of the farmers intermingled. Both sides lost cattle and horses and killed rival intruders. As Moshesh would observe no boundary, the Free State attacked him. But it had not the resources to sustain a long war against a people who could always retire to impregnable natural defences, and always emerge from them to lay waste the farms as soon as the weary commandos dispersed with the cry of *'huis-toe!'* The Free State abandoned the struggle. Grey intervened and laid down a new boundary which he knew would not be respected.

Many Free Staters thought that the only way to recruit their strength was to federate with the Cape Colony. Grey encouraged the idea, and urged a general federation upon the Colonial Secretary and upon the Cape Parliament. In doing this he disobeyed express instructions, and was recalled, to return for a short time after undertaking to do nothing more of the kind. Britain had withdrawn from the troubled lands north of the Orange, and was resolved not to court trouble and expense in that region again. The Free State then turned to the north. A union with the Transvaal might serve the purpose. Pretorius, President of the South African Republic, was elected President of the Free State as well. The personal union might lead to something more. At this point the Colonial Office showed the other side of its dual personality.

The two republics owed their independence to the Sand River and Bloemfontein Conventions. Both had, in these agreements, undertaken to forbid slavery in their territories. There were dark and partially substantiated stories of the existence of that institution in the Transvaal under the name of 'apprenticeship'. If the charge could be proved, there would be grounds for denouncing the Sand River Convention as having been broken by the Transvalers them-selves. This idea had been entertained in London, though not very seriously. But the annexation of the Free State by its northern neighbour might bring the abuses and the responsibility for them right down to the Orange. Determined not to allow this, and fearful of a big republic in the interior, the British authorities informed both republics that their union might give rise to doubts whether, or to what extent, the Conventions were still valid. The Transvaal was too tenacious of its independence to take this risk, and even the Free State would cling to the bird in its hand till it knew what the alternative would be. Moreover, while Pretorius was at Bloemfontein, his other country dissolved into warring factions, so that it was clear that he could not fill the two posts at once. He resigned the Free State presidency, crossed the Vaal again, and the experiment of a personal union came to an end.

The Orange Free State was too weak to cope with the problems that had been thrust into its unwilling hands in 1854. One reason for the weakness was its inadequate revenue. Young communities depend much more upon indirect than upon direct taxation to fill their coffers. At this time about half the revenue of the Cape Colony came from customs duties. Imports to the Free State were brought through the ports of the Cape and Natal, where duties were paid; but neither colony would concede any part of this money to the country for which the goods were destined. It was alleged that such a concession would give the Free State the means to undertake policies harmful to the colonies, or over which the British, who granted the money, would at any rate have no control. This difficulty was one of the strongest inducements to the Free State to federate with the colonies.

Foiled in two attempts to escape from its impossible position, the Free State then elected as President J. H. Brand, a Cape advocate and member of Parliament, son of the Speaker of the House of Assembly. In 1865 war broke out again on the turbulent Basuto frontier. The strain on the little republic was very great, but it was fighting for its existence and made a tremendous effort. The existence of the Basuto nation also was at stake. The Boer commandos, however, destroyed their enemy's crops, captured cattle and stormed several mountain strongholds by a ruse which was successfully repeated on various occasions. In 1866 Moshesh was brought to accept a peace in which the Free State took all the fertile lowlands, more even than the area in dispute.

If this treaty stood, the Basuto would cease to exist as an independent force, being deprived of their economic basis. To break them up was frankly Brand's purpose. But what would happen to them then? They were already pouring into the lands bordering the Cape Colony. No British Governor with a sense of responsibility could allow this. Moshesh appealed for British protection, begged to become a British subject. Shepstone, Secretary for Native Affairs in Natal, coveted Basutoland for his colony. The legislators there saw in the Basuto some useful potential taxpayers. There was a widespread realisation that the lands left to them could not support the Basuto. The Colonial Office, pushed along by events, pulled back by the thought of the budget, agreed to the acceptance of Moshesh's offer if either Natal or the Cape would annex him and bear the expense.

What the Basuto wanted was British protection, not annexation to a colony; but if it must be a colony, then to the Cape rather than Natal. Unless the Free State were deprived of lands it had long held there would be no link between Natal and Basutoland, divided as they were by an almost impassable mountain range. But Wodehouse, the Governor, had had such difficulties with the Cape Parliament that he saw little value in an annexation to that colony either. And there was so much sympathy for the Free State there that no approval of a policy of robbing the victor of his spoils could be expected. Wodehouse's way out of the difficulty was to annex Basutoland to the Empire; thus disregarding his instructions, as so many of his predecessors had done before him.

The Free State felt itself cheated. Britain had annexed that country against its will, then made it independent against its will, then refused it the support of the Cape and forbidden its union with the Transvaal. Even the raising of volunteers in British territory had been prohibited. Now that victory over the Basuto—which Britain had refused to seek because of the expense—was almost complete, Britain stepped in to undo its effects. On the other hand the break-up of the Basuto people was a serious menace to the peace of the British colonies. And the Free State had weakened its position by expelling from the annexed territory the Paris Evangelical missionaries, the chief civilising agents among the Basuto. Like their colleagues of the L.M.S. in earlier times they were accused of being 'political', of giving aid and encouragement to the enemy. The expulsion was ordered by the Volksraad and deplored by the President; it made a very bad impression in England and France. A Free State deputation went to London; but the annexation stood.

The boundary had still to be defined. In negotiating this at Aliwal North Wodehouse recovered for the Basuto some of what they had lost at the time of their defeat, but not nearly as much as they claimed. The outline of Basutoland was drawn as it remains today. When the terms were known the legislators in Bloemfontein were pleasantly surprised; it was the chiefs and missionaries that protested.

The moral of this story of vacillation is as important as the facts themselves. The annexation of Basutoland has been represented as a treacherous blow, as an unprincipled seizure of the fruits of another's efforts. Further, Great Britain in the Bloemfontein Convention denied any 'wish or intention' to make a treaty with any native tribe north of the Orange. The words do not imply an obligation; but did they not have a certain moral force? From various points of view the annexation may appear a breach of faith. Yet under the circumstances of 1868 it was the obvious course of statesmanship. The fault lay not there, but in the impossible undertakings of 1854. The self-denial of that year could not be sustained unless Britain removed herself from South Africa altogether. If the scuttle were not to be completed it should never have been begun. As a British junior minister said in 1871, 'we are reaping the fruits of our folly in ever abandoning the authority over the Orange River Territory'. The evil that men do lives after them.

Such as it was, the settlement of the boundary caused an exodus from Basutoland. The Free State farmers got plenty of labour. The citizens of Bloemfontein complained of an excess of idle natives in the capital. But the dry diggings of Kimberley were opened the year after the treaty of Aliwal North. Labour was wanted there, and when that territory, too, was annexed by Britain, the labourers at the diggings could buy guns and powder with their wages. The Basuto found the second annexation a useful complement to the losses which were consecrated by the first.

First Basutoland, then Griqualand West. A punch at the Free State from the right was followed up with a blow from the left. Both can be defended on the ground that the peace and security of the British colonies demanded them. Neither was a great disadvantage to the Free State. One gave her additional territory, a secure border and a labour supply, the other a market; yet the tactless handling of the situation had led to the breach of at least the moral implications of a treaty, and left behind a sense of wrong which turned the Free State from an outlier of the Cape Colony into a self-conscious and increasingly anti-British republic.

It is hardly necessary to point out that neither annexation was the result of any greed of territory or imperial urge in England. The Colonial Office gave permission for annexations to Natal and the Cape, but Wodehouse and Barkly departed from their instructions. They took steps which they regarded as indispensable for the maintenance of peace and order in South Africa as a whole.

When the new government of Griqualand West tried to introduce order into the land tenure of the colony and investigated the basis of land titles, it discovered that the claims of Waterboer could not be sustained. Thus Arnot's house of cards collapsed, but only after the harm had been done. By that time there was a British population at the diggings which, if it had been incorporated in the Free State, would have been enough to decide the issue in presidential elections. Brand realised this, and agreed to accept £90,000 and regard the question as closed. The Colonial Secretary did not ask the Chancellor of the Exchequer for this money; it was charged to the account of Griqualand West.

Great Britain, having burnt her fingers in the South African fire, would have been glad to keep clear of it in future. In her attempts to get clear she was burnt still more severely. It was now apparent in London, as it had formerly been to Sir George Grey, that the situation might be eased if all the colonies and republics could be federated. In Grey's time the Cape and the Free State at least had shown signs of moving in that direction. If this movement could be started again, a strong and united South Africa might be created to relieve British governments of heavy and costly responsibilities. It was the tragedy of the 'seventies that the attempt to bring about this union produced friction, suspicion and disunity that have left permanent marks on the country.

The examples of Canada, Italy and Germany gave a great impetus to the movement for federation. In 1874 Lord Carnarvon returned to the Colonial Office, where he had sat when the Dominion of Canada had been brought into being. It was his ambition to repeat this achievement in South Africa. But obstacles stood in the way, and Carnarvon's methods were not of the kind that would remove them.

The annexations of Basutoland and Griqualand West stiffened the attitude of the Free State; Brand would have nothing to do with confederation. The constitutional dilemma in the Cape Colony had been resolved in 1872 by the grant of responsible government. Molteno, the Prime Minister, depended largely on the support of Dutch votes, and these supporters had strong sympathies with the Free State. The Cape therefore approached the confederation question very warily. The Easterners tended to welcome the idea in the hope that their province might form a separate unit in the federation, but opposition to eastern separation was one of the chief planks in Molteno's platform.

Natal would welcome the financial and military support of the rest of South Africa in dealing with the Zulus and her own Africans, but commercial motives had the opposite effect. Her trade with the interior was helped by a lower customs tariff than that of the Cape, and federation would remove this advantage. Moreover, Natal was in 1875 smarting under the sting of a reproof administered by the Colonial Office. The Hlubi tribesmen, followers of Chief Langali-balele, were returning from the diamond fields with guns, which they were not allowed to possess in Natal without permission from the Lieutenant-Governor. The chief refused to appear when summoned to account for the breach of this regulation. A punitive expedition brought him in, punished another tribe as well as his, and Langalibalele was tried by a specially appointed court unknown to the constitution. The Lieutenant-Governor was judge as well as prosecutor. The accused was condemned to life imprisonment on Robben Island, the traditional prison of African chiefs who were neither swimmers nor navigators. As Robben Island happens to lie in Table Bay, it was necessary for the Cape Parliament to pass an act enabling the Natal court's sentence to be carried out. This was done, but all the proceedings were so irregular that the Colonial Secretary had no hesitation in ordering them to be reversed. Both the Cape and Natal were hurt. There was no chance of converting the Transvaal to federation; her part in the story will appear later.

Under these circumstances it was tactless of Carnarvon to take the initiative in so important a matter. He not only proposed a conference, but nominated the delegates to attend it, and included the leader of the eastern separatists in the list. Molteno, tenacious of the self-governing privileges of his colony, stood upon his dignity. So did the Free State. Natal had, in the Langalibabele affair, shown itself incapable of self-government, so Sir Garnet Wolseley was sent there to coax the colonists and their legislature into an abandonment of their existing privileges. The elected members, hitherto two-thirds of the Council, were left with a bare majority of one; as they were unlikely ever to be unanimous, the nominees were now in effective control. This arrangement lasted for five critical years.

Carnarvon made matters worse by sending Froude, the historian, on a speech-making tour of South Africa. Froude stumped the Cape Colony in the interests of the parties opposing Molteno, a proceeding which the latter thought odd for an agent of the British government. Carnarvon then summoned a federation conference to London; only delegates from Griqualand West and Natal, which were fully controlled from London, attended. The British Parliament passed a permissive act, but no response came from South Africa.

Only one territory remained to be cajoled—the South African Republic. Carnarvon thought he saw a gleam of hope in that direction. It was not that the Transvalers were likely federalists—they were the principal isolationists of the whole country. But their government was breaking down. After the removal of Pretorius they followed the example of the Free State and elected a Cape Colonist as President. T. F. Burgers was a Dutch Reformed clergyman with liberal tendencies which had got him into trouble with his church. But he had an ingratiating manner and seems to have had a close connection with the Cape Commercial Bank. This bank afterwards lent him £60,000 to straighten out the finances of his state. Yet the credit of the republic remained so low that he was unable to raise in Europe more than a small part of the money needed for a railway to Delagoa Bay. In April, 1877, the cash in the Transvaal treasury amounted to twelve shillings and sixpence.

The President's religious views were regarded by puritanical citizens as certain to bring calamity upon the country. Some migrated across the Kalahari and did not stop till they reached Angola. When the Bapedi chief Sekhukhune rebelled and the President took charge of the operations against him, few of the Boers were willing to follow such a leader. The expedition was a failure; and Sekhukhune's land was needed for purposes connected with the Delagoa Bay railway.

In the eastern districts of the republic, near the disturbed area, gold mining had begun and British and other immigrants had established themselves. Some of these called for British intervention. Shepstone, the Secretary for Native Affairs in Natal, feared that a war between the Zulus and the Transvaal, arising out of a boundary dispute, was imminent. Here were all the factors that had caused Britain to intervene on other occasions, and they might do so again. If the Transvaal could be brought under British control, the Free State might be unable to hold aloof from the federal plan, Natal and Griqualand West had no voice of their own, and the Cape could hardly remain out of a union embracing the rest of the country.

Shepstone was therefore sent to the Transvaal to investigate the possibilities, and to annex the country if public opinion were favourable. He was accompanied by twenty-five policemen and was given a great welcome by the largely English population of the villages. After getting no satisfaction out of President or Volksraad he ran up the Union Jack at Pretoria. The Sand River Convention had been treated as a scrap of paper. Shepstone's proclamation had been read beforehand by Burgers, who in turn submitted to Shepstone the protest which he was to issue with the latter's secret permission. When this play-acting was over, Burgers returned to Cape Town, accepted a pension, and attended a ball at Government House.

Behind the scenes of the Transvaal stage moved the Cape Commercial Bank, whose directors were mainly Cape Afrikaners. Finding Burgers a bad debtor they had stopped all credit to him, demanded security for their past loans, got some members of the republican Volksraad to move for an embarrassing statement of accounts, and appealed to the High Commissioner to save them. The annexation of the Transvaal was something more than a final gamble for federation by a desperate Colonial Secretary.

Even in April, 1877, when the deed was done, it was not too late to make a success of the existing situation. Shepstone had promised the Transvalers self-government, but the fulfilment of this promise was postponed. Paul Kruger, the ex-Vice-President, twice went to London with other emissaries to see the Colonial Secretary. When Carnarvon showed that he believed the annexation to have been in accordance with popular feeling, Kruger saw his chance. It was clear that if Shepstone had fully obeyed his instructions, he would have got the Volksraad to ratify his action and so justified the annexation. But that had not been done. Burgers had been allowed to make a formal protest and the Volksraad had gone home. Public opinion, in fact, had still to be tested, and on his return to South Africa Kruger

D

organised meetings and drew up petitions for and against the annexation. This informal vote showed the Boer population to be almost unanimous in demanding the restoration of independence. So, on his second visit to London, Kruger was able to show that the popular support on which Shepstone was supposed to have based his action did not exist. But the British government would not undo what had been done, and under these circumstances hesitated even to grant an elected legislature. A new Volksraad would not be co-operative.

One of the chief reasons for the annexation had been the danger of war with the Zulus; and it was a really formidable danger. After the defeat of Dingaan his brother Panda had ruled under the patronage of the Boers. As Panda grew old the real power fell into the hands of his son Ketshwayo, who at last succeeded his father in 1872. The new king followed the paths marked out by Shaka and Dingaan. He restored the old military system, with regiments composed of young braves who could not marry till they had 'washed their spears' in blood. Shaka's warriors had done this in the blood of the Bantu tribesmen living anywhere within reach of Zululand, but Ketshwayo could not cross his own border without invading the territory of Natal, the Transvaal or Portugal. The existence of the Zulu military system was therefore an obvious threat to one or more of these countries, but especially to Natal and the Transvaal. After 1877 this meant, in either case, Britain.

Apologists of the Zulus, like Bishop Colenso, admitted that the existence of a Zulu army of some 30,000 fearless, highly disciplined warriors was a 'standing menace' to the white population of Natal, with a great multitude of Africans in their midst and a long and unprotected frontier. Fear of a Zulu invasion deepened in the course of 1878 when repeated and protracted drought had sent a wave of hungry restlessness moving through all the Bantu tribes. But despite one or two nasty border incidents a war with Zululand on the Natal front did not seem inevitable. The most likely *casus belli* was the boundary dispute with the Transvaal, whose outlying farmers had long been pursuing their traditional technique of encroachment on native territory. In this dispute Shepstone, while in Natal, had supported the Zulu side; but when, after the annexation, he examined the Boer documents at Pretoria he changed his mind. The Natal government appointed a commission to decide the question. Its verdict to everyone's surprise was in favour of the Zulu claim. To Sir Bartle Frere, the very able 'pro-consul' whom Carnarvon had sent out as Governor of the Cape and High Commissioner in the hope that he would be able to put through federation and become the first Governor-General of a united South Africa, the verdict was embarrassing; to give effect to it without qualification was bound to have two awkward consequences. It would encourage Zulu aggression and it would finally alienate the Transvalers. Frere was well aware that Disraeli's Government wanted to avoid war with the Zulus, since war was imminent with the Afghans and war with Russia would be likely to follow. But he had made up his mind that a Zulu offensive might come at any moment and that the safest course was to crush the Zulu power in one quick campaign before the crisis in Europe came to a head. When explicit orders to avoid a war arrived, he had already combined with the announcement of the boundary award an ultimatum to Ketshwayo, requiring him among other things to break up his military system and allow all men to marry when they chose. To go back on this ultimatum was impossible, and when its time-limit expired early in January, 1879, three British columns crossed the Zulu border. Lord Chelmsford, the Commander-in-Chief, accompanied the force that crossed the Buffalo at Rorke's Drift. A few miles beyond that point the column encamped at a hill called Isandhlwana. In spite of the advice of Boer leaders, no laager or defence work of any kind was made round the camp. A Zulu force appeared some miles away and then retreated, drawing part of the British troops, under Chelmsford himself, after them. The main Zulu *impi* then surrounded the camp, pounced upon it and all but wiped out its defenders.

This disaster might have been followed by an invasion of Natal but for two circumstances. The Zulu losses at Isandhlwana had been so heavy that the surviving warriors, content to have 'washed their spears', dispersed to their homes. And this impulse was confirmed when, on the night after the battle, a section of the Zulu army attacked the makeshift fort at Rorke's Drift and were repelled by its heroic little garrison again with heavy loss.

Isandhlwana took several months to avenge. In the course of the campaign the Prince Imperial of France, who insisted on serving in this war as a volunteer, was killed. 'A very remarkable people, the Zulus,' was Disraeli's comment. 'They defeat our generals; they convert our bishops [a reference to Colenso]; and they have settled the fate of a great European dynasty.' The Prince was killed in a small skirmish. Operations on a larger scale brought converging columns to Ketshwayo's capital, Ulundi. There Chelmsford, just as he was about to be superseded by Wolseley, finally defeated and destroyed the Zulu military power.

The Transvaal Boers, with a few notable exceptions, played no part in this war. Britain had taken their country, so Britain, they felt, could defend it. But upon them the defeat of the Zulus had an effect like that of the defeat of France in Canada upon the American colonists. The Zulu danger was a reason, not altogether unappreciated, for Britain's continuing to rule the Transvaal. That reason having ceased to exist, the mounting resentment of the Boers became less controllable. And after Ketshwayo the British subdued Sekhukhune also.

One consideration caused Kruger to stay his hand. When in England he had heard Gladstone attack the government for its Transvaal policy. In 1880 Gladstone came into power, and might be expected to reverse the decisions of Disraeli. When this was not done the Transvaal Boers prepared to fight. The outbreak was precipitated by a significant incident. The British authorities, as short of money as their republican predecessors, pressed for the payment of taxes. The people replied that they would do so only under protest, so that the payment would not be taken to show willing submission to the government. The latter would not recognise the protest, and proceeded to enforce unconditional payment by seizing the wagon of a defaulter at Potchefstroom. The person thus distrained upon was, of all people, P. Bezuidenhout, whose name recalled the Slagter's Nek rebellion. A crowd of farmers came into the village, forcibly removed the bailiff from the wagon and took it back to its owner's farm.

Other events followed quickly. One more popular assembly was held at Paardekraal—since called Krugersdorp—where the resolution to fight for independence was taken, and a triumvirate of Kruger, Pretorius and Joubert elected. On December 16, 1880—Dingaan's Day—this government took possession of the Landdrost's office at Heidelberg and hoisted the republican flag.

The British were unprepared. Small detachments of troops were scattered about the country. One such force, marching from Lydenburg to Pretoria, was surprised at Bronkhorstspruit and overwhelmed. While skirmishes and sieges were continuing in various parts the British forces in Natal prepared to enter the Transvaal and relieve their countrymen. The Boers, too, concentrated at Lang's Nek where the road from Natal crossed the border. Colley, the British general, bears the main responsibility for what followed. The Free State President had intervened with such effect that Kruger suggested to Colley an armistice and a Royal Commission to settle the dispute. The British government cabled its approval.

But Colley had suffered more than one reverse, and was determined to win a victory before fighting ceased. He neglected to inform Kruger of the British answer till it was too late to stop the move on which he had resolved. So he was able to lead his men by night to the summit of Majuba Hill which overlooked the Boer positions. On the morning of February 27, 1881, the Boers bravely climbed the hill and drove the defenders from it; Colley himself was among the slain.

The two sides then negotiated the armistice which could have been settled before the battle. Gladstone had opposed the annexation policy from the beginning, and, though he had failed to reverse it in time, he did not feel justified in continuing the war merely for the vindication of military honour. If independence were to be restored anyway, it had better be done without further sacrifice of life and without adding to the existing causes of bitterness.

The Convention of Pretoria did not give the Boers all that they wanted. According to the preamble, they were to have 'complete self-government, subject to the suzerainty of Her Majesty'. Suzerainty was a vague word, but the articles of the convention gave it some substance. There was to be a British Resident at Pretoria, and all the relations of the Transvaal with foreign states were to be conducted through him and the High Commissioner. In particular, he was to report to the President on cases of ill-treatment of Africans; to report to the High Commissioner on the observance of the convention, and on the encroachment of Transvalers upon native lands beyond the borders; and to share with the President the responsibility of marking out locations for the Africans within the state. In case of alleged encroachment on native lands 'the decision of the Suzerain will be final'. The Resident was to be the only channel of communication between the Transvaal government and native tribes outside its territory. Laws affecting Africans were not to be valid without Her Majesty's consent.

The reader will not be surprised that the convention carefully and comprehensively specified the debts for which the new government would be responsible, nor that the claims of the Cape Commercial Bank were the first to be named in the list. There were also many administrative details of the transfer of authority to be provided for. And the restored republic was 'hereinafter called the Transvaal State', not the South African Republic. Its boundaries were defined.

The convention combined the two aspects of British policy which Rhodes enthusiastically described as 'philanthropy plus five per cent'. Though the interest on the debt was actually three and a half per cent, it would have been wiser as well as more practicable to

have concentrated entirely on the philanthropy, since the encroachment of the Transvaal on the lands of native tribes was a danger to
the future peace and harmony of South Africa which it was absolutely
necessary to check. But the republic was too poor to pay the debt
with which it was saddled. The convention had to be modified.

Needless to say, all these events put an end to the confederation
scheme. And whereas the various annexations gave an immense
impetus to Afrikaner nationalism, as will be shown in another
chapter, the abandonment of the Transvaal after Majuba was a bitter
humiliation for the whole British population of South Africa. The
Boers were filled with contempt for Britain's military power, and
were led by their confidence into incautious policies that were factors
in a later disaster.

In 1884, on the request of a Transvaal delegation to London, a
new convention was substituted for the old. The functions of the
Resident were limited to those of a Consul and there was to be no
British control over legislation affecting Africans. The debt was pared
down. The country was once more called the South African Republic,
and its borders were enlarged on the west. It could still make no
treaties with foreign Powers—except, now, the Free State—without
the consent of Her Majesty; but otherwise the conduct of foreign
affairs was in its own hands. The Transvalers wanted to get rid of the
'suzerainty'. On this there was a compromise. Suzerainty had been
mentioned, along with self-government, in the preamble of the old
convention. In the new certain articles were substituted for the
articles in the old. Did the preamble therefore remain in force?
Stricly speaking, a preamble is not part of a law and has no force
whatever. But the preamble of the Pretoria Convention was in form
not so much a preamble as an un-numbered article. Lawyers disputed
whether it was abrogated in 1884 or not.

On these doubtful terms the South African Republic entered the
New Year of 1885, and a new crisis. The two conventions had so
hedged the republic about with boundary lines and restrictions on its
dealings with Africans that the steady expansion of the past had
become impossible. Yet the land-hunger was as great as ever. It was
assuaged in a new way. The Transvaal could not expand. But
Transvalers could emigrate from their country and colonise on their
own responsibility. The Zulu power had been broken and Zululand
carved up into thirteen petty chieftainships. In this direction the
Boers began to push forward in 1882, and to occupy land on which
the New Republic was set up.

On the western frontier the Africans themselves gave them an opportunity. In the Mafeking area two Barolong chiefs, Montsiwa and Moshete, fought. Further south there was a struggle between Mankorwane and Masau. All four called for volunteers and offered lands. Moshete and Masau were assisted by Transvaal Boers, and their rivals asked for British help. The latter were soon defeated and the victors gave out land to their allies. These set up two little republics, 'Stellaland', with its capital at Vryburg, and the 'Land of Goshen' to the north. They lay right across the Missionaries' Road which had so long been regarded as the route for British trade and influence to the interior.

It was clear that the South African Republic could not annex these states without British permission. To Cecil Rhodes, a member of the Cape Parliament from the newly incorporated Griqualand West, it seemed that the future paramountcy of Britain in southern Africa depended on their annexation to the Cape. He was taking up the torch formerly borne by Moffat, Livingstone, Arnot, Southey and others. But the Cape, with its Dutch vote, was sensitive to Transvaal opinion, and Britain was unwilling to annex.

The London Convention gave a part of the two republics to the Transvaal; but what remained was, as Rhodes said, 'the Suez Canal of the interior', 'the neck of the bottle'. It is impossible to say what would have happened if Britain, the Cape and the South African Republic had remained the only claimants. The intrusion of a fourth precipitated decisions. The fourth was Germany.

German missionaries and traders had for years operated in the lands on the west coast between the Orange River and Angola. It was a turbulent country in which Bantu tribes, Hottentots and 'Bastards' from the Cape Colony perpetually struggled. The slow expansion of the Cape northwards made it appear natural that these territories also—Great Namaqualand and Damaraland—would ultimately fall to her lot. Bismarck had even enquired whether Britain would not undertake to protect German subjects and interests there. But apart from the annexation of Walfisch Bay and the Guano Islands nothing was done.

It must be remembered that in those days the existence of great savage territories which could be penetrated at any convenient time in the future was taken for granted. No one foresaw that the whole of Africa would shortly be partitioned among European powers and that opportunities not seized at once would be for ever lost.

Britain and the Cape allowed time to pass, and were startled when the German flag was run up at Lüderitz Bay in 1883 and the whole of South-West Africa proclaimed a German protectorate the following year. The Germans immediately surveyed a route for a railway to the east. They took an interest in the coasts of Zululand and Pondoland on the other side of the continent. Kruger, after the London Convention, was fêted in Berlin. As the French had once threatened to hem the English colonies to the North American coast, now there appeared the threat of a German belt across Africa to block the expansion of Britain from the Cape.

Under these circumstances the missionary John Mackenzie was sent to Bechuanaland as British Commissioner. Rhodes, who criticised Mackenzie's handling of the situation, was soon sent to take his place. Rhodes was followed by 5000 troops under Sir Charles Warren. But when Warren insulted and antagonised the Boers, Rhodes resigned his post. He wanted the expansion of the Cape with Afrikaner support; Warren proposed to exclude all Dutchmen from the new territory. Rhodes was critical of the methods and refused to share the responsibility for them; but the primary object of his appeals was attained. Bechuanaland, south of the Molopo River, was proclaimed a Crown Colony; north of that river, and up to 22° South latitude, a British protectorate. The road to the north was now in British hands and the Transvaal nearly encircled.

The Union Jack had already been hoisted at St Lucia Bay, the only harbour on the coast of Zululand; though it was not till 1887 that the whole of that country was annexed to the British Crown. Thereupon the New Republic, set up in the manner of Stellaland and Goshen by emigrant Boers, was absorbed by the Transvaal. This was cold comfort to Kruger, now President, who had hoped that expansion in that direction would lead him to the sea. He wanted a port in his own or at least in German hands. Except for the narrow sector of Tongaland, Britain now held that coast.

Further south another gap remained. Attempts to extend the authority of the Cape Colony beyond the Kei had been frustrated by orders from London. But the congestion in that region had led to a tribal fight in 1877 which developed into the Ninth Kaffir War, and in the following year provoked a rebellion of the neighbouring Bantu within the Colony. Their suppression was followed by the gradual annexation of all the territory, except Pondoland, up to the borders of Natal. In 1885, while Sir Charles Warren was in Bechuanaland, a British protectorate over the coastline of Pondoland was declared also. So quick and comprehensive was the British response to the intrusion of Bismarck upon the South African scene.

8

THE UITLANDERS

In January, 1885, a conference was held at Fourteen Streams to discuss the Bechuanaland situation. President Kruger headed the Transvaal delegation. Cecil Rhodes was one of the British representatives. The 'Colossus' and the 'Lion of Rustenburg' faced each other for the first time.

So long as they lived, these two were to fight a duel which would be the dramatic expression of the whole political struggle of their age. Their personalities made so deep an impression on their followers that South African politics still tend to move along the lines which these men marked out. This has been a great misfortune. There were more beneficial forces at work than those which either of them represented. There were fundamental problems to be solved on which there was no great disagreement between Kruger and Rhodes and to which therefore their conflict made no contribution. Had Brand still been living in the 'nineties—he died in 1888—his influence would probably have changed the course of events immensely for the better. The rest of the story would have been more inspiring, too, if there had been a colossus in the party of Joubert, Schalk Burger, Esselen and Eugene Marais in the Transvaal or among the Merrimans and Schreiners of the Cape. But these groups produced no one of the stature of Kruger and Rhodes.

Kruger was a product of the Trek and a descendant of trekkers and pastoralists. Rhodes, the son of a Hertfordshire parson, descended from a line of farmers. Both were men of inflexible will and determination. Each fought for the principle of nationality, British or Afrikaner. For that reason each is revered by later

generations which cling to their national identity and traditions on
either side. Yet neither can be regarded by a cool observer as a
representative of the best traits in his national character.

In most ways they were in startling contrast. Kruger belonged to
the Dopper Church, the most rigidly puritanical of Afrikaner sects;
he regarded the singing of hymns as wicked levity. He was a
Fundamentalist, sought his science in the Bible and believed the
world was flat. He was at home in the world of cattle and big game
and ox-wagons and farmhouses out of sight of their neighbours'
smoke. Rhodes was a millionaire, a diamond magnate who controlled
vast corporations with millions of capital. He dreamed of expanding
British rule northwards right through the heart of Africa, of a railway
from the Cape to Cairo, of consolidating the British Empire and
linking it with the United States to dominate the world. He knew
that money meant power. There were times when he seems to have
thought there was nothing it could not do.

Both, therefore, had serious limitations. But they would not have
won the devoted loyalty of thousands without other qualities. Both
had great courage. Kruger, for all his puritanism, had a rugged and
sometimes grim sense of humour. Rhodes had a gift of attracting
not merely the friendship but even the love of men who knew him
intimately. It can be said that he pursued wealth not for its own sake
but for the political ends it would serve. His own personal tastes
were simple. Yet money corrupts. Neither Rhodes nor Kruger had
a lofty or discriminating sense of honour. Yet both were great men.
Kruger, himself a child of the Great Trek, personified the spirit
of that movement, its strength as well as its weakness, its passion for
freedom as well as its narrow isolationism. Rhodes not only gave to
British South Africans an inspiring vision of their rôle in history,
but, except for one short lapse, kept them consistently to the path
of co-operation with their Afrikaner countrymen. His statesmanship
rose far beyond the chauvinism which the Jameson Raid has caused
to be associated with his name. His friendship with Hofmeyr was
one of the great forces drawing the two nationalities together.

Rhodes had come to Natal in his youth to improve his health.
The diamond fields soon attracted him and he made a fortune. That
enabled him to go to Oxford for a pass degree; he attended to his
mining interests at the same time as his studies. Returning to
Kimberley, he found mining operations at a critical stage. So long as
diamonds were to be scratched from the surface of the ground, every
digger could attend to the few square feet of his own claim. But the
busy throng on the surface disappeared from view as a great hole

sank into the earth. Roadways between the claims fell in and the sides of the hole collapsed on to the diggers below. Claims had to be amalgamated. Rhodes proved his financial genius in his response to this challenge. He formed a company which controlled a whole mine; he defeated rival amalgamators and by 1890 his De Beers Consolidated Mines, Ltd, had united the whole of the South African diamond industry into one concern. Its property was worth £14,000,000 and it controlled the diamond market of the world. Big Business made its first appearance on the South African scene since the fall of the Dutch East India Company.

By that time Rhodes had used De Beers to promote the British South Africa Company, of which he was Managing Director in South Africa. It received an imperial charter and became the means of colonising and conquering Rhodesia. That story lies outside the scope of this book, but it had repercussions on the countries to the south. The Pioneer Column entered Mashonaland in 1890; in the same year Rhodes became Prime Minister of the Cape.

He had, by then, his finger in another pie also. Since the days of the first diamond discoveries, gold was known to exist in the Transvaal. Mines were developed, principally in the eastern districts. In 1886 prospectors on the bleak uplands south of Pretoria, the Witwatersrand, discovered what proved to be the greatest goldfield in the world.

From Kimberley and elsewhere miners and financiers came to see. The galvanised iron shanties of the new mining camp of Johannesburg were the beginnings of a miraculous growth. Within a decade the town had 100,000 inhabitants. Along the line of reef, over a length of sixty miles, smaller towns grew up beside the mines. By 1895 it was known that this would not be an ephemeral gold-rush camp. The reef seemed inexhaustible and could be mined at deep levels. It had two distinguishing characteristics. The gold was very thinly distributed in the rock and it was very evenly distributed. There were no nuggets to make a digger rich overnight. The extraction was difficult and required expensive machinery. But since the reef was so uniform and reliable, and labour cheap, the investment of big capital in the mines, which the difficulties made necessary, was not unduly risky. The Rand was obviously a field for the experienced financiers of Kimberley.

Rhodes was one of these, but not the most important. His company, the Consolidated Goldfields of South Africa, gave him a share in the new wealth and a connection with Transvaal politics. But in Johannesburg even greater interests were represented by J. B. Robinson, Lionel Phillips, and others.

Rhodes was in a position which made it almost if not quite impossible to reconcile his various duties and interests. He was responsible for the Cape government, De Beers, the Consolidated Goldfields, the Chartered Company and Rhodesia. As is the way with financial magnates, he used one of these rôles to ease his task in another.

His greatest single objective was the unification of South Africa under the British flag. Here he was following in the footsteps of Grey and Carnarvon. He rightly regarded the South African Republic as the chief obstacle in the way of this achievement. Kruger would have union on his own terms—the absorption of the rest of the sub-continent by his own state—but on no others. It was not for nothing that the Transvaal was called the South African Republic. The name was calculated, like that of the Soviet Union in later times, to smooth the way for the annexation of neighbouring states.

Before 1886 Kruger was in a poor bargaining position. He had even suggested a customs union with the Cape, a proposal which was turned down and was not to be repeated after the gold discoveries. Kruger, like every Transvaler since the days of Louis Trichardt, thought that the independence of his country would not be secure without a seaport of its own. The annexation of the New Republic, on the way to the sea, had been accompanied by a British annexation of Zululand. There still remained one small stretch of available coast—Tongaland, just south of the Portuguese border. Between this and the Transvaal High Veld lay the turbulent region of Swaziland, whose independence was guaranteed by the London Convention. Three times, between 1890 and 1895, Kruger negotiated with the British over Swaziland. The first time he had a good card to play. One of his burghers had got a concession from the Matabele Chief Lobengula. This came at the moment when Rhodes was preparing to send his Pioneer Column to Mashonaland on the strength of another of Lobengula's concessions. Kruger was prepared to hold back his men at the Limpopo if he could have a *quid pro quo* on the east. What he got was a joint Anglo-Transvaal administration of Swaziland, and the right to a corridor to the sea, provided the Transvaal joined the Customs Union which the Cape and the Free State had just formed. The price was considered too heavy and the Volksraad never fulfilled the terms of this arrangement. When the republic was finally permitted to declare a protectorate over Swaziland, Kruger had just made a speech in which he announced that Germany could be called in to counterbalance British power in South Africa. Britain therefore annexed Tongaland and the Transvaal was finally cut off from the sea.

There could be no Transvaal port and no German port. The remaining alternative was Portuguese. Railway connection with Delagoa Bay would free the republic from dependence on British colonial ports. Even in the days of President Burgers this railway had been a favourite republican scheme. The presence of the tsetse fly in the low country made ox-wagon traffic to Lourenço Marques impossible. But the funds for a railway could never be raised before gold came to strengthen Transvaal credit. Then the Dutch and German financiers came forward with alacrity.

The Netherlands South African Railway Company, which was given a monopoly of Transvaal railway connections with other states, was floated in Holland. Dutch subscribers provided 29 per cent of the capital but kept to themselves more than two-thirds of the voting power. A greater number of shares was held by the republic itself, and a much greater number in Germany.

Kruger did what he could to prevent the Cape and Natal railways crossing his border before the Delagoa Bay line was completed. Long before any through connection was established it was necessary to build a line along the Rand to link the mines with their source of coal at Springs. The Railway Company was later able to boast that the traffic on this short line paid the interest on the construction of its whole system. In return for a railway loan Kruger allowed the main line from Port Elizabeth, which ran through the Free State to Viljoen's Drift, to be continued to the Rand. This was in 1892. It was not till two and three years later that the connections with Delagoa Bay and Natal were complete.

The railway company was the object of bitter attacks, and not only by the mining magnates. It was complained that construction was three times as expensive as it need have been; that the company provided 'jobs for pals' and lucrative contracts for subsidiaries; that the Komati bridge, in the midst of country abounding in stone, was made of stone imported from Holland—of all countries! The company's profits were greater than its working expenses, and its dividends ten per cent and more. It was allowed to collect the customs duties on the Portuguese border and keep them for itself.

Recent investigations have taken much of the sting out of these and other charges. The construction of the line through difficult and unhealthy country from Komatipoort to the High Veld was necessarily expensive, and it was this line that Kruger very naturally regarded as a political necessity. The capital was difficult to raise in Europe; most of it had to be loan and not share capital, and the profits on the Rand line had necessarily to compensate for the expense of the route to Delagoa Bay. As for the Komati bridge, the local stone was unsuitable and the means to work it were lacking on the spot. Nor could personnel be recruited locally. The collection of customs duties was a consequence of the republic's guarantee of minimum profits to the company.

From the point of view of the foreign population on the Rand, these considerations were irrelevant. If the Cape Government Railways could provide, for whatever reasons, cheaper communications with the outside world, the Rand consumers saw no necessity for the Netherlands Company at all. Its tariffs were much heavier than those on the Cape railways. The latter cut their rates so as to capture the Rand traffic. It became cheaper to bring goods from the Cape to the Rand than over the much shorter line from Lourenço Marques. The company, to keep the traffic to its own routes, therefore trebled the rates on its short line from the Free State border to Johannesburg. The people concerned tried to escape this charge by unloading goods at Viljoen's Drift, on the Free State side of the Vaal, and bringing them to the Rand by wagon. Kruger then closed the drifts (fords) over the river to this traffic. But he had gone too far. A firm stand by the British government made him retreat. And he had united the Free Staters, the Cape Colonists (Dutch and English) and Great Britain against him.

There were many grounds besides its railway policy on which the Transvaal régime could be criticised. Monopolies were granted to favoured people. The dynamite monopoly, of vital concern to the mines, caused the price of dynamite to be three times as high as it would have been with free importation. This monopoly cost the mines £600,000 a year. Legal quibbles were used to deprive the mining companies of property and bring profit to officials and their friends. Eugene Marais, editor of *Land en Volk*, regularly exposed cases of bribery and challenged the people he named to sue him for libel. They never did so with success. One member of the Executive, who had supported the dynamite concession, was said to draw £10,000 a year from it thereafter for his pains. In connection with the Selati railway concession bribes were distributed to officials and legislators, and the President said he saw no harm in it.

Laws were passed with retroactive effect. When a Field-Cornet was convicted of ill-treating an African the government paid his fine. Taxes were specially devised to fall mainly upon the Uitlander (foreign) population, which claimed that it contributed at least nine-tenths of the public revenue. In the critical years before the

Boer War the Chief Justice claimed the right to test the constitution-
ality of laws, and for this he was dismissed.

The Uitlanders thus had serious grievances. They hoped to
qualify for Transvaal citizenship and elect representatives who
would redress them. The frustration of this hope produced the
greatest grievance of all. It had formerly been very easy to become
a burgher in the Transvaal, as it continued to be in the Free State.
But the sudden influx of a large alien population produced a change.
The naturalisation and franchise laws were tightened up. Petitions
by many thousands of people, asking for easier terms, were treated
with scorn and derision by President and Volksraad. One legislator
challenged the foreigners to fight for the vote. At last it became
impossible for an immigrant to get it till he had been fourteen years
in the republic, twelve years a naturalised subject (having lost his
previous nationality) and at least forty years old; and even then he
would not vote in presidential elections. In effect, citizenship was
impossible to acquire, though the government could always grant
it to any favoured person.

Most of the aliens were British subjects, though there were many
Germans and Americans. Of the British, a good many came from
the Cape Colony and Natal. These felt their exclusion from political
rights much more bitterly than the others. The great capitalists
'did not care a fig for the franchise' (they preferred working with
'electoral funds'), but the bulk of the immigrants, intending to make
permanent homes on the Rand, were very serious in demanding it.
Moreover, while denied the rights of citizenship, they were expected
to shoulder its obligations. When some of them, called up for
military service, refused to go, this was treated as evidence of their
unfitness for the franchise.

Now consider Kruger's case. His people had won the Transvaal
with blood and tears. They had moved great distances and made
great sacrifices to find a country where they could be themselves
and preserve their way of life. Now they were suddenly invaded
by a horde of cosmopolitan fortune-seekers whose outlook and
civilisation were poles apart from their own. In a few years the
newcomers were believed—it seems wrongly—to outnumber the
old burghers. If he gave them the vote, Kruger said, he might as
well haul down the republican *Vierkleur*.

One of the Uitlanders' demands was for state support for English-
medium schools. This was an inconsiderate demand, since the
preservation of the Dutch character of the state was a fundamental
condition of its existence. It was reasonable to expect new citizens

to conform to this character. As for paying nine-tenths of the taxes and having no representatives, Kruger's attitude was bluff and logical: if they didn't like it, they could go. If they stayed, he might take that as a sign that they were doing well enough.

The mining companies were not doing badly, though it may be significant that the profits were made chiefly by the older companies working near the surface, and the complaints mainly by the newer mines working at deep levels. In any case the more vociferous protests came not from the magnates but from the rank and file of the Uitlander population. These formed the Transvaal National Union to demand redress of their grievances. The successive chairmen of this Union were South African by birth, as were many of the members. These were, as a rule, more serious than the British-born immigrants in demanding the rights of citizens. Nevertheless their refusal to act when the day of revolution came is one reason—and there are others—for the suspicion that they were not so much principals in the dispute as pawns in a game of power politics which was being directed from elsewhere. However this may be, many of their grievances were substantial and much of the discontent was genuine enough.

The demands of the National Union fell on deaf ears. Feelings were embittered by folly on both sides. The republican flag was torn down and trampled on by a Johannesburg mob. Kruger spoke of the Uitlanders in rough and sometimes unprintable terms. 'Go back and tell your people', he said to a deputation, 'I shall never give them anything: I shall never change my policy, and now let the storm burst.'

It did. The National Union began to organise a revolution, and Rhodes took a hand in it; partly, it has been said, because he was disappointed in his hopes of a 'New Rand' in Rhodesia, and wanted to bend the old Rand to his purposes. Many successful revolutions have had less justification than this one. Though the old Boer patriarchs, struggling to preserve what was dear to them, may win our sympathy, their case was weak. The wise conservative achieves something by making concessions to the spirit and needs of a new time. The late nineteenth century was not a time in which half the people of a country (not counting Africans, whom all disregarded), paying nine-tenths of its taxes and owning a third of its land, could be kept indefinitely in a state of subjection. When it is remembered that the rulers were a simple people unversed in the ways of the world, and that the subjects could enlist the support of what was still the greatest of the Great Powers, Kruger's obstinacy seems still more foolish. If he were to preserve the old Transvaal unchanged, his only logical course was to follow the methods of Afghanistan or old Japan. He should have put up a notice at the Vaal River like that formerly on the Khyber Pass, which said, 'It is absolutely forbidden to cross this frontier.' But the London Convention forbade this; and if it had been done, the state revenue would not have multiplied twenty times in ten years.

Plotting therefore began in Johannesburg. Rifles and machine-guns were smuggled in under loads of coke or concealed in oil-drums with oil dripping deceptively from the taps. Most of these loads came from the sidings of De Beers Consolidated at Kimberley. There was a plan to seize the arsenal in Pretoria. Would the revolution be a purely domestic one, or carried out under the British banner, with a demand for British annexation? The plotters were so divided on this point that at the last moment they postponed 'flotation of company', as it was called in their cryptic telegrams, and the movement seemed to have fizzled out. Quite apart from divisions in the ranks of the 'shareholders', they had not nearly enough arms or ammunition for their purpose.

But on the hot afternoon of December 30, 1895, when the leading conspirators were gathered together, they received a telegram which made their blood run cold. It read: 'The contractor has started on the earthworks with seven hundred boys; hopes to reach terminus on Wednesday.' Thus was announced a 'flotation' for which the subscribers wanted no responsibility and which would bring some of them within sight of the gallows.

The contractor was Dr Jameson, intimate friend of Rhodes and Administrator of Rhodesia. He had been brought into the conspiracy because it was thought necessary to have support from outside the Transvaal to make sure of success. The Chartered Company was then building a railway from Mafeking to Bulawayo. On this excuse Rhodes got the Colonial Office to transfer to the Company's administration a 'railway strip' through the Bechuanaland Protectorate. Down this strip Jameson brought a force of Mashonaland Mounted Police, and encamped them at a spot on the Transvaal border not far north of Mafeking. It was, of course, for this purpose that the Company had acquired the conveniently placed railway strip.

Rhodes and the Johannesburg plotters had provided this force in order to give outside support if anything should go wrong with the revolution. Jameson was given an undated letter from the leaders in Johannesburg calling him to come in to save their women and children from the Boers. When it appeared that the revolutionaries were divided in their aims and insufficiently armed, they sent two

messengers as well as telegrams to Jameson to 'postpone flotation'.
All the messages reached him. Rhodes, too, tried to stop him, though
his telegram arrived too late. But Rhodes had once said to another
officer: 'You cannot expect a Prime Minister to write down that you
are to seize ports, etc. But when he gives you orders to the contrary,
disobey them.' He reaped the bitter fruit of this seed when Jameson
disobeyed the explicit orders reaching him from all sides.

Two years earlier, Jameson had fought a war with the Matabele
and added their territory to that of Mashonaland. Because of the new
weapon, the machine-gun, the war was a walk-over. Jameson became
too confident. He had, too, been reading about Clive. 'You may say
what you like,' he said, 'but Clive would have done it.'

Fortified by these thoughts he led his band across the Transvaal
border and made a dash for Johannesburg. The Boers were quite
capable of handling this sort of situation. Their commandos
assembled with great speed and stood between the invader and his
goal. The High Commissioner, on hearing the news, repudiated
Jameson's action and sent a messenger to order him back. The order
was disobeyed. On the fourth day Jameson was trapped. When
further resistance was hopeless, a white apron was seized from an
African woman and hoisted in sign of surrender. The same night
the invaders were all lodged in Pretoria gaol.

De Kiewiet says of the Raid that 'it was inexcusable in its folly
and unforgivable in its consequences'. No one would now question
this judgment. The folly was so great as to be almost unbelievable.
A British force, operating from British territory, invaded a country
with which the Queen was at peace. It did not do so in sufficient
strength to have any chance of success. The Raid was supposed to
assist a revolution organised in Johannesburg, yet the revolutionaries
had given Jameson the most emphatic orders not to move.

It was pointed out at the time that the Transvalers under Pretorius
had conducted a supposedly (though not really) analogous raid into
the Free State in 1857. Kruger had been one of the invaders, though
he had not approved of the policy. He used his influence to avert
hostilities and cause a withdrawal of the Transvalers. The analogy
is significant, but does not excuse Jameson's crime.

The leaders of the movement in Johannesburg were compromised.
Sixty-four of them were arrested. Of these, four were condemned to
death. But although a patriot chose this moment to bring from
Somerset East to Pretoria no less an historical relic than the beam
from which the Slagter's Nek rebels had been hanged, the penalty
was commuted to a fine of £25,000 each. Rhodes and his friend

Beit paid on behalf of the prisoners. The others were punished by imprisonment for which also a fine was substituted. With great wisdom Kruger handed Jameson and his raiders over to the British government for trial. They got very light sentences.

A committee of the House of Commons and another of the Cape House of Assembly enquired into the responsibility for the Raid. The London 'Committee of No Inquiry', concerned for Britain's international position, failed to push to a conclusion the charge that the Colonial Secretary was implicated. Recent research leaves no doubt that both Chamberlain and the High Commissioner were fully aware of what was going on. That they could not foresee Jameson's independent action is beside the point. Their failure to take control of events was a grave dereliction of duty. Interesting as these revelations are, however, the blame for the Raid must remain essentially where it was placed at the time, on the shoulders of Rhodes. He encouraged and financed the movement, yet failed to control the people he had stirred up. He had so often supported irregular political and military proceedings that Jameson might naturally suppose he would support this one.

Of the consequences of the Raid, direct and indirect, we have not yet seen the end. The immediate results were serious enough. The Kaiser sent Kruger a congratulatory telegram which began the estrangement of Britain from Germany. Rhodes parted company from Hofmeyr and most of his Afrikaner friends (this was a revolution in Cape politics), resigned his Premiership and his seat on the board of the Chartered Company. A stop-gap ministry took office in the Cape Colony, where Briton and Afrikaner drew apart in hatred and suspicion. Many of the British colonists, of whom Merriman was the outstanding representative, felt that their flag had been besmirched by the underhand dealings of Rhodes and Jameson. Others thought that the Uitlanders on the Rand, by failing to rise, had betrayed Jameson and his brave boys. J. C. Smuts, a young Cape advocate just back from Cambridge, abandoned his British nationality in disgust and settled in the Transvaal, where he was soon to become State Attorney. The Free State turned its back on the Cape and formed a defensive alliance with its republican neighbour. Up in Rhodesia the Matabele, followed by the Mashona, took advantage of the absence of the police to rise in rebellion. Rhodes himself played a brave and dramatic part in the pacification. In the Transvaal there had been, among the old burghers themselves, considerable opposition to Kruger. This was now almost silenced, and the president was re-elected for a fourth term in 1898. For a century there had been suspicion of British motives and fear of British treachery. The suspicion and fear seemed now to be confirmed beyond a shadow of doubt, and all the earlier policies of Britain were thrown into darker relief. Even Natal drew apart from the Cape. The Garden Colony had received responsible government in 1893, and now wished to take advantage of its low customs tariff to trade with the Transvaal. Throughout South Africa there were fear, bitterness, recrimination and broken friendships.

What did the future hold? In less than four years from the Raid the British Empire and the Republics were at war. One asks whether the war was inevitable. Underlying its immediate occasions there appeared to be a fundamental antagonism. There were some resemblances to the Civil War in America. Britain, like the American Union, represented a modern industrial civilisation; the republics, like the Confederacy, an antiquated and static rural society. Was there an 'irrepressible conflict' between them? The American conflict came because both sides shared a common country, and the national policy had to take one line or another. But South Africa was not one country. Could the separate parts not agree to differ? It might be said that they could not, because the conflict was not a difference of policy between the states, but a struggle for power in one of them. This is a half-truth. Milner's essential object was British predominance, 'paramountcy', in the whole subcontinent. It was not so clear that Kruger had a corresponding ambition for his republic, but he was becoming the focus of the loyalty of many Cape Colonists, while the loyalty of his Uitlander subjects was given to Britain. Neither side could be indifferent to the threat which the other presented to its own power. The conflict was irrepressible; but that is not to say that it had inevitably to be resolved by war.

Within the Transvaal two different civilisations came to grips. Their quarrels related to every aspect of the state's affairs: taxation, railway and customs policies, monopolies, police, the administration of justice, the method of legislation, the official language, education. There can be no doubt that the Uitlanders, if enfranchised, would never have been content till these questions were settled to their own satisfaction. Such a change would have destroyed the republic of the Boers, whether the Vierkleur continued to wave or not. Therefore the old burghers were determined to prevent it. Their attitude was as natural as that of their opponents; but which side was right? The best answer is perhaps that the Boers were supported by the letter of the law, but the Uitlanders by the principles of historical development and by every historical analogy.

It was assumed that Kruger would not make any concessions on the mere demand of the Uitlanders. 'I shall never give them anything.' Most of them, being British subjects, then naturally turned to Britain for assistance. Had Britain either the right or the duty to interfere? Her right to do so depended partly on the articles of 1884, partly on the disputed 'suzerainty'. But the articles of the Convention did not cover the case, and nobody could say what suzerainty meant. The problem seemed insoluble in theory; but in April, 1899, it became a question of practical politics, and a solution had to be found. Some 20,000 Uitlanders petitioned the Queen for protection. This was 'the appeal to Caesar'. Many British colonists in South Africa regarded it as a test case which would show whether their attachment to the Empire guaranteed to them the Mother Country's protection or not, whether Palmerston's *civis Britannicus sum* was a sham or a reality. Chamberlain persuaded himself that the same anxiety was felt in Canada and Australasia.

As a matter of practical politics, Britain's disregard of the Uitlanders' petition might have cost her the loyalty of thousands of her own people; so that Kruger would have had it both ways. On the moral side there is a point of vital importance to be remembered. Up to August, 1899, every Transvaal proposal on the subject of the franchise contained a curious provision. There was to be a long interval between the Uitlander's naturalisation and his getting the right to vote. During this time—it was twelve years by the existing law—he could have no voice in the affairs of his adopted country and would have cut himself off from the country of his birth. Had it not been for this circumstance the Uitlander might have chosen one allegiance or the other and been expected to abide by his decision. But in fact there were no alternatives: he must be protected by his native country or not at all. World opinion today would not admit that a law-abiding person ought to renounce the privileges of one nationality without gaining those of another; nor did this seem right in 1899.

Chamberlain therefore took up the cudgels for the Uitlanders. A new High Commissioner, Sir Alfred Milner, took the initiative appropriate to the 'man on the spot', but worked in harmony with the Colonial Secretary. Milner believed that, as long as it remained united, the British Empire was the mainstay of peace and freedom in the world, and that South Africa was a vital link in the chain that held it together. That meant that the British and those Afrikaners who were willing to share this allegiance to the Crown must be the dominant element in South Africa, not Kruger's republicans. For the task in hand he had all the qualities of a first-rate civil servant, but by temperament and training he was more an administrator than a diplomatist. But, since neither he nor Chamberlain thought war to be inevitable at this stage, they had agreed to make the most of diplomacy first. Their principal aim was to get a reasonable franchise for the Uitlanders, after which Britain would accept no further responsibility for them. Milner met Kruger at the Bloemfontein Conference and this question was stiffly discussed. No agreement was reached.

In the Transvaal an important change of personnel had taken place. Several of the Hollanders whom Kruger had placed in the highest executive posts were removed and their places taken by Afrikaners. J. C. Smuts, the young advocate from the Cape Colony, became State Attorney, and F. W. Reitz, ex-President of the Free State, became State Secretary. These men brought a more realistic and progressive spirit into the negotiations, and they were helped by outside influences that were brought to bear on the President. Sir Henry de Villiers and J. H. Hofmeyr came up from the Cape to counsel moderation. The result was a change in Transvaal policy which put a very different complexion on the whole dispute.

A new dispatch from Reitz offered a five years' franchise which was to be retrospective; the price demanded was the tacit abandonment of the British claim to suzerainty, and no further interference in the internal affairs of the republic. Any remaining points in dispute could be settled by arbitration in which the Transvaal would not ask that foreign Powers should take part. Chamberlain saw several snags in this offer. The South African Republic had often repealed laws by the simple process of a resolution passed by the Volksraad at a single sitting. And its previous franchise laws and proposals had been hedged about by administrative complications which took back with one hand what had been given with the other. Britain could not pay the price asked unless the concession were to be effective and permanent. But Chamberlain's despatch, which he afterwards described as a 'qualified acceptance', was so tactlessly and obscurely worded as to make it seem like a refusal. The Transvaal thereupon withdrew its offer. If the despatch had been worded as a clear acceptance, and the necessary qualifications tactfully introduced, there might have been no war. Chamberlain had had the power to prevent it. Kruger's régime would have been undermined from within, but that would have worried nobody but his own clique.

This possibility was even closer to the Uitlanders' grasp before the Raid. At that time most of South Africa was hostile to Kruger. Had the Uitlanders waited, and Jameson never left Rhodesia,

Kruger was likely to lose the next presidential election as well as control of the Volksraad. The margin would not have been great, but the victors would have regarded Kruger's party as their main enemy, and this would have been a strong inducement to add Uitlanders to the electorate. After the Raid even the 'liberal' Boer leaders, Joubert and Burger, were very chary of concessions. In 1895, and again in August, 1899, there was a prospect of a peaceful solution. But it must be repeated that the overthrow of the narrow oligarchy of the republic was the essence of that solution. Given the forces that were at work, the old régime could never have survived in peace. But its overthrow by peaceful means would have had very different results from its going down in a blaze of patriotic glory before superior force.

After the misunderstanding of August the continued interchange of despatches served little purpose. Both sides had to prepare for the possibility of a breakdown. Milner had ceased to believe in the possibility of peace; and, since he thought that war would bring about the unification of all South Africa under the British flag, he was ready to face it. Maybe his full, clearly argued despatches stiffened Chamberlain. But several Boer writers have believed that Kruger's intransigence was also to blame. 'The only *casus belli*,' Lord Bryce wrote, 'has been the conduct of the two contending parties during a negotiation, the professed subject of which was in no sense a *casus belli*.' In the end the guns went off almost of themselves.

Kruger had been buying German artillery and building fortifications ever since the Raid. Britain now ordered troops from India and the Mediterranean to Durban, and prepared to despatch an army corps. Republican commandos assembled on the Natal border, within sight of Majuba. British troops were held back from the borders, but the shadow of that mountain still fell across the whole British army.

If there was to be war, the only chance for the republics—the Free State stood by her ally—was to start it before the British forces had arrived in strength. Reitz therefore despatched an ultimatum: all troops on the borders of the republic to be withdrawn; troops that had arrived in South Africa since June 1 to leave the country; troops now on the high seas not to land. Chamberlain replied that the conditions 'are such as Her Majesty's Government deem it impossible to discuss'. On October 11 the Boer War—to the Boers the Second Freedom War—began.

Very serious mistakes of strategy were made on both sides, but as the chances of a Boer victory depended on rapid success their mistakes were fatal; time was on the side of the British. In the whole course of the war the British Empire mobilised 448,000 men, the Republics about 87,000. But on the day hostilities began the Boer forces outnumbered their opponents in South Africa by two to one. As the Afrikaners of the Cape were in sympathy with the Republics, the correct strategy for the latter was to overrun that colony as quickly as possible and to draw its rural population into rebellion. This could probably have been done, and Britain would have faced the task of reconquering almost the whole of South Africa. That it was not done was partly due to historical tradition. The urge towards the sea, the memories of the loss of Natal in 1843 and of the victory of Majuba, drew the main Transvaal force into the Garden Colony. Above all, the British troops, the Boers' natural target, were concentrated in Natal. But even this policy was not part of an overall strategy. There was no unified command for the two republics, and in each army the local commanders tended to make their own strategic decisions. On the western front the principal Boer forces, on their own local responsibility, undertook to besiege Kimberley and Mafeking. When the British in Natal fell back to Ladysmith, Joubert (the Transvaal Commandant-General) insisted on sitting down to a siege of that town instead of making a bold dash for Durban.

For a time the Boers retained the initiative, forcing their opponents to attend to the relief of the besieged towns. The British commander allowed his policy to be dictated by the enemy. Where a competent general would have concentrated his limited forces for victory at one decisive point, Sir Redvers Buller dispersed his men all over the front. The result was 'Black Week' in mid-December: Methuen, advancing to the relief of Kimberley, was defeated at Magersfontein; Gatacre was thrown back from Stormberg by Free Staters invading the Colony; Buller himself, facing the main Boer army along the Tugela in Natal, suffered at Colenso the defeat which proved him as bad a tactician as a strategist.

These experiences roused the British people to a sense of the magnitude of their task. Reinforcements were sent with despatch and Lord Roberts came out as Commander-in-Chief, with Kitchener as Chief of Staff. Canada and Australia made their contribution. That Roberts directed his attention first to the relief of Kimberley was partly due to the insistence of Rhodes, who was in that town constantly bickering with the military commander. But from the moment of its relief the initiative passed to Roberts. The Free Staters under Cronje were too reluctant to abandon what they had wrongly made their principal objective, and too slow in getting away from the neighbourhood. Roberts pursued Cronje, surrounded him and his 4,000 men at Paardeberg, and there on February 27—the anniversary of Majuba—Cronje surrendered.

From that point events followed rapidly and logically. The Free Staters who were helping to besiege Ladysmith immediately abandoned their positions and crossed the mountains to defend their homes, with the result that Ladysmith was relieved and the Transvalers had to abandon Natal. In the Free State itself there were panic and demoralisation which gave Roberts the road to Bloemfontein. Though the sickness and exhaustion of the troops caused a long pause at Bloemfontein, when the advance was resumed it brought the Tommies rapidly to Johannesburg.

Louis Botha had become Commandant-General after the death of Joubert. It was he who frustrated an attempt by some Boers to destroy the gold mines before the arrival of the British. Johannesburg was intact, though almost deserted, when it fell into their hands. The Boer leaders, to the disgust of their followers, decided also not to defend Pretoria. Kruger and his administration retired down the Delagoa Bay railway, and the British marched into the capital past the forts that had been built at great expense against this very contingency.

The Free State was annexed under the title of the Orange River Colony. When Kruger had crossed the Portuguese frontier and the British entered Komatipoort the Transvaal, too, was annexed, and Roberts thought the war was over. Yet only eleven months had passed, and it was to last two and a half years altogether.

The first phase had seen a British victory in the field and the acquisition of two new colonies. But the second phase, the guerrilla war, was to be still more important in its ultimate effects. One of the principal reasons for the British success had been the excellent discipline of the regular troops and the indiscipline of the Boers. Their armies were a reflection of their social system. The officers were elected and were treated as equals by their men. Every man had his own views on tactics and felt himself free to disobey orders which did not accord with them. When he thought it time to go home on leave he stood not upon the order of his going. There was one rank, that of General, which had been instituted at the beginning of the war and went by appointment and not election. When this rank was conferred the new officer would debate in his own mind, or even with his subordinates, whether to accept it or not.

These, however, were but the defects of the Boer's qualities.

When large-scale operations ceased and commandos broke up, every man was prepared to take responsibility and show initiative, whereas the British soldier was too often helpless without orders. In the second half of 1900, when Roberts went home and left Kitchener in command, this reversal of the situation became apparent. All over the former republics guerrilla bands were active. Their operations continued throughout 1901 and into the next year. All this time the governments of the republics remained in being, though chased from pillar to post over the wide spaces of the High Veld.

This indefinite prolongation of the war led the British into policies which have had lasting consequences. Along every railway line, and across the spaces between railway lines, stretched continuous barbed wire, with blockhouses sometimes only 200 yards apart. This was to divide the country into compartments which could be cleared one at a time. The Boer commandos met this threat with great daring and resource. They often crossed the lines, but always with difficulty. When closely pursued, they melted away, only to rejoin their commandos when the danger had passed. Every farmhouse provided them with supplies and intelligence. It is to be noted how this was a consequence of the racial difference between town and country. Had the Boers lived on the Rand and the British on the veld, the capture of a few centres would of course have ended the war. But *Boer* means *farmer*. How was Kitchener to defeat this semi-civilian army which wore no uniform (except, when its clothes wore out, captured British uniforms) and was supported by the civilians of the farms? It is significant that Kitchener, who favoured reconciliation and easy peace terms, was responsible for a harsh policy which he justified by military necessity; whereas Milner, who preferred unconditional surrender and subjugation, thought Kitchener's policy a mistake for political reasons. Military considerations were allowed to carry more weight at the time.

The policy followed was to destroy all farms that might be suspected of giving aid and comfort to the enemy. But it was carried out indiscriminately, so that by the end of the war there was hardly a farmhouse left standing in the annexed territories. Buildings and their contents went up in flames, stock was driven away, standing crops destroyed, and the troops encouraged to loot. What was to become of the women and children whose homes were destroyed? Camps were prepared to receive them, 'concentration camps', an institution that had recently become notorious in Cuba. Some, though a minority, of the women and children sought these camps voluntarily as places of refuge. Most were brought to them under compulsion. Large numbers of African labourers, too, were taken to them—a fact almost completely forgotten in later controversies. Since the farms and their inhabitants were supporting the burghers in the field, the policy of concentration in camps was justifiable from a military point of view. The policy itself may even be called humane. When peace came, Botha was to thank Kitchener for the care that had been taken of the women and children. President Steyn, who wanted to continue the war, supported his opinion by pointing out to the burghers that their dependants were in safety and would not be made to suffer by further military operations.

The farm-burning was much less defensible. It is true that the combatants drew supplies from the farms, but the destruction of the houses and their contents was quite a different matter from the burning of crops and the removal of stock. The burning of houses and the wrecking of pianos was meant as a deterrent punishment. In that object it failed completely. It is arguable that if the farms had been left alone, and the combatant burghers had been responsible for the women and children within their lines, they would have given in sooner.

So much for the policy itself. What damns it, however, is not so much its conception as its execution. Farms were destroyed before many questions were asked. People were poured into concentration camps that were not ready to receive them. There was a shortage of beds, of food, of sanitary and medical facilities. It is true that many of the women had the most primitive ideas of medicine and hygiene, but that does not relieve the military authorities of their responsibility. In all the camps together the deaths in October, 1901, reached a rate equal to 344 per thousand per annum. The child mortality was much worse, in some camps reaching and surpassing the rate which, if continued throughout the year, would have extinguished the whole child population.

Some camps were in much better condition than others, and the efforts of Emily Hobhouse, who came from England to probe into this unhappy subject, were effective in bringing about an ultimate improvement everywhere. But by the end the concentration camps had been the deathbeds of some 26,000 Boer women and children. They form the last and the most terrible item in the indictment against England that remains indelibly printed on many Afrikaner minds.

But this memory is not the only enduring relic of the guerrilla war. National sentiment is not felt with equal intensity by all the people of any country, and in a mixed community it appears in a complicated shape. There were people of British birth or descent who had become loyal citizens of the republics, especially of the Free State. These fought devotedly and even fanatically for the countries of their adoption. Judge Hertzog, who became a Free State General, was so moved by this that he never afterwards felt any hostility towards people of British origin as such; but he expected of them a political attitude which had no meaning whatever for the great majority of British South Africans, and much mis-understanding and confusion was to follow.

In the Cape Colony there were people of Dutch descent, Afrikaans-speaking, who fought loyally for the British. Others of the same group rebelled against their government and gave either political support or active military assistance to the republics. Blood, they said, was thicker than water. Finally there were the Uitlanders who fled from the Rand before the outbreak of war, formed the Imperial Light Horse and other units, and fought with especial bitterness against the Boers. All these were men who took their stand on a principle from the beginning and gave their allegiance where they thought it due.

There were others in a more compromising position. When the Boer resistance seemed to have collapsed many citizens of the republics surrendered to the British and took an oath of neutrality. Some of these afterwards rejoined the commandos in the field. The British treated them as oath-breakers; the Boers held that the British, by pressing these men for information of Boer movements and otherwise demanding their support, had failed to respect their neutrality and had therefore released them from the oath. Others who surrendered—'hands-uppers'—thought the continued resistance madness and felt that the 'bitter-enders' would be responsible for the ruin of their country. Some even offered active support to the British and were enrolled in an organisation called the National Scouts. Some formed a Peace Committee to spread peace propaganda among the men who still fought. The chairman of the committee ventured into the Boer lines, was arrested, tried as a traitor, and shot. Though the words 'Quisling' and 'collaborationist' could not be used, they correctly describe the 'hands-uppers' and National Scouts as seen through the eyes of the 'bitter-enders'.

This division of Afrikanerdom gave rise to various hopes and fears. Had the war lasted much longer, and had it been possible to build up political institutions before the peace came, the collaborationists might have become the leaders of an Afrikaner people that had broken its ties with the commandos and the memory of the republics.

The 'bitter-enders' would have hung about the fringe of politics, outside its main stream. This was Milner's hope.

Kitchener, a soldier, felt more respect and sympathy for the men who fought him to the end. He wanted the guerrilla war to stop. In April, 1902, he gave permission for the leaders of the two republics to meet at Klerksdorp. Out of their discussions arose a negotiation with the British authorities. The Boers insisted on independence. Chamberlain insisted that the annexations must stand. The Boer leaders believed that they had no power to accept this condition, which only the sovereign people could do. Representatives elected by the commandos, and regarded as representing the people as a whole, then met at Vereeniging. Among the Transvalers the prevailing opinion was for peace. The Free Staters were bitterly resentful. They had espoused a quarrel which was no concern of theirs, and now the principals in the dispute asked them to abandon their independence. Behind this argument lay the fact that the Free State would remain Afrikaner whatever happened, whereas the Transvaal was with every month of the war falling more into the hands of the English and the 'hands-uppers'. Of the Free State leaders, only President Steyn resisted to the last. Generals Hertzog and De Wet came round to the Transvaal point of view represented by Botha and Smuts. The Peace of Vereeniging was signed on May 31, 1902.

Thus the leaders in the field had made a great personal sacrifice to save their nation from collapse. Collaborationists no longer appeared as the natural leaders of the Afrikaner people. National sentiment crystallised round the heroes who had fought to the bitter end. For the next half-century the leading Boer generals and statesmen and their sons would dominate South African politics. If they had all been of the same political persuasion, historians might have spoken of a Family Compact. As they ultimately moved into opposing camps, their old comradeship in arms may have been the cement that has held the country together through all its feuds.

By the peace terms, the burghers in arms surrendered and accepted King Edward as their lawful sovereign. The British government gave £3,000,000 to repair farm damage and restore the people to their land, and, in addition, loans free of interest for two years. The colonial rebels were not given any guarantee by the treaty. The south-eastern part of the Transvaal—the former New Republic —had already been annexed to Natal before the peace. The new colonies were promised self-government in due course, and there was to be no enfranchisement of Africans before that stage was reached.

Two months before the peace, Rhodes had died in his cottage at Muizenberg. He was a chastened man; and since even Jameson came to be forgiven by many Afrikaner leaders, Rhodes if he had lived might have made greater contributions to the common good than he ever did before 1896. But the weak heart which led to his premature death (he was in his forty-ninth year) was a double misfortune. It gave him a sense of urgency—'so little done, so much to do'—and tempted him to short-cut the paths of history. The publication of his will made known the great benefaction with which his name will ever be associated, the scholarships to bring to Oxford young men from all over the English-speaking world.

The war was over when Kruger followed Rhodes to the grave. Having bequeathed a political testament to his people, he died in Switzerland, 'far from the land to which he had devoted his life'. His burial with great ceremony in Pretoria coincided with the political revival of the Afrikaners.

The five years that followed the peace were the period of 'Reconstruction'. The term reminds us once again of the American Civil War, but in leniency to the conquered the comparison is very much in favour of the British reconstruction of South Africa. In America twelve years elapsed before the last of the Southerners were free to govern themselves, and by then the rights of the Negro were enshrined in the federal constitution. In South Africa the period was five years, and political rights were not given to Africans. Had they been given, the Boers could not have risen with new political strength from the grave of the republics; and Milner thought this concession in the treaty the greatest mistake of his life. But he had not acted merely out of tenderness for the feelings of his defeated enemies. On this question there was no difference between Boer and Uitlander. Milner was not a Lincoln, and the British South Africans were not New Englanders.

The burghers returning from the field, and their wives from the concentration camps, to their ruined homesteads were in no mood to praise the administrative efficiency of the new government. Yet Milner, who had been tactless as a diplomatist and one-sided as a politician, carried out the administrative task of reconstruction with great credit. Agriculture had to be revived during two seasons of drought; the railways repaired and used for civil purposes when they were strained by the loads of troops and homecoming internees and prisoners of war; a brand new administrative organisation created; and the mines brought back into operation. All this was done. The money granted in accordance with the peace terms, and more besides, was quickly distributed. The plan to flood the new colonies with British immigrants failed, though a few hundred were placed on the land; the genius of South African history worked steadily against the growth of a rural British population.

Milner wanted immigrants, anglicisation and prosperity before the time should come for parliaments and elected majorities. The only force that could bring these things quickly was gold. The derelict mines had to be got to work as rapidly as possible. But the large African labour force on which they depended had melted away. The wages offered at first were even lower than before the war, and other means of livelihood had in the meantime become available to the African. It was impossible to recruit the required number of miners by traditional means.

Two alternatives suggested themselves. One was white labour, which one mine manager thought he had proved to be practicable. This manager, F. H. P. Creswell, was destined to play a political rôle in which his white labour idea was dominant. But other mining authorities disagreed. As for bringing poor immigrants from Europe, it was thought very bad policy to have Europeans alongside Africans, doing the same work, and for wages 'little if any higher'.

There remained the proposal to introduce Chinese coolies. If this immigration were to follow the plan of the importation of Indians to Natal, South Africa would have a new racial problem on her hands to complicate the already over-complicated situation. On this point there was general agreement. But the plan was to import the coolies for a limited time and a special purpose, to prevent them from entering any other occupation but the unskilled mining work for which they were intended, and to guarantee their repatriation to China when the work was done. This was just traditional 'native policy' in an extreme form. The labourers were to be brought from further afield than the Transkei or Mozambique, but like Africans they were to serve the white man's purposes without being allowed to become a part of his society.

The opposition to the scheme—in South Africa—arose from doubts whether the repatriation would in fact be achieved. The advocacy of the scheme, not only by the mining magnates, is explained by the urgent necessity to develop the gold industry as a basis for general economic recovery and expansion.

The Chinese began to arrive in 1904, and gold mining did rapidly develop. But the political effects were at least as great as the economic. The Liberal party in Britain took up the cry of 'Chinese slavery' as an electioneering weapon, and partly because of it

achieved the landslide electoral victory of 1906. While the British
Liberals complained that the coolies were shut up in compounds like
slaves, the Transvaal people protested that they were not fenced in
at all, but wandered about the Rand to commit crimes. The new
British government took steps to release them from their slavery, but
the coolies regarded repatriation as the rude awakening from their
most cherished dream—to remain in South Africa. By 1910 the last
of the Chinese had departed.

The Liberal victory in England had a momentous effect on South
Africa. After the war the Boer leaders had, apart from the visit of a
few deputations to Europe, lived in retirement, attending to their
farms and the practice of the law. They refused to sit on the nominated legislative councils of the new colonies. They protested at
some of Milner's financial arrangements, and still more at the
anglicising policy of the new education departments, which allotted
too little time to the Dutch language in the schools. But it was the
Chinese question that gave the final stimulus to political action.

Under the leadership of Botha, the Transvaal Boers formed a
party called *Het Volk*, The People. Its principal demand was
responsible government, from which all other blessings would
flow. A minority of the Transvaal British, who supported this
demand, organised a Responsible Government party, which was
later called Nationalist and worked in alliance with Het Volk. The
British who inherited the Uitlander-Milner tradition became the
Progressive Party. This bore the same name as the pro-British party
organised in the Cape Colony after the Jameson Raid. In the Orange
River Colony Hertzog and De Wet were the chief organisers of the
Orangia-Unie, analogous to Het Volk.

The British elements in all the colonies but Natal now faced
strong Afrikaner parties (everywhere supported by small British
minorities) which had good prospects of success at the polls. In the
Cape the Progressives were in a better position than before the war,
because the rebels had been disfranchised for five years. An attempt
had been made to suspend the constitution of the colony, to give
further security to the British during the reconstruction period; but
the opposition of other parts of the Empire, as well as of the
parliamentary feelings of Chamberlain himself, frustrated it. In
1904 elections were held, and a narrow Progressive majority brought
Jameson, of unhappy memory, into power.

His allies in the new colonies were uneasy. The Conservatives in
Britain planned a representative system, without a responsible
executive, for those territories. But the Liberals would go further.

They had opposed Chamberlain, Milner and all their works for ten years. Now Smuts, the Boer General, came to London to ask for responsible government. Campbell-Bannerman, the Prime Minister, was convinced. Smuts put in writing what he and Botha had resolved when peace was signed: 'Let it be clearly understood once and for all that the Boers and their leaders do not wish to raise the question of the annexation of the new Colonies or the British flag. They accept accomplished facts.' On this basis Campbell-Bannerman resolved to trust the Boers. He carried his cabinet with him at a meeting in which at least one member was moved to tears. Full responsible government was given to the Transvaal and, shortly after, to the Orange River Colony.

To Botha and Smuts the undertaking about the annexation and the British flag became a debt of honour. They regarded, as many others have done, the concession to the so recently defeated republics as the noblest act in British history. It wiped out the past, the 'century of wrong'. But in the Orange River Colony a different view prevailed. Hertzog regarded the grant of responsible government as merely the fulfilment of one of the terms of the peace treaty; others of its terms, as for instance the status of the Dutch language, he (wrongly) thought Britain had shamefully failed to honour. He had put his name to no document accepting the annexations as irrevocable; he had only signed the peace treaty, which Smuts had not done. These differences of opinion were destined in time to rise to the surface of politics.

In 1907 elections were held in the new self-governing colonies. Het Volk and its British allies won a large majority in the Transvaal, while in the neighbouring state the Orangia-Unie made very nearly a clean sweep of the constituencies. Botha became Premier of the Transvaal, with Smuts as his principal lieutenant; Fischer Premier of the Orange River Colony with Hertzog as second in command. The Boers had lost the war but won the peace.

E

9

NATIONALISM

The emotional forces that were to move the various peoples of South Africa after 1907 had already become clearly apparent by then.

The Afrikaner people, formed in the eighteenth century, was a self-conscious nationality by the twentieth. This consummation was long in coming. Though Afrikaners were conscious of their differences from other people since the time of W. A. van der Stel, their feeling could not for many generations be called a national one. Even the republics formed after the Great Trek lacked this sentiment. The Free State had many English-speaking citizens, and many colonial Afrikaners, to whom state boundaries meant little. President Boshof came to Bloemfontein from Natal, and after his term of office returned to Natal, to his British allegiance and a political rôle in that colony. Brand came from the Cape, and while President accepted a British knighthood. The English language was generally spoken in Bloemfontein, even by many people of Dutch descent. Free State farmers owned other farms in the Cape or Natal, and British colonists had farms in the Free State.

This easy intercourse with the British was less noticeable in the Transvaal, but that country was for many years so deeply divided by faction that it lacked even the elements of a national consciousness. In the Cape Colony the anglicising process went on through the nineteenth century. School and Kerk were filled with Scotsmen. Dutch Reformed services were often conducted in English. Portraits and effigies of Queen Victoria were venerated even in farmhouses where English was not understood. The Cape Afrikaners were led and represented by the partly anglicised squirearchy and townsmen of the Boland, between whom and the pastoralists of the interior there was a gulf dating back for generations. These leaders in Church and State deplored the Great Trek and all its consequences.

The diverse elements were moved towards a common sentiment and national unity by British policy. The annexation of Basutoland and Griqualand West started the process. The feeling that the Free State had been wronged made Afrikaners everywhere aware that the Free Staters were their own people. In the Cape Colony this feeling merged with another, that the Afrikaners there were subjects of a régime not their own. English being the official language, people who could not speak it fluently were excluded from public life. Few Afrikaners sat in the Cape Parliament or held positions in the civil service. To the simple Boer of the *platteland* the whole apparatus of State appeared as an alien institution imposed on him from without. But it must not be forgotten that his ancestors had felt much the same about the East India Company.

The Dutchman was almost as much a foreigner as the Englishman. When the Afrikaner put pen to paper he struggled to express himself in a language which he encountered chiefly in his ponderous *Statenbijbel*, but which as a spoken language was quite foreign to him. If the use of the Dutch language was required, most Afrikaners felt as uneasy and inferior as if they had to use English. Many used English more naturally than Dutch, and preferred it even for their love-letters. But the feelings of their souls could be properly uttered only in the despised *patois* which did not yet rank among the languages of the world.

After the middle of the century this difficulty gave rise to a movement in favour of Afrikaans as a written language. Homely poems were published. In 1875 the launching of the 'Society of True Afrikaners' at Paarl brought this 'first language movement' into the limelight. Rules of spelling and grammar were laid down and a newspaper founded. The protagonists of Afrikaans had a long row to hoe. Most of their educated countrymen clung to the language of Holland. But a new literary life was given to the popular tongue after the Anglo-Boer War, when the 'second language movement' produced poetry and other writing of a higher order, and the *taal* began to show signs of approaching maturity.

In the meantime national sentiment developed independently of the language movement. The British annexation of the Transvaal did much to foster it, but the War of Independence and the victory of Majuba still more, starting a thrill of pride and a blood-is-thicker-

than-water feeling all over the Afrikaans-speaking world. In the
Cape two organisations came to life during the British occupation
of the Transvaal. One, the Afrikaner Bond, was begotten by the
same parents as the language movement. Its object was to cultivate
national sentiment among the Afrikaners, and its tone was republican
and anti-British. The other, the Farmers Protection Union, was
a response to an excise duty which was greatly resented by the
wine farmers. But J. H. Hofmeyr—affectionately known as Onze
Jan, Our John—had much wider objects in view for this body. It
was to be a means of stimulating the political consciousness and
activity of the Cape Afrikaners. When the two organisations merged
under the name of the Afrikaner Bond and the leadership of Hofmeyr,
the latter weaned the movement from its republican tendency and
inculcated loyalty to the Crown. The fostering of national self-
respect among Afrikaners and of a South African nationality
embracing people of all races whose primary allegiance was to South
Africa remained its principal objects.

The Bond was as highly organised as an army; it was not only for
many years the only political party in the Cape, but the lineal
ancestor of more than one party existing at the present day. It
procured the election of Afrikaners to Parliament; got the Dutch
language recognised, first in parliamentary debate, then to an ever
increasing degree in education, the civil service and for other official
purposes.

Though functioning as a political party and represented by a
solid phalanx in Parliament, the Bond as such never formed a
government. Hofmeyr felt that a Bond government would provoke
the British colonists to counter-organisation and so produce political
division on racial lines. His policy was therefore to support an
English-speaking Premier on his own terms, and to withdraw that
support when it was no longer deserved. During the 'eighties and
early 'nineties there developed, therefore, a rough and unstable
division of the English-speaking politicians into a pro-Bond and an
anti-Bond group. The former justified its position to its own people
by claiming that the Bond was loyal to the Crown and the British
connection, while the latter gained strength whenever that loyalty
appeared to be doubtful. Rhodes, who became an intimate friend of
Hofmeyr, was pro-Bond, and was kept in office by Bond votes.

Had Cape politics not been affected by events outside the colony,
the Bond and its allies might have become and remained an ordinary
political party. But the focus of all South African politics was
situated in the Transvaal, and the reaction to the British annexation

there determined the political feelings of Afrikaners everywhere. In the course of 1879 a series of mass meetings was held in the annexed republic, bringing together the great bulk of the burghers of the whole country. For the first time these farmers, who lived in isolation, realised that they had a common cause and became aware of a national sentiment. Out of that awareness sprang the War of Independence. When it ended in victory at Majuba a passionate excitement and rejoicing stirred both the republicans and the colonial Afrikaners, and from that time a feeling of identity united them all.

In the following years the friction between Britain and the Transvaal—not the Free State—kept the South African Republic in the foreground of the Cape Afrikaner's vision. His heart beat in sympathy with the Transvaal over Bechuanaland, Swaziland, the outlet to the sea, and other controversies. Yet his feelings were mixed, for loyalty to the Queen and attachment to his own economic interests often prompted him to oppose Kruger's policy. His feet were set on the road to complete identity with the republican Transvaler, but further shocks would be needed to impel him forward on that way.

In the republics themselves nationalism was fostered by an outside influence. The burghers of those countries being farmers, and the population of the small towns largely English, the republican governments looked to Holland for the trained officials needed to run the machinery of State. This was done to a very slight extent in the Free State, but in a big way in the Transvaal. The Hollanders came from the nation-conscious Europe of the nineteenth century, and were shocked by the easy-going indifference to state boundaries which they found in South Africa. They used their influence to inculcate national feeling, which as they saw it should be not very different from Dutch national feeling. Even in the early days of the Trek emissaries from Holland had brought such notions to the laagers of Natal and the interior, where there was much hoisting of Dutch flags and emphasis on the common Netherlandish traditions.

This was the background of Afrikanerdom when it heard the news of the Jameson Raid. Everywhere people who had come under English influence and were forgetting that blood is thicker than water received what was described as an electric shock. A wave of national feeling swept over the people, a more powerful wave even than in 1881.

During all these years, the sentiment of nationality was giving rise to concepts in the sphere of practical politics. Such slogans as 'a united South Africa under its own flag' and 'Africa for the

Afrikaners' showed the aspirations which national feeling had provoked. The flag envisaged was the Transvaal Vierkleur, the Union an enlarged South African Republic. Kruger became the hero of many a colonial Afrikaner.

It was natural therefore that such a man, British subject as he was, should regard the Anglo-Boer War as an attack by Britain on his 'own people'. The influence of Hofmeyr kept the Bond, as such, formally loyal and practically neutral. But numbers of Bondsmen felt it their duty to take up arms for the republics, and many more used political means to hamper the British effort or mitigate the consequences of the republican defeat. Colonial Afrikaners felt this defeat as if it had been inflicted on themselves, and those who had not fought actively on the Boer side were none the less bitter for that.

In the aftermath of the war Afrikaner sentiment was embodied in three separate but now parallel and sympathetic organisations: the Bond in the Cape, Het Volk in the Transvaal and the Orangia-Unie in the Orange River Colony. But in each of these there was a division of feeling and opinion. While all had the same sentiment of nationality, they did not agree on their attitudes to the British flag and allegiance and the British population in their midst. Hofmeyr and a section of the Bond persisted in their aim of uniting the two white nationalities, and accepted the British flag at least for the time being. Botha, Smuts and their followers in Het Volk felt that the grant of self-government to the Transvaal imposed the same opinion on them as a matter of honour. But other members of Het Volk and the Bond and a larger proportion of the Orangia-Unie clung to the hope of a republican restoration and maintained the attitude that had been general before 1899. For the time being the two opinions continued side by side without splitting the party organisations.

It was inevitable that the growth of Afrikaner nationalism should stimulate British sentiment on the other side. The rise of the Afrikaner Bond, the recognition of Dutch as an official language, the defeat at Majuba and the retrocession of the Transvaal all led to protest and indignation on the British side in the Cape Colony. Then as always the British attitude was conditioned by the fact that the Afrikaners were a majority of the white population. The colony had become accustomed to an English-speaking Parliament and the British section had regarded the gradual anglicisation of the Afrikaners as pointing to the future unity of the colony on an Anglo-Saxon basis. While these conditions remained the British section could fight for responsible government, condemn the interference of the 'imperial factor' and even, at times, apply the name 'Afrikander' to itself. But the rise of the new nationalism—'a new force that affects the imagination like a nightmare with silent horrible pressure'—led to a change of heart. The imperial factor came to be thought of as a bulwark against the dangers of 'Africa for the Afrikaners' and their 'own flag'. Thus the sentiment which was in essence a British nationalism acquired the name of imperialism and often led to exaggerated emphasis on Empire and British Supremacy. After Majuba, and during the struggle for the possession of Bechuanaland, British colonists formed the Empire League for the defence of the imperial connection. But this passed away with the crisis which had given it birth. The need for such a league was not widely felt, since every Cape government had English-speaking leaders and the Bond always remained in the background. Attempts to extend the Bond to the republics failed there for the same reason: the Afrikaners were in power and saw no need for a Bond.

The crisis of the Jameson Raid, which sent an 'electric shock' through the Afrikaners, did much the same for the British. The group of anti-Bond members of Parliament, who had come to be called Progressives, now formed a well-organised party under that name. Behind it in the constituencies stood the South African League, successor to the Empire League and a counterpart of the Bond. The Progressives lost the bitterly fought election of 1898 by the narrowest of margins; won that of 1904 equally narrowly when the rebels were disfranchised; and lost in 1908 when the rebels voted again. In the meantime, in 1903, the Bondsmen in Parliament and their English-speaking allies had adopted the name of the South African Party.

The British were quicker to organise in the Transvaal, where they were Uitlanders, than in the Cape Colony. But the Transvaal National Union could play no part in legitimate politics. After the war that body was succeeded by a Progressive Party in which the personnel of the National Union played a leading part.

Everywhere but in Natal the organised forces of British nationalism confronted the still stronger forces of Afrikaner nationalism. That a British minority supported the latter side was due to several factors. Such support was given always on the understanding that the Bond or Het Volk accepted the British flag and allegiance, and this understanding was always honoured by a part, though not the whole, of those bodies. This obstacle removed, the pro-Bond British took their stand on the principle that the two white national-ities must be drawn together, and that the Progressive Parties with their frankly anti-Afrikaner attitude could not do this. Rhodes, except for a brief moment before the war when he 'came out strongly as a Progressive', consistently supported the view that co-operation between the white sections was a necessary basis of politics. He expressed this opinion even to a very Jingo audience in the midst of the war. Lastly, this British section was antagonised by the flamboyant chauvinism of the Progressives, and by what they thought the shameful acts, culminating in the Raid, done in the British name. But they were no less insistent than their opponents on the maintenance of the British connection; a fact to be remembered if later political developments are to be understood.

A nation is held together by a common historical tradition. By the first decade of the twentieth century the Afrikaners had developed such a tradition and embodied it in historical literature. The machinations of the early missionaries, the Black Circuit, Slagter's Nek, the great romance of the Trek, the embattled laagers standing against Zulus and Matabele, England's pursuit of the Trekkers and her unjust appropriation of Natal, Basutoland, Griqualand West, the Transvaal itself, Zululand, Rhodesia; the Uitlanders undermining the South African Republic from within, then the Jameson Raid, the Boer War, the farm-burning and the concentration camps, the anglicising policy in the Cape and later in the annexed republics —all this formed the single track of history that gave Afrikaners a sense of common sufferings and a common destiny.

But in the year 1907 such history was not taught in schools. There the emphasis was still on the greatness of the Empire and the glory of its conquests. The Afrikaner schoolboy, reading *ad nauseam* of '1066 and all that', Wolfe and Clive, turned in repulsion to what he thought was his own tradition. Descendants of Western Province landlords and Scottish predikants who had revered Queen Victoria and condemned the Trek came to feel as if their own ancestors had been murdered by Dingaan or beaten him at Blood River.

When the Afrikaner version at last penetrated the school-books and was patronised by education departments, it would be the turn of the British child to be repelled and to cast about for a tradition that he could feel to be his own. But in 1907 that day was still far off.

10

UNION AND DISUNITY

That the two old British colonies and the two former republics of South Africa should have merged in a close legislative union on the eighth anniversary of the treaty of Vereeniging is often regarded as one of the miracles of political history. In fact it is not more remarkable than that the union, so quickly achieved in outward form, has not been realised in the hearts of men to the present day.

The causes of the unification were both sentimental and practical. The Afrikaner people were, after 1902, acutely aware of their common national identity. Before the war there had been clumsy attempts to federate South Africa, but Grey and Carnarvon had failed. Rhodes faced the apparently insuperable obstacle of the independence of the republics on the one hand and the British allegiance of the colonies on the other. How could both be preserved in a single union? The war removed this obstacle. All South Africa now owed allegiance to the same crown and flew the same flag. In the bitterness of defeat many far-seeing Afrikaners thought that a new ideal ought now to be substituted for the old. Republican independence was lost, but a union of all Afrikaners—together with the British—in one state had now become technically possible, and might lead to greater things than the republics had ever had in their grasp.

Among the British federation was an old political tradition, now sanctified by the memory of Rhodes. He had bequeathed his home, Groote Schuur, to the government of a united South Africa as the official residence of its Prime Minister. Union under the British flag had been the main object of his life's work. The examples of

Canada and, more recently, Australia were a challenge to British colonists in Africa.

Had the problem been one of uniting purely British and purely Afrikaner states it is safe to say that it would not have been solved in 1910. But the populations were mixed; the Afrikaners were in great strength everywhere outside Natal, the British everywhere outside the Orange River Colony. A union of states might therefore come with a great flourish of trumpets and mutual felicitations, yet leave the fusion of the two white nationalities as far off as ever.

As this was well understood by many men, some approached the question with ulterior aims in view. Could the union be so contrived as to give predominance to British, or to Afrikaner, ideals and power? In 1906 the Progressives governed the Cape, Natal of course was British, and the other two were crown colonies. A union under Progressive auspices might be made. But the Liberals had just come into office in Britain, self-government was to be given to the ex-republics, and neither the Bond nor Het Volk would support a move while crown colony administration remained. By the end of 1907 the picture had changed. There was responsible government everywhere, the Dutch governed the Transvaal and Orange River Colony, and though Jameson was still in power in the Cape he was willing to work with Botha and Fischer. F. S. Malan, a former Bond extremist who had been led to the ideal of conciliation by his deep religious convictions, made the first move, supported by Jameson, in the Cape Parliament. Lord Selborne, High Commissioner and Governor of the inland colonies, gave the weight of his name to a memorandum drafted by Lionel Curtis, one of Milner's young Oxford men in the Transvaal administration. The High Commissioner was determined to avoid Carnarvon's mistake of thrusting an ideal upon unwilling South Africans, and did not publish the memorandum till invited by the Cape government to do so. Thus the question of unification was brought before the public. By 1908, when the National Convention met in Durban to draw up a scheme, Merriman and the South African Party were in office in Cape Town; the Union would be under Afrikaner auspices after all.

The Selborne memorandum had said little about the sentimental aspect. Without that, there were enough practical reasons to make union an urgent necessity. In 1903 all British South Africa had at last been united in a customs union; but the competition between Natal and the Cape for the Transvaal trade, the preference of the Transvaal for the Delagoa Bay route and its ability, because of its wealth, to dictate terms to everybody threatened to break the union.

The question was one of railways even more than customs tariffs. Although the railways of the two former republics were now run by a common administration, which therefore profited by all traffic north of the Orange instead of only north of the Vaal, the Lourenço Marques route was still more profitable to it than the others. It was an advantage also to the Portuguese, and they made the adequate use of that line a condition for the recruitment of African labour in Mozambique for the Rand mines. With the departure of the Chinese the mines were dependent on Mozambique labour. Without a political union, and particularly a union of the railways, the customs union might break up and the paths of the four colonies diverge.

A Zulu rebellion in Natal in 1906 revived memories of Langalibalele, of Shepstone and the Zulu War, and pointed the need for uniformity of native policy. Still more serious was the position in Europe. Ex-President Steyn insisted that South Africa must be united before a great war in Europe came to divide the country more profoundly than ever. What kind of unity he had in mind was obscure at the time but became clearer in the sequel.

These and all the other advantages of unity, such as drove the Americans, Canadians, Germans and Australians into federation, were in the minds of the constitution-makers who assembled in Durban in the insufferable heat of October, 1908. Further meetings in Cape Town and Bloemfontein rounded off the work in 1909. The lead was taken by the Transvalers. Smuts drew up a draft as a basis for discussion, and had the advantage that his party and its Progressive opponents had reached agreement before they went to Durban. The Transvaal had the further advantage of being the rich relation. The other colonies would gain financially by union, and the financial sacrifice of the Transvalers entitled them to a respectful hearing. But Botha, Smuts and their party did not represent the 'moneyed interest' of their colony. The Progressives were the party of the mining magnates. It is conceivable that if they had been in power they would have driven a harder bargain.

It was perhaps the dominant position of the Transvaal, and the dominance of Het Volk in that colony, that decided the Convention in favour of the close union that was adopted. Natal was strongly federalist and in the Cape Colony the principle of federation was supported by Hofmeyr and Schreiner. Their chief motive was to safeguard the liberal native policy of the Colony. But neither Hofmeyr nor Schreiner was in the Convention, and other leaders took a different view. In the end the Union constitution was ratified by three Parliaments and by a referendum in Natal.

In some ways the agreements in the Convention were due to misunderstandings. Different men expected different results from the same arrangements. Hertzog and his political friends would not have accepted these arrangements if they had known that five years hence the Union would fight at Britain's side in a European war. The British generally would not have accepted them if they had known that, in fifteen years, Hertzog and his Nationalists would be in power. De Villiers, Merriman, Sauer and others would have made very different arrangements if they had foreseen that, in twenty-seven years, the Cape native franchise would be abolished.

But hope is greater than fear. When the South Africa Act was passed by the British Parliament in 1909 everyone saw in it such possibilities as he wanted to see. Many of its provisions were similar to those which other Dominions had adopted from the British constitution: a Governor-General, Senate and House of Assembly; a Cabinet of ministers responsible to Parliament; a single supreme court with provincial and local divisions and an appellate division (here South Africa differed from the federal countries); a permanent civil service. The Senate (here was a trace of federalism) represented the equality of the provinces, the eight Senators from each province being elected by the provincial councillors and the province's members of the House of Assembly. There were in addition eight nominated Senators, four of whom were to be acquainted with the wishes of the Africans. As Senators held their seats for ten years, their house might come to be of a different complexion from 'another place', whose life span was five years. Hertzog later obtained power for a government to dissolve the Senate after a general election for the lower house.

The composition of the House of Assembly was a controversial matter. The franchise laws of the colonies differed, and none would give way to the others on this point. They therefore agreed to differ. The Cape kept its property and literacy tests and no colour bar; the colour bar in the other colonies, frank in the ex-republics and decently clothed in Natal, remained. But non-Europeans, who remained eligible for the Cape Provincial Council, could not sit in the Union Parliament. As a concession to the Cape the non-European vote there could not be abolished without a two-thirds majority of both houses sitting together. Since the extension of that system to the north required no special procedure, it seemed obvious to the Cape liberals that their ideas were destined to spread.

How were seats to be apportioned among the provinces? The north would not allow the coloured voters of the Cape to be taken nto account. But if only white voters were counted, the Cape would suffer through having many Europeans who did not qualify for the franchise. Hence the next compromise: seats apportioned among the provinces in proportion to the adult white male population, but apportioned within each province according to the number of registered voters.

It was an Afrikaner tradition, realised both in the republics and the Cape Colony, that the rural areas should be more strongly represented than the towns. The urban British countered this, which they thought a racial stigma upon themselves, with 'one vote one value'. As a compromise the commission of judges, which was to delimit the constituencies every five years, was empowered to depart 15 per cent either way from the provincial quota, so that a 'sparsely inhabited', i.e. rural, constituency might have a smaller electorate and an urban one a greater.

The provinces were completely subordinated to the Union Parliament, the ordinances of the provincial councils being valid only if not in conflict with a Union statute. These councils were given control of education 'other than higher', of hospitals, municipal institutions and a few other matters, their taxing powers were limited and their executive committees were subordinated to Administrators appointed by the central government.

The equality of the Dutch and English languages for all official purposes was guaranteed, and like the Cape franchise could be altered only by a two-thirds majority of both houses sitting together. As a happy concession to old feelings, the name of the Orange Free State was restored, and 'House of Assembly' was rendered into Dutch as *Volksraad*.

All these hurdles surmounted, the Convention was nearly disrupted by the question of the capital. The solution represented by Washington, Ottawa and Canberra was entertained but rejected in favour of a judgment of Solomon: Pretoria to be the executive capital, Cape Town the legislative, and Bloemfontein the judicial; Pietermaritzburg to have monetary compensation. Thus ministers and a host of civil servants would have to migrate, like storks or swallows, with the parliamentary seasons.

A democratic constitution is like a machine which requires a force— steam, oil, electricity—to work it. Public opinion expressed through a party system is that force. The makers of a constitution seldom trouble themselves about this noisy but indispensable adjunct to their machine.

Could the statesmen of 1909 have devised a party system suited to the working of the constitution? Could they have grouped them-

selves into two parties differing on questions of tariff, railway rating
policy, provincial powers and the like, while agreeing on the essential
constitutional questions? It is very unlikely. In the Afrikaner tradition
the ideal party, to which the development of any party must tend,
was an organisation embracing the whole Afrikaner nation and
expressing its national sentiments: thus the Bond, Het Volk, the
Orangia-Unie. The opponents of these had formed analogous parties
with the slogan 'Vote British'. The British who rejected this sentiment worked with the Afrikaner parties. That was the tradition of
the country. It did not extend to Natal, where there was no developed
party system but a rough division between the trading and sugar
planting interests of the coast and the farming interest of the
interior, Durban against Pietermaritzburg.

When Botha was called upon to form the first Union ministry,
he put it together out of the existing ministries, which were all of the
same complexion except in Natal. The members elected in that
province were mostly non-party independents. Botha's followers then
came together to merge their parties into one. The South African
Party and its Afrikaner Bond, Het Volk and the Orangia-Unie
flowed together into one South African National Party, from whose
name the 'national' was shortly dropped.

The principal opposition came from the 'Vote British' Unionist
Party, the successor of the Progressives. At this stage, two years
after Union, the party division was substantially what it had been
in the Transvaal since the war and in the Cape for a generation. But
the divisions within the South African Party were about to become
more significant. A split was brought about by General Hertzog,
Botha's Minister of Justice.

Hertzog had, before 1910, been Minister of Education in the
Orange River Colony. There he had introduced into the schools a
system of compulsory bilingualism and of instruction through both
media for the same pupils in different subjects. This measure produced a violent reaction among the British throughout South Africa.
Apart from the educational issue involved, it was fashionable for
the British to despise everything 'Dutch', to regard the learning of
that language as a waste of time, and to assume that English, even in
the Orange River Colony, must become increasingly dominant. This
attitude was the chief cause of the great emphasis on language rights
by the other side. But 'Hertzogism' became such a bogey to the
British that Botha was nervous of including Hertzog in his cabinet.

The Union Parliament being supreme and unhampered by federal
restrictions, the school question was raised in it almost from the

beginning, even though schools were a provincial matter. The tact of Botha, Malan and others procured a report which condemned the purely English-medium system of the other provinces as well as the element of compulsion in the Free State, but Hertzog felt aggrieved. Tension increased till in 1912 he made a series of speeches announcing the principles of 'South Africa first', Empire second, and the 'two streams' in which the two nationalities should flow separately for a time. In the distant future the two streams might flow together, but then the stream which had its origin in the soil, history and traditions of South Africa would be dominant and would absorb the other. 'The Afrikaner must be the master in South Africa.' In the term 'Afrikaner' he would include English-speaking people, but only those whose national sentiments were the same as his.

This was 'Hertzogism' with a vengeance, and the British section reacted sharply to it. A minister from Natal resigned from the cabinet. As Hertzog refused to do likewise, Botha himself resigned and re-formed the cabinet without Hertzog. By 1914 the latter and his followers had set up the National Party, based on the principles Hertzog had announced. It was not formally a republican or secessionist party, but Afrikaner national aspirations were its driving force. Its strength lay mainly in the Free State, where it soon became dominant. The memory of 1902, of the Free Staters' resentment against Botha and his Transvalers, was not dead.

The new party was hardly, as its members would say, 'dry behind the ears', when the expected crisis broke upon Europe. Against such a possibility the Union had just established its Defence Force, of which Beyers, Boer War veteran, was Commandant-General. Botha informed the British government that the Union could take over its own defences, setting free the imperial forces for service elsewhere. Britain, while gratefully accepting this offer, asked the Union to invade German South-West Africa and capture the wireless stations. Botha would do it. But knowing his countrymen he called a meeting of the rural commandants to test their feeling. Personal loyalty to Botha proved to be their predominant feeling.

With equal caution and tact the Prime Minister resolved to use only volunteers for the expedition. But rumours to the contrary had already spread. War for England against Germany was more than many 'bitter-enders' could stomach. Some thought, like the Irish, that England's difficulty was the Boers' opportunity. Now was the chance to 'throw off the yoke' and restore the republics. A well-known 'prophet' in the Western Transvaal had encouraging visions. In that area and in the Free State an ill-co-ordinated rebellion broke out. Famous Boer veterans supported it. Steyn refused to use his influence against it. Hertzog did so, but cautiously, afraid of losing his influence altogether. Beyers resigned his command, rebelled, and was drowned while crossing the swollen Vaal River. De la Rey was accidentally shot before the fighting started. De Wet was captured. One commander went over to the Germans with most of his men, and was followed by escaping rebels. But Botha, using almost exclusively Afrikaner troops, put down the rebellion, and meted out very mild punishment. Only one rebel, who had neglected to resign his commission before he went over to the revolt, was shot.

The Union could then play its part in the war. Botha rapidly conquered German South-West. South African troops then went to Europe and to German East Africa, where General Smuts took command of the whole imperial force and soon ousted the Germans from their main positions. Smuts then went to England, to the Imperial War Cabinet, to the British War Cabinet itself; was offered and refused the Palestine command; played a prominent part in negotiations on the continent, in Ireland, and with Welsh strikers, and in founding the League of Nations. Botha and Smuts went to the Peace Conference, but memories of Vereeniging taught them that the vindictive peace was a disaster. Only with great difficulty could Botha persuade Smuts to sign it.

That Smuts should have played so great a part on the world stage, that South Africa with the other Dominions should have been a signatory of the peace treaty and a member of the League of Nations, and been entrusted by the League with the government of South-West Africa under mandate, all meant a new and honourable status for the Union. But it was not good enough for the Nationalists. Their party had been given a great fillip by the 1914 rebellion. At the election of the following year it made a considerable show, though its main strength was still confined to the Free State and the south-western Transvaal.

While Botha and Smuts went to Paris to make peace, Hertzog with a Nationalist delegation went unofficially to take advantage of the new principle of the rights of small nations. They wanted republican independence for South Africa; failing that, the restoration of the former republics, or of the Free State at least. Lloyd George told them, in effect, that South Africans were masters of their own house, in which neither he nor anyone else could interfere, His attitude was apt, and constitutionally correct, but glossed over tbe fact that South Africa was not yet one house, and that there were still 'no South Africans'.

Worn out by war and peace-making, Botha died soon after his return from Versailles, and was succeeded by Smuts. In 1920 Smuts faced the third general election, and with unhappy results. As against 41 S.A.P. seats, plus 3 pro-government independents, the Nationalists won 44, the Unionists 25 and Labour 21. The Unionists had supported the government on the war issue, and would do so now against the Nationalists; but if Labour supported the Opposition the government's majority would be negligible. The S.A.P. obviously needed a closer rapprochement with some other party. It approached Hertzog first, but these negotiations broke down on the question of republicanism, on which the Nationalists were now insistent. Smuts then turned to the Unionists, who accepted his terms and merged with the South African Party. This produced results at a new election in 1921: S.A.P., 79; Nationalists, 45; Labour, 9; and 1 independent.

Here was a change in the party system. Whereas a purely British party had up to 1915 provided the main opposition to an Afrikaner party with some British support, now all the British outside the Labour movement had merged with the moderate Afrikaners, and were opposed by a militant, republican and rising Afrikaner Nationalism. It was almost as if Rhodes and Kruger were facing each other again, and across the floor of a common chamber. The natural swing of the pendulum against the government would lead Afrikaner 'Saps', but not British, to go over to the opposition. The South African Party would become increasingly British, and the dividing line between parties would come near to coinciding with the division of race and nationality. The other obvious prospect was that, when the Nationalists had increased a little more, Labour would hold the balance of power. Against this background the sudden growth of the Labour movement in 1922 can be seen in its significant proportions.

Trade unions, socialism and 'Labour members' had burst upon South Africa after the Boer War. The white miners on the Rand were mostly Englishmen, largely Cornishmen. Their background was the long struggle of British trade unionism, culminating in the recent setback of the Taff Vale decision. But in the Transvaal their movement acquired a new feature. They fought not only against capitalists, but against the encroachment of cheap African labour on their own profitable preserves. Their leader in the Transvaal Parliament was F. H. P. Creswell, the mine manager who had preferred white to black or yellow labour. In 1922 Creswell was still their leader, now in the Union Parliament. As the Nationalists were at first confined to the Free State and Western Transvaal, so Labour drew almost all its support from the Rand, with a much smaller following in Durban and Cape Town.

The industrial atmosphere of the Rand, like the physical atmosphere, was highly charged with electricity. Before 1914 Johannesburg householders grew accustomed to keeping stocks of candles, and baths full of water, against the chance of strikes. The miners had a way of bringing other workers out in sympathy with them. But though one writer describes this period under the heading 'Karl Marx Comes to Town', the strikes on the mines were inspired by something far removed from Marxism. As the old frontiersmen of Graaff-Reinet in 1795 had spoken the language of the French Revolution when they rebelled against Equality and Fraternity, the Rand miners used Marxist jargon and unfurled the socialist banner when they fought for white privilege against black encroachment. They took their stand on certain ratios between white and black workers, and on the exclusion of the black from skilled work. To the mine-owners an increase in the proportion of Africans meant lower working costs—wages being about half their total expenditure. To humanitarians, the exclusion of Africans from skilled work was oppression. If the struggle was between Capital and Labour, it was Capital and Labour Through the Looking-Glass.

Both sides were highly organised. The Trade Unions were federated, and the Transvaal Chamber of Mines was dominated by the handful of great holding companies, which controlled the individual mines. Any local clash was liable to involve these two concentrations of power. In July, 1913, a strike on the East Rand led to rioting in Johannesburg. There was shooting in the streets; the railway station and a newspaper office were burnt down; Botha and Smuts came to the Carlton Hotel, their lives seriously in danger, to negotiate with the strike leaders. The government and the mine-owners gave way. Within six months another strike threatened to become general. Commandos of the new Defence Force were then mobilised, order quickly restored, and the strike leaders deported to England without trial before their followers knew what was happening. The government obtained indemnity from Parliament for this irregular proceeding, but it lost ground in the country. The Labour Party got control of the Transvaal Provincial Council.

When the Great War was over the Rand was troubled again. A fall in the price of gold, in relation to currency and to other prices, made it necessary for the mines to cut their costs if many of them were not to close down. Costs could be cut by increasing the proportion of African workers. Out of this situation arose the strike of March, 1922, which winds blowing from Russia fanned into Revolution. The Council of Action at the head of the strikers included leading members of the new Communist Party. The exclusion of Africans from skilled work can hardly have been part of their policy. They aimed at social revolution and thought that the hour had struck. The rank and file of miners were now no longer Cornishmen but largely Afrikaners from the countryside, who knew as little of Marx as the old Graaff-Reinetters knew of Rousseau. But together these elements organised commandos, drilled and armed, hoisted the red flag, and called on the workers of the world to 'unite and fight for a White South Africa'.

The government, rather belatedly, struck. Battle raged in the suburbs of Johannesburg and along the Reef. The revolt was crushed. The Chamber of Mines imposed its terms. The whole Labour movement turned bitterly against Smuts. Many of the Labour rank and file were Afrikaners, though the leaders were English. What more natural than that they should draw closer to Hertzog, who also demanded that 'Smuts must go'? Hertzog believed in white supremacy; so did Creswell. To achieve common aims they formed an electoral pact, the Nationalists agreeing to keep their secession policy in cold storage while the agreement lasted. The government, after losing a series of by-elections, went to the country in 1924 and was defeated. Smuts held 53 seats, the Nationalists gained 63 and Labour 18. Hertzog formed a joint Nationalist-Labour cabinet, the 'Pact' government. The fall of the South African Party had not, after all, produced a pure and unadulterated Afrikaner ministry.

I I

RACE RELATIONS

The relations between white men and black, during the greater part of South African history, can be expressed in military terms. But the long tradition of warfare across an ill-defined frontier did not cease to be an active force in politics after the last tribal warriors had suffered final defeat.

The advancing white settlement had pushed the Bantu back, but this process was not carried to its logical completion. It could not be, for the Africans continued to increase, and they had to live somewhere. The tide of white colonisation therefore swept round the rocky black islands on which the Africans crowded too densely for comfort. In these territories that remained to them they carried on as well as they could the old tribal life, with chiefs administering native law and allotting land for the use of tribesmen. Traditionally, the chief owned the land in trust for the tribe. His powers of distribution remained, but the legal ownership passed to the white man's government in various forms. Over the chiefs the governments placed officials with superior authority, both administrative and judicial, and Parliament or Volksraad assumed powers of legislation. Generally speaking, the land in native 'reserves' and 'locations' was protected against European encroachment.

The existence of the reserves indicates one aspect of the white man's policy, adopted from the beginning in colonies and republics: the safeguarding of European settlements against the flood of barbarians that would be overwhelming if no space were provided for it. On one side of a frontier, as in the days of the border wars, lay the white man's country; beyond were the hills of 'Kaffirland'.

Yet no European ever proposed that the whole African population should be accommodated in reserves. Native policy had its other side, the provision of a labour supply for farmers and other employers. European colonisation had from the first been based on coloured labour, slave and Hottentot. In the western parts of the Cape the 'Cape Coloured' continued to supply the labour for farm and town, but elsewhere the Bantu were the only source. From their confined territories they were driven out by economic pressure, and looked to the white man for employment. Thus the farmers of the Eastern Province took on many who fled from starvation after the 'suicide' of 1857, and those of the Free State were well provided for at the end of the Basuto wars, when Basutoland was too small to keep its people. Very often the African did not have to move away to work; the European farm was superimposed on him where he stood. 'My grandfather,' says a petty chief in the Transvaal, 'woke one morning at his own kraal and found a white man who said, "You are living on my farm and you must work for me".'

It suited the pioneers well to have African families living on their farms, so long as there were not too many of them. The Republic of Natalia in its short existence laid down a policy in this matter that was afterwards adopted by the other republics: no farm to have more than five African families resident on it. In the South African Republic this law, like some others, was honoured mainly in the breach, but it stood on the statute-book as a reminder of the double aim of the authorities: enough Africans in white areas to provide labour, but not so many as to threaten the white man's control and supremacy. Further, in times of labour shortage, no farmer was to engross the available supply to the detriment of his neighbours.

In Natal the arrangements made by the Republic broke down during the interregnum between the British annexation and the setting up of an effective British administration. From north and south the Bantu poured into the delectable land where no Dingaan or even Panda could tyrannise. By 1854 there were 100,000 of them, and the Boer pioneers found themselves surrounded on their isolated farms or even jostled off them. Shepstone, without the help of a single soldier or policeman, persuaded these unwelcome immigrants to move into certain areas, scattered over the colony, which were set aside as locations for them. Yet every European farm retained its resident families.

The system that developed on the Natal and Transvaal farms, and to a smaller extent in the Free State and the Eastern Province, reminds students of the medieval manor. The heads of the resident

African families were obliged to labour for the farmer during a part of the year that varied from three to six months, and might be either a continuous period or a broken one extending over the year. Their dependants did occasional service too, the women in the house and the boys with the herds. In return these 'labour tenants' were given land to cultivate for themselves and grazing rights on the farm for their stock.

Between this system and that of wage labourers, who were given food and quarters, old clothes and an occasional sheep (more rarely a small cash wage), there was a great variety of intermediate gradations. In the Orange River Colony after the Boer War the 'half shares' system was common: the labourers cultivated the farmer's land and paid him half the crop. This system and labour tenancy sprang naturally from the circumstances of both white farmers and Africans. Both were accustomed to something like a subsistence economy and had no use for cash transactions. One wanted labour and the other land. So they came to an arrangement.

But at the same time there were white landowners with a different tradition and different needs. Speculators had bought up much of the land of Natal without occupying it. Uitlanders in the South African Republic, often through the medium of companies which might be offshoots of the mining companies, did the same. Individual farmers, Briton and Boer, often owned several farms, some of which would be unoccupied and might be in low-lying and malarial districts. When the Africans overflowed from the reserves on to these farms and on to Crown or government land, farmers, companies and governments took advantage of the circumstance to charge a rent. As such tenants crowded densely upon the farms, this was a profitable arrangement, often more profitable and always more dependable than working the land directly. 'Kaffir-farming' seemed as though it might drive white occupants out of the countryside altogether, leaving only absentee landlords.

In the republics no African might own land; he could occupy it on any of the terms that have been described. In the British colonies, however, nothing but poverty prevented an African from buying and occupying any farm whatever. And after the Boer War the Transvaal courts ruled that the same principle applied to that country. This was the position of Africans in regard to land and agricultural labour at the time of Union.

Before that date an inter-colonial commission on Native Affairs had sounded a note of warning to which the first government of the Union immediately gave heed. The spread of 'Kaffir-farming', the increasing number of labour tenants and share-croppers, and the legal possibility of land-purchase by Africans all seemed to point to the extinction of the white race in rural areas. To avert this, limits had to be set to all these processes. Broadly speaking, the Natives Land Act of 1913 attempted to freeze the existing distribution of ownership as between the races (no European land to be sold to Africans or vice versa); to stop the share-cropping system in the Free State at once; and to put an end to cash tenancy ('Kaffir-farming') as the existing contracts ran out. Obviously so many tenants could not be removed without putting them somewhere else. The act was supposed to be a temporary measure, to be followed by a new demarcation of areas for African ownership and occupancy, so that a complete segregation of black from white farmers could be achieved. Pending this demarcation, the Governor-General was given power to grant exemptions from the operation of the law.

When steps were taken to follow up this act as had been intended, an insuperable obstacle was met. While all European farmers were strong supporters of the principle of segregation, none would allow his own district to be included in the African area. Though a commission had made recommendations, the government therefore refused to carry them through Parliament. But the Governor-General's dispensing power was used to allow acquisition by Africans, and also cash tenancy, in the areas which the commission had recommended. Moreover, the Supreme Court ruled that the act did not apply to the Cape Province. There were, therefore, several loopholes for escape from its harsh restrictions. But when Smuts fell in 1924 the promise of 1913 had not yet been fulfilled.

Up to about 1870 the reserves and the European farms together accounted for all the significant part of the African population. The diamond fields then introduced a new factor, which was to increase in importance till it became the central question of 'native policy'. The diamond diggers were skilled Europeans, mostly immigrants. They needed the services of unskilled labourers. The pressure in the reserves had become acute (one remembers the recent constriction of Basutoland), a tide of work-seekers was flowing towards the farms, and a part of it was naturally diverted to Kimberley. A trivial wage, for which no European would work, was quite enough to attract these men whose only alternative was the subsistence economy of villeinage on the farms. By accepting the small cash wage they could leave their families at home on the land, and return there shortly with guns and ammunition. As the individual white diggers gave place to companies, and ultimately to one big company, white men too became employees. But they did skilled work for which high wages had to be paid if competent men were to be attracted to it. Only Europeans, with their high standard of living, could do this work. Africans, with a low standard and willing to accept a low wage, could be obtained in any numbers for unskilled labour. Thus the coming together of two races at very different levels of civilisation in the same industry created a great gulf between the wages of skilled and of unskilled labour.

Johannesburg was the child of Kimberley, and the same dualism grew up on the gold as on the diamond mines. Between them they created the railway system, and that too distinguished between the high wages of the skilled and the low wages of the unskilled, between white and black. In the other jobs available to Africans in the towns—domestic service and the menial work in connection with incipient industries, local and central government, business—the standard set by mines and railways prevailed.

In the first instance these arrangements were the result of natural forces. But vested interests were created which thereafter struggled to resist these forces. A generation of Africans grew up in the towns and knew no other environment. It followed, though at a distance, the white man's way of life, became conscious of new wants and needed money. It progressed from unskilled to semi-skilled work, and was on the way to acquire skill. These Africans came into conflict with various forces. In unskilled occupations they had to compete with the migrants whose homes and families and land were in the reserves, and who could accept a wage which would not support a family that had no other resources. Labour tenants from the farms, during their free time, came to town and left their families to cultivate their plots. These, too, could accept something less than a living wage.

On the other hand the fully urbanised African who did skilled work, though he needed more money than his rustic brother, could accept a wage that would be too low to support a white family. The entry of such people into skilled occupations therefore threatened to oust Europeans from them altogether, or else reduce them to a barbarous standard of living. The skilled white workers formed trade unions, very largely for the purpose of meeting this danger. The strikes of 1913, 1914 and 1922 were concerned with it.

Outside the Cape Province the trade unions generally confined their membership to Europeans. When governments came to terms with the trade unions, therefore, they gave the organised white workers legal means of preserving their monopoly. The strike of

1922 precipitated important legislation. An Apprentices Act regulated apprenticeship in such a way as to require a standard of education which few Africans had a chance to attain. Two years later, just before the Smuts government fell, an Industrial Conciliation Act provided excellent machinery for negotiation between employers and workers, but it excluded 'pass-bearing natives' (almost all Africans outside the Cape) from its operation, and therefore from membership of trade unions recognised by the law. White workers could strike, though this act provided an alternative which made strikes rare after 1924; African workers were prevented from striking by the Native Labour Regulation Act of 1911, which made it a criminal offence for them.

Another act of 1911 provided that certain skilled operations in the mines could be performed by Europeans only, but this touched a very small part of the industrial field. The industrial 'Colour Bar' was maintained less by direct legislative means than by trade unionism, differences of educational opportunity, and the preference of white employers for white workers where they were prevented from paying lower wages to Africans.

The Colour Bar acquired a new importance during the first decade of Union because of the sudden growth of secondary industries. Before 1914 these were insignificant in comparison with agriculture and mining. But the First World War cut South Africa off from many of her sources of imports, and gave the encouragement of a natural protection to local industries. The money value of industrial production increased nearly sixfold between 1911 and 1921 and the number of employees nearly trebled. The slump that followed, and helped to cause the strike of 1922, affected secondary industry as well as mining. The disappearance of the natural protection afforded by the war led industrialists to demand an adequate protective tariff. But this had not been introduced by 1924.

The complicated policy which these facts illustrate—the direction of African labour to farm, mine and town, its exclusion from skilled work, and the retention in the reserves of all Africans whose labour was not needed elsewhere—gave rise to administrative problems which were dealt with largely by pass laws, methods of taxation and the regulation of African residence in towns.

Pass laws, as we have seen, made their appearance very early in the Cape Colony. By requiring a travelling Hottentot to carry a pass Lord Caledon hoped to prevent vagrancy and to ensure a labour supply to the farmers. The fiftieth ordinance of 1828 abolished this system, and it never returned to the Cape Colony. Passes were indeed demanded of all persons entering or leaving the Transkeian Territories or British Bechuanaland, and as this rule was not in practice applied to Europeans there was in effect a native pass law in those cases. But it was a light burden in comparison with what the republics imposed.

After 1902 the system in the ex-republics was revised, and then amounted to this: every African man (but not woman) in the two colonies travelling from his home or place of employment had to carry a pass signed by his employer, his chief or an official. No railway ticket could be issued to him unless he produced this pass. In the Orange River Colony he required a residential pass, showing that he was entitled to live and work where he did, even when not travelling. In the Transvaal an African entering a town to look for work was given a temporary pass allowing him to do so, and when work was found his contract was registered on another pass. In the Transvaal, too, no African man in an urban area could be abroad at night without a night pass signed by his employer. In Natal the system was simpler. Every African employee who was not working on the farm where he resided had a permanent identification pass, and another was needed for entering or leaving Natal.

It will be seen that the pass system was designed to retain labour on the farms and the mines where it was wanted, to permit migration to the towns while excluding those who failed to find employment, to keep in the reserves those who were not wanted elsewhere, and to safeguard the white townspeople against criminals at night. In keeping with these principles, Africans who had reached a certain standard of education and who practised a skilled trade or profession, and with whom therefore farms, mines and police were not concerned, could claim exemption from these laws. They had, however, to carry a certificate to prove their exemption.

At various times in the nineteenth century the shortage of African labour was acute, and the labour-supply aspect dominated the native policy of various governments. One solution of this problem was to impose on the Africans in reserves a direct tax in money, which could be obtained only by working for Europeans. Thus was established, in the Cape and Natal, the hut tax. Huts were easy to assess, and the number possessed by an African was an indication of the number of his wives and therefore his wealth. Squatters on Crown land in Natal paid a rent, hut tax being payable only in the reserves. In the Cape encouragement was given, especially by the Glen Grey Act of 1894, to tribal Africans to convert their communal land tenure into individual tenure on perpetual quit-rent.

The quit-rent gave exemption from hut tax. When Natal tried to impose a poll-tax as well as the hut tax, the rebellion of 1906 broke out. But the principle of a poll tax, which touched every adult male African wherever resident, was soon generally accepted as the basis of direct taxation of Africans. This, and the growth of mines, industries and towns, drew the whole African population into the cash economy of the Europeans.

Lastly, the conditions of the industrial age led to special methods of controlling Africans in towns. The Land Act of 1913 did not apply to urban areas, where no restriction was placed on the ownership of real property. But the Natives (Urban Areas) Act of 1923 provided for restriction of occupation or residence. Municipal authorities were to set aside 'locations' for Africans, to build houses for them to hire, to establish elected advisory boards in these locations, to confine Africans (with certain exceptions, notably those living with their employers) to residence in them, and were given powers to exclude unwanted Africans from the municipal areas.

Except for this last act, few of the restrictions described here applied to the Cape Province. Its exceptional position was due to the liberal legislation of the colonial period, and in particular to the franchise. The Cape franchise knew no Colour Bar, but was based on a valuation of property owned or occupied, or wages received; since 1892 on a higher value and a literacy test as well. After 1896 the parties in the Cape Colony were highly organised and fairly evenly balanced, and there were seven constituencies where the African vote was enough to hold the balance between parties. This circumstance secured the Cape Africans against the discrimination shown elsewhere. But after 1910, though the Cape franchise remained, the balance of parties was altered and could no longer be decided by seven Cape constituencies. It is important to note that both parties in the Cape Colony solicited the support of the African voters.

In Natal a handful of Africans was given the franchise, but on conditions so difficult that there was nothing that could be called an African vote; in the republics they were frankly excluded. In the reserves of the three northern provinces local administration was in the hands of the chiefs, subject to control by European magistrates. The Cape Colony, however, had never favoured the chiefs. They were in most areas effectively supplanted by magistrates, and the Glen Grey Act of 1894 began the process of associating with them the elected representatives of the people. The district council thus established was ultimately reproduced in all the districts of the

Transkei, where a General Council, partly elected by the district councils, was given advisory functions in all local matters, such as education, agriculture and roads. Something was done there to improve African methods of farming. Agricultural schools were set up and demonstrators sent round the districts.

Education for Africans was provided mainly by missionary bodies, and, though their schools received government aid, attendance at them was neither free nor compulsory. Yet some progress was made. The proportion of Africans of school-going age who went to school rose between 1905 and 1925 from about 12 to about 21 per cent. In 1914 the South African Native College was founded at Fort Hare, in the Eastern Province, to provide university education for Africans. By 1924, therefore, the black race had made considerable progress towards civilisation, but suffered serious restrictions to its movements and to its social, economic and political opportunities.

South Africa's population includes two important non-European groups which are not classed as native or African. One is the Cape Coloured people, 8 per cent of the total. Living as they did mostly in the Western Province of the Cape they benefited by the liberal policy of that colony and were not discriminated against by law. Even in the other provinces they came to be exempted from the pass laws, though not to be granted the vote. They were not given the same educational advantages as the Europeans in any province, but their disabilities were mainly those which they shared with the poorest strata of the white population, together with the social discriminations which lay outside the sphere of public policy.

The other group is the Asiatic, which in practice means Indian. It came to Natal at the demand of the sugar planters, who in 1860 found that African labour lacked the stability and persistence that sugar planting required. A reluctant Indian government gave its consent to the migration of indentured coolies (and their families) to Natal. At once the sugar industry, and with it the Garden Colony, flourished. When their contracts expired the coolies had the alternatives of return passages to India and land grants in Natal. They usually chose to remain. They became market gardeners, waiters, domestic servants. They were followed to Natal by 'passenger Indians', more prosperous men who paid their own passages and established themselves in wholesale and retail trade. These were commonly Gujarati-speaking Moslems from Bombay, whereas the indentured coolies were usually Hindus from Madras who spoke Tamil or Telegu.

As the Indian population grew and prospered the white Natalians took fright. Land and trade were passing into Indian hands. Even the franchise was not denied them. After the introduction of responsible government the colony took steps to limit the numbers and power of the Indians. The franchise was withdrawn from people 'who (not being of European origin) are natives or descendants in the male line of natives of countries which have not hitherto possessed elective representative institutions founded on the Parliamentary Franchise'. By this thinly disguised method the Indians, who now nearly equalled the Europeans of Natal in number, were deprived of the vote. Rioters at the Durban docks then tried to stop further immigration by preventing the passengers of two ships from landing. Subsidised immigration was in fact stopped, though indentured labourers continued to come at the expense of their employers till this too was stopped in 1911 by the government of India. .

There were Indians in the Transvaal as well as Natal. They were absolutely excluded from the Free State, and the small numbers in the liberal Cape Colony constituted no problem. But the South African Republic had been compelled to admit them by the London Convention. After supporting Britain in the Boer War many returned to the Transvaal, but new immigrants were excluded by Milner. Those formerly resident could return. Over the measures taken to distinguish between these two classes the Indians fell foul of the government. M. K. Gandhi, who began his career in South Africa, led the Transvaal Indians in this struggle, and Smuts was his opponent. The Union Parliament dealt with the problem by prohibiting the migration of Indians from one province to another. Officials discriminated against them in the issue of trading licences and in other ways. They suffered also, like other Non-Europeans, from social discrimination—in hotels, on trains—and in education.

Gandhi's principle of passive resistance was first practised in South Africa. He led a resisting band from Natal to the Transvaal. All were imprisoned. In 1914 Smuts and Gandhi ended this deadlock by an agreement on various minor questions, but the Indian problem was then overshadowed by the war. Fear of commercial competition from people with a low standard of living on the one hand, and resentment at all the restrictions on the other, were still acute when the government changed in 1924. But the Indians were little more than 2 per cent of the population.

The social and economic systems which this contact between races had produced weighed heavily on a part of the white population as well as on the other groups. As the country filled up, and new land ceased to be available, the old crude methods of farming became inadequate. Capital, machines and efficient organisation were needed on the land. To make matters worse, the Roman-Dutch principle of equal division among heirs cut many farms into pieces too small to work. Bad methods of cultivation, grass-burning and overstocking started erosion which began to turn fertile areas into desert. A class of landless men developed as *bywoners*, hangers-on of their wealthier neighbours, to whom they stood in a relation like that of the African labour-tenants. The destruction of the Boer War carried the process further. Many families, almost all Afrikaner, were driven off the land altogether. Coming to the towns, they found themselves unfitted for skilled labour; in unskilled occupations they would have to compete with raw Africans, whose race and whose 'Kaffir work' they despised. Among these 'Poor Whites', for whom there seemed no place in South African society, hatred of the black race became more bitter than in any other section of the people. They drifted into the urban slums, to live cheek by jowl with the depressed classes of all races and colours. Some were still *bywoners* on the farms; others woodcutters in the Knysna forest. The Dutch Reformed Church tried to rehabilitate such people by placing them in agricultural colonies of small-holders under strict control. But even this praise-worthy effort had limitations, as a considerable number of the Poor Whites had degenerated both physically and mentally. The degeneration was partly a cause and partly a result of their condition.

This unfortunate class was politically as well as economically outcast. Many of the National Scouts of 1901 were drawn from it. In 1924 its resentment was to be vented against the Smuts government. Had not the Pact promised a 'white labour policy'?

12

HERTZOG

From 1924 to the outbreak of the Second World War General Hertzog was Prime Minister of the Union. In world history that period is divided sharply by the depression which began at the end of 1929 and spread wider and deeper in the following years. South Africa, too, was affected by it both economically and politically. The year in which Hitler came to power in Germany, and the United States turned to Roosevelt and the New Deal, produced in South Africa a coalition government; that led, under circumstances that will presently be seen, to a fusion of the main political parties. But Hertzog remained, and 1933 marked no profound revolution in policy. The old aims were still pursued, though under cover of a new banner. The period can therefore be treated as a continuous whole.

The Nationalists, who were the predominant partners in the Pact Government, had two principal lines of policy in view. One was to bring the constitution and the machinery of state into line with their own national aspirations, short of the republic which the terms of the pact forbade; the other, to 'solve the native problem'.

Among the factors which had inclined the electorate towards the Pact candidates had been the census report of 1921, which had given an alarming interpretation of the figures for the African population. It appeared that the Bantu were increasing a good deal faster than the Europeans. Later censuses have not shown the alarm to be justified; but at the time the danger assumed even larger proportions in the popular than in the official mind. Fears that the white population would in time be engulfed in a black flood played a large part in shaping government policy and in securing public support for it.

Hertzog determined to secure the dominance of the white man against every threat from the black.

The main principles of his policy were embodied in a series of bills introduced quite early in the life of the new government. But reference to select committees and obstruction in the Senate held them up for ten years. It was not till 1936, under changed political circumstances and after much modification, that they were passed. Opposition to such policies now came from a new quarter. In 1916 F. S. Malan had fathered an Act to establish universities. On the foundation of the old colleges he built two (soon increased to four) teaching universities, as well as a federal examining university that incorporated the remaining colleges. Some of these catered for the Afrikaner, some for the English-speaking population. In the latter group, and to a slight extent in the others, the liberal spirit of eighteenth-century philanthropists, nineteenth-century missionaries and enlightened Cape politicians blossomed into new life. Here the ancient race prejudices encountered the most persistent opposition.

The famous bills and many of the speeches about them were the product of experiences and prejudices reaching far back into history, yet recognised by many people in 1936, and by still more today, to be largely irrelevant to modern conditions. The basis of Hertzog's policy was Segregation, which has been called a 'magic word' in South African politics. A century earlier the Natal republicans had limited the number of African families allowed to live and work on European farms, and had tried to hold back the rest of Bantu Africa at a boundary line. Africans had for generations been regarded as foreign enemies whose penetration into the white man's lands was hostile and should be punished. Even in the modern cities they were thought of as birds of passage who came from 'the reserves' for a season, and returned there to bask in the sun when their purses were full. For many years this opinion accorded with the fact. The African was thought of as a foreign visitor, not a part of the white man's society.

Hertzog's policy was to give a comprehensive legal basis to this exclusion of the black man from the white man's world. Within the limits of the segregation policy he was anxious to be just to the black man. An extension of the reserves in which Africans could own and occupy land had been promised in 1913, but never undertaken. The Native Trust and Land Act 'released' additional areas, established a Trust with power to buy land in them and to own it in trust for the Africans. Much of the land so acquired was crown and company land already occupied by them as cash tenants, so that there was not in fact a significant extension of the land in African occupation. Even when all the released areas had been acquired for this purpose, the Africans, two-thirds of the population, would have no more than one-eighth of the surface of the Union.

Most of this, it is true, lay in the more fertile and better watered parts of the country, and it was estimated at the time that the reserves with the new areas contained about 56 per cent of the African population; while 30 per cent lived on European farms, and the rest in the towns. But these figures were deceptive. The reserves could not support the primitive peasant population which the revenue officers attributed to them. About half the adult males of the Transkei were, at any one time, absent from that territory earning money elsewhere. While more state expenditure on the agricultural and industrial development of the reserves might have stopped this migration and the disruption of families, it was not practical politics: it would have cut down the labour supply which European employers already thought insufficient.

The Native Trust and Land Act was, therefore, a belated tribute to the tradition that black and white should live apart. While it sought to carry out a promise made in 1913, it aimed also at a stricter enforcement of some of the principles of the act of that year. The 1913 act had tried to stop cash tenancy, but had left loopholes; it had not touched labour tenancy. Yet laws limiting the number of labour tenant families to five had been on the statute book, and had been regularly broken, for decades.

In 1936 the government was given power to eliminate 'squatters' or cash tenants by a system of registration, licences and a rising scale of fees; and to allow as labour tenants only those who worked at least half the year for the farmer. This would mean driving many families off European farms, and increasing the services of most labour tenants by 50 per cent, while it was notorious that the reserves and the released areas had no room for more. In due course this provision of the Act was applied, by proclamation, to one district of the Transvaal. After a few years' trial the policy was found to be unworkable, and the proclamation withdrawn. But the last had not yet been heard of this notion.

Much more controversial were Hertzog's political arrangements. To him and to most other white South Africans it seemed that the advances made by the Africans in civilisation would before very long make them a majority of the electorate in the Cape Province. Before such a force the whole system of defences set up by the white man would collapse. The Cape franchise had therefore to be

F

attacked. In face of vehement resistance by African leaders and
European liberals the original measure was watered down. Africans
in the Cape Province retained the old franchise, but not on a common
roll with Europeans. The Africans were formed into separate
constituencies to return three members to the House of Assembly
and two to the Cape Provincial Council. The Coloured people of
that province remained on the same roll as the white; in everything
but social intercourse Hertzog classed them with the Europeans.

Next, the Africans of the whole country, including the Cape,
were given a complicated system of indirect election by which they
returned four senators, in addition, of course, to the four nominated
senators who were supposed to represent their interests. Lastly there
was the Native Representative Council, whose elected members
were chosen by the same method as the four senators. This Council
was to be a purely advisory body; its elected members, unlike those
in the two houses of Parliament, were to be Africans.

The Native Representative Council had, before long, to complain
that no notice was taken of its advice. The new parliamentary
representatives, however, were a great gain to the political life of the
country. They were drawn, as was natural under the circumstances,
from the most liberal, humane and highly educated class of
Europeans in South Africa. Yet some of them said that the best
service they could render was to abolish the system under which
they had been elected. The system was one more aspect of the
segregation principle which had broken down in the economic
sphere. In due course it was, indeed, abolished, but only to make way
for a segregation still more extreme.

The policy of which these acts were the most dramatic expression
was the basis of many other measures also. Special courts were set
up to administer native law in cases where it applied. The power of
legislating for the African areas was given by Parliament to the
government. This was not a 'new despotism', since ministers were,
as a rule, more sympathetic to African demands than the European
public or its immediate representatives. But another measure,
passed at the beginning of the Hertzog period, produced an angry
reaction from the Africans and came to be regarded by them as a
symbol of oppression. It was popularly known as the 'Colour Bar
Act'; securing the existing monopoly of skilled operations to white
workers in the mines, it provided for an extension of this principle
to other industries by proclamation.

This applied to skilled operations. But the government wanted to
solve the Poor White problem by introducing Europeans to unskilled

labour. This it could do directly on the railways and other state enterprises. Its 'civilised labour policy' was imposed also on the provinces and local authorities, and indirect pressure was applied to private employers to bring them into line. White labourers in considerable numbers then took the place of Africans, though they were not, of course, paid at African rates. State subsidies were given to municipalities to cover some of the difference in wages between white and black unskilled labour.

Segregation for the Africans, and legal equality with the whites for the Cape Coloured, left a third racial problem to be dealt with: the Asiatics. An attempt was made to apply the segregation principle to them also. The proposal in this case provoked opposition from something more powerful than a racial minority in South Africa: opposition from the Indian government. A conference met and the Cape Town agreement was made. The bills were dropped, and an undertaking given to help the South African Indians to raise their standards of living and of civilisation. The Indian government was to assist in the repatriation to India of such of its people as were willing to leave South Africa, and to appoint an Agent-General in the Union. The contact of South African society with the cultured men who successively filled this office had an important effect on the opinions of many. A little was done to honour the terms of the agreement. And there the Indian 'problem' remained till after 1939.

Fundamental as these questions of race and colour are, they attracted less attention from politicians and public on either side than the 'national' question. This had many aspects, and the handling of it passed through phases in which subtle but important differences of emphasis can be detected.

Most Afrikaners in 1924 still suffered from a sense of inferiority in the presence of the English. Their language and culture were new and were often treated with contempt. The defeat of 1902 and the support given to Britain in 1914, not to mention all the grievances of the nineteenth century, still rankled. Afrikaners felt themselves to be a defeated nation which had to retrieve its lost independence and to show the world that the defeat had been wiped out. South Africa, they thought, was their country; yet its governments in the past had imposed alien forms on the people and compelled them to serve foreign interests. They could not hold up their heads in their own land.

A minority of Afrikaners, which supported the South African Party, did not share these emotions. But it was now in opposition. The Nationalists had their opportunity. One by one they removed the symbols of the British connection, and in various spheres of power raised their own people to dominant positions. New postage stamps appeared, and the King's head was not in the design. The House of Assembly requested the King to confer no more titles on South Africans. The Afrikaans language took the place of Dutch for official and educational purposes, and its literature entered a new period of rapid development. Its equality with English in official use was rigidly insisted on; municipalities as well as Union departments were made to conform to the rule. Civil servants, even those who had no contact with the public, were required to be fully bilingual. As the Afrikaners were generally better qualified in this respect than the English, their numbers increased rapidly in a service that had formerly been left to English-speaking and often unilingual men. Before long it began to look, to the latter, like an Afrikaner preserve.

These Afrikaners, who at last were coming into their own—were they an independent nation? Hertzog's main concern was to be able to give them that assurance, and he went to the Imperial Conference of 1926 determined to get it. He played a leading part in drafting the Balfour declaration, which, putting into words what had been a matter of practice since the war, defined Britain and the Dominions as 'autonomous communities within the British Empire, equal in status, in no way subordinate one to another in any aspect of their domestic or external affairs, though united by a common allegiance to the Crown, and freely associated as members of the British Commonwealth of Nations'.

Hertzog came home to tell his people that this meant full, unfettered independence. That being so, he was content to retain the common allegiance as long as it was in South Africa's interest to do so. In 1931 the Statute of Westminster gave legal sanction to the principle of the Balfour declaration, and three years later the Union Parliament passed a similar act to establish the principle in South African law. The status of the Union was then different from what it had been before 1926, when the Imperial Parliament still had the theoretical right to apply legislation to the Dominions; when the Governor-General, who could refuse his assent to bills, represented the British government and received instructions from it; when the King acted in the name of the whole Empire, but on the advice of his British ministers only; when the Union had no power of extra-territorial legislation or control over foreign relations. Now the Governor-General came to be the personal representative of the King, who appointed him on the advice of the South African ministry. The British government was represented by a High Commissioner, distinct from the Governor-General. The Union could legislate extra-territorially, appoint ministers to foreign capitals and otherwise act as an independent state. The common allegiance to the King, and the common status of the people as British subjects, remained.

As soon as the Balfour declaration had given the Nationalists the status they wanted, they began to devise outward forms to advertise it. The Union must have its distinctive flag, and its people a nationality distinct from that of British subjects. When it appeared that the flag was to have no Union Jack in its design, there occurred among the British South Africans an outburst of bitter hostility which would seem strange to one who was ignorant of their historical background. A flag was a mere symbol, a piece of bunting; the bitterness was aroused really by the changes in the balance of power, and in the political tendency of the country, which the new flag was to symbolise. The government paused in its advance, and agreed to a compromise: a small Union Jack, with the banners of the old republics, was placed in the centre of the flag; and in addition to the national emblem the Union Jack would be flown officially to symbolise membership of the Commonwealth. There were two languages, two capitals, two flags and two nationalities. All 'South African nationals' were still British subjects, while British immigrants acquired South African nationality by a period of residence.

In the later phase of Hertzog's government there were more disputes of the same kind. The Union Jack was one of the official flags, but attempts were made to cut down the list of occasions on which it could be flown. *God Save the King* was not to be regarded as the national anthem, a rôle reserved for *Die Stem van Suid-Afrika*. Place-names were changed. Roberts Heights, the military headquarters outside Pretoria, was a reminder of the Field-Marshal who defeated the Boers; it was to be changed to Voortrekkerhoogte. Again an outcry, and a compromise: different names for the military college, the post office and the railway station. A South African, though English-speaking and British-born, was appointed Governor-General. His successor would be of Afrikaner descent and South African-born.

Much of this nationalising policy was regarded with tolerance by the moderate section of the British. The Afrikaners and their language had occupied an inferior position in the state, and an advance on their part would seem to be due. And many Afrikaners, even among the Nationalists, felt that they had now been given their due. Why should the two white races quarrel any more?

In 1929 Smuts made a speech referring to the ultimate amalgamation of the Union with territories to the north. The Nationalists took this as a threat to drown the white race in a black flood. Their 'Black Manifesto' enabled them at the general election to gain an absolute majority in the House of Assembly. Labour was eclipsed. It was largely discredited among the British by its pact with Nationalism, while the Afrikaner workers tended to support the latter party. The fortunes of Nationalism reached their zenith; yet even in that election, it is important to note, they polled fewer votes in the aggregate than the South African Party.

Then came the depression. Britain went off the gold standard in 1931. South African farmers, whose best customer was Britain, received lower prices for their products. The gold mines found their margin of profit severely cut. Unemployment and bankruptcy mounted. Speculators, convinced that the Union must go off gold, sent their money abroad, to bring it back when the exchange rates had altered. Yet the government stuck to its guns. There were some, in South Africa as elsewhere, who felt that to devalue the currency was to break faith with creditors. But the essential motive of Hertzog and of Havenga, the Minister of Finance, was political. If South Africa should devalue merely because Britain had done so, what became of sovereign independence? Here was the chance to prove that Afrikaners were masters in their own house. Unfortunately for Hertzog, his followers in the countryside were not prepared to destroy themselves economically even for this ideal. Smuts had a heaven-sent opportunity to sweep the government out of office. Hertzog said he would rather resign than yield on the gold question. Tielman Roos, a judge and former Nationalist minister, returned to the political arena with the cry that the gold standard must be abandoned. Such a political portent, with all its disturbing economic effects, was decisive. At the end of 1932 the Union went off gold; but Hertzog did not resign.

Smuts, who had the premiership within his grasp, now rose above the level of party politics. He offered to serve under Hertzog in a coalition. After much manœuvring Hertzog accepted the outstretched hand. An opportunity had come to bury the outworn hatchet of racial strife and bring the parties and nationalities together. The coalition government went to the country and swept it almost clean of opposition. The tide of prosperity rose, as a result of the devaluation, with tremendous force. Mines, farms and factories flourished with an activity never before known. Johannesburg, the mushroom city, grew so rapidly outwards and upwards that its appearance changed more radically in four or five years than it had in the previous forty.

The atmosphere was favourable for a further development, the fusion of the two great parties. Thus was born the United South African National Party—United Party for short—in which, among other things, the members were to be permitted a free vote on Hertzog's 'Native Bills'; hence the two-thirds majority at a joint sitting in 1936. In 1938 the party won an overwhelming majority in the elections. Many believed that the day of racial peace, so often heralded by false dawns, had broken at last. But even in 1938 there were signs that this might not be so.

The constitution and aims of the United Party were so similar to those of the old Nationalists that it took an acute eye to distinguish between them. Some of the British supporters of the South African Party thought that fusion meant nothing less than the complete triumph of all that they had opposed since Briton and Boer had first come into conflict. Unable to accept it, they walked out and formed the Dominion Party, successor to the Progressives and Unionists of former days. But for various reasons this got little support among the British. Being a national minority—about 40 per cent of the white population—they knew that their salvation depended on co-operation with a section of the Afrikaners. A purely British party could never hope for power. Secondly, the issue on which the Dominion Party took its stand was one that gave it a poor case. It fought against the independent status of the Union, which had been established by the Mother of Parliaments herself. Hair-splitting about the divisibility and indivisibility of the Crown meant nothing to the electors. Thirdly, a section of the Nationalists—much bigger than the Dominion Party—also rejected fusion. Thus Hertzog might be not so bad after all.

After the breakdown of intricate negotiations, Dr D. F. Malan (not to be confused with F. S. Malan), leader of the Cape Nationalists, broke away from Hertzog and spurned the fusion movement. With his followers he formed the 'Purified' Nationalist Party, and became, to the amusement of many, the leader of 'His Majesty's Opposition'.

Behind the feud between Hertzog and Malan, and the uneasy alliance between Hertzog, Smuts and the British, lay differences of outlook which are easily recognised by those familiar with the past. The Hertzog-Smuts alliance was full of misunderstandings, suspicions and agreements-to-differ which it was hoped time would heal. Hertzog, throughout his career, had firmly defended the equality of the Afrikaans and English languages, and the equal rights of Boer and Briton to share in political power and the benefits of government. Of the British he asked one thing: to 'feel as Afrikaners' and forget their ties with their mother-country. He did not understand how big a thing this was. But within the limits of an exclusive South African allegiance he was scrupulously just. On this basis the British supported, though with some misgivings, the United Party.

The Afrikaners of the 'purified' party were of a different opinion. The iron of defeat and inferiority had eaten more deeply into their souls. They would be satisfied with nothing less than a purely Afrikaner state in which the English and their language could remain only on sufferance. All the compromises on constitution, language, status and the rest they treated as mere temporising measures to be swept away as occasion offered. They were not hopeful, as Hertzog was, of 'converting' the English. Any contact with the English they thought dangerous to the survival of their own culture and way of life. They had the feeling, which arose from experience in history, that the Englishman always outwitted the Afrikaner and undermined his exclusive allegiance to his own national tradition. They were deeply influenced, too, by the Calvinist principles of their religion. The doctrine of predestination combined with a belief in the curse on the children of Ham to suggest that the Elect could be identified by their white skins; with more certainty, by their use of the Afrikaans language; with more certainty still, by their profession of the Nationalist ideology. It would be impossible to understand the Nationalist point of view without feeling the force of this Calvinist idea, overflowing from religion into politics, of an eternal distinction between Saved and Damned.

The influence of this idea was felt beyond as well as within the field of politics. Afrikaners seceded from the Boy Scout organisation and formed one of their own called the Voortrekkers. The National Union of South African Students was broken, Nationalist students forming a separate body. The same tendency appeared in the trade union world. Then it spread to business. The Afrikaners in the towns, once a very small minority, were by 1936 about as numerous as their cousins in the country. But they came to the towns as refugees from a farming industry that could no longer support them. They had to start at the bottom of the ladder, the upper rungs of which were all occupied by the British. Afrikaans was spoken in the poorest quarters of the cities, English in the more prosperous. To remedy this, Nationalists organised to give financial backing to Afrikaners setting up in business; banks, insurance societies, industries of every sort, shops and wholesale warehouses with a Nationalist political bias arose. So did separate social, sporting and cultural organisations. All these were integrated together, one supporting another. Consumers and employees, all Afrikaner, were drawn into the system, which aimed at Afrikaner independence of the 'British money power' which had vigorously survived the breakdown of the old-fashioned Empire.

That this movement greatly helped the Afrikaners in the process of urbanisation and on the road to prosperity will probably be marked to its credit by future historians. But it is equally true that its greatest object was to withdraw the Afrikaner from contact with the British. It was a new phase of the Great Trek, a 'withdrawal into the interior' on a new plane, a turning of the back on the ever-dreaded Uitlander and his ways.

The movement had begun before 1938, but in that year it was given an immense impetus by the celebrations to honour the centenary of the Trek. This was no casual act of respect to the calendar, but an elaborate and heart-stirring pageantry in which the special history of the Afrikaner nation was enacted again to revive and strengthen the self-conscious unity of the people. Out of the pageantry was born the *Ossewabrandwag*, the ox-wagon guard, which began as a cultural organisation but soon became a disciplined political phalanx on the Nazi pattern.

From this unity the British were excluded. Nor would they have had it otherwise. Their aim and hope had always been unity on an individual basis, with everyone pursuing cultural aims, wealth and political power according to fair and equal rules. Into the mystic unity of an exclusive Afrikaner *volk* with its special historical self-consciousness they could not and would not enter. Hertzog expected them ultimately to do so, and particularly to break their sentimental ties with Britain. But this they could not do either.

Had Whitehall retained some control over the Union, it is possible that Briton and Boer would have been united, in opposition perhaps to the negrophilist policies of British governments. But precisely because that control had long been no more than nominal, and Hertzog had laid even its ghost, there was no point at which the British of South Africa and those of Britain could possibly conflict. On the other hand Afrikaner nationalism was the traditional enemy of the British South Africans. Having yielded with the best grace they could before its steady advances, they were now faced with a party whose avowed aim was to reduce them, their language and traditions to a position of inferiority and dependence in South Africa. The natural effect was to strengthen their sentimental bonds with their mother-country, and to make them cling to the imperial connection, tenuous as it was, as to a life-line. The British, too, being concentrated in the cities (nearly three-quarters of them in the big towns), were keenly aware of the contacts with the outside world which pervaded their social, cultural, political and business life. So had the Dutch of eighteenth-century Cape Town been, when their country cousins were turning their backs on Europe. Thus these metropolitan-feeling citizens not only felt distaste for what was provincial and of the earth earthy, but were repelled by the suspicious, defensive, inward-turning and circumscribed mentality of the Nationalists. Many of the Afrikaners shared this repulsion. But in 1938 it was not clear how far such feelings had spread.

The centenary, the creation of separate Afrikaner organisations in every sphere of life and their integration together strengthened Malan's rather than Hertzog's hand in politics. The tide of history seemed to be flowing now towards the Afrikaner-dominated and exclusive republic of which the Nationalists dreamed. Yet the National party, when, undivided and at the height of its power, had failed to secure a majority of the popular votes. How could it do so against Hertzog and Smuts together?

This difficulty, the problems inherent in an exclusive and doctrinaire régime, and the course of events in Europe all helped to turn the thoughts of Nationalists away from the parliamentary system and towards the new ideology of Germany and Italy. Anti-semitism, hitherto unknown to the Afrikaner, sprang into being, encouraged perhaps by the fact that the hated 'money power' was Jewish as well as British. The Jews, a very small minority of the population, were largely concentrated in Johannesburg and Cape Town and were conspicuous in business and the professions. They, too, seemed an obstacle in the way of the pure Afrikaner republic.

Curiously enough, Hertzog and some of his followers in the United Party were likewise dazzled by the brilliance of Nazism. Not only were the German race-theories very convenient in a country with the structure of South Africa, but the bitter attacks of Malan had caused Hertzog to lose faith in the party system itself and to grope about for an alternative. Pirow, Minister of Defence and a man of German descent, afterwards admitted that he was a National Socialist before the war, and he became one openly when it began.

These tendencies were alarming not only to the whole English-speaking population, and to those Non-Europeans who knew what they meant, but to a great many United Party Afrikaners, former Nationalists as well as former 'Saps'. Some of them publicly denounced the Fascist propaganda that the Italian Minister was allowed to spread.

The political trend in a Nazi-Fascist direction gave, for some people, a sinister meaning to the favourable trade agreements with Italy and Germany. When the city of Port Elizabeth accepted a British tender, though a lower tender had been received from a German firm, Hertzog tried to force it to change its mind. The mayor stood firm and Hertzog apologised to the German Minister. He severely reprimanded newspapers for attacks on Hitler.

Such was the background of the final crisis. For South Africa, as for the world, it might have come in 1938. When war seemed likely over Sudetenland, the Prime Minister proposed to the cabinet a policy of neutrality, and even Smuts was constrained to accept it. Sudetenland, after all, was a German-speaking country, and it could still be maintained that Hitler wanted no more than the unity of all Germans. South Africa, with its hair-trigger animosities and its memories of 1914, could not dare to treat this as a *casus belli*.

The invasion of Czecho-Slovakia changed the situation. Some of the British section in South Africa wondered why the Nationalists did not think of Germany as playing the part of Britain in 1899, and Czecho-Slovakia in the rôle of the Boer republics. They did not, because Britain was Britain and Germany was Germany; because they felt some sympathy with the German régime; because of 1914; because of the Kaiser's telegram to Kruger; because some of them, it was said, could 'not see past an Englishman'.

When, after all the preliminaries, Britain declared war on September 3, 1939, a strange chance decreed that the Union Parliament was due to meet in special session the next day to prolong the life of the Senate. Had this not happened, Hertzog might not have consulted Parliament on the critical decision he was to make. On receiving the news from England he met his cabinet and proposed a policy of neutrality for the Union. Smuts opposed him and spoke for war against Germany. The cabinet split, six for neutrality and seven for war. The fusion government, then, had come to an end, but it would rest with the House of Assembly to give power to one faction or the other.

As a matter of course, the Dominion Party would be for war; so would Labour, but a small remnant of its former self; and Malan's much bigger party would be for neutrality. But the decision rested with the United Party members, the great bulk of the House but no longer united or disciplined. The vital question would be decided, outside the small parties, by a free vote. The debate, which would be dramatic in any circumstances, was made doubly so by the knowledge that speeches could sway votes, and any convert might decide the issue.

Hertzog and some parliamentary experts expected a small majority for neutrality. The Prime Minister spoke. As he warmed up he turned from the neutrality question to a defence of Germany, the Germany of Versailles and now of Hitler. He, too, the Prime Minister said, had known the bitterness of defeat. What Germany was doing was merely to wipe out the stain of 1919. At this point, according to later calculations, a small number of Hertzog's followers determined to vote against him.

Smuts spoke, and others spoke, for the cause of freedom and democracy. They denounced the tyranny of Nazism. Mr. Nicholls thought that South Africa was automatically at war when it was declared by Great Britain, so that the debate was unnecessary. At this point, it has been thought, several members who were for war may have decided to support Hertzog, since South Africa's independence had to be vindicated.

Mr Long saw the danger and got up to repudiate Mr Nicholls' views. While defending the sovereignty of the Union Parliament, he pleaded for support of the democracies against Nazism. All day the battle continued, while the public outside waited in a state of extreme tension. The loyalty of the British to the Crown and to their own wider world, their feeling that Britain was their own mainstay in an immediately hostile environment, and that if Britain fell in the world they themselves would collapse in South Africa, was countered by a Nationalist hope that the fall of Britain would give the Afrikaners unlimited domination of the Union. More, they had for years believed in Hertzog's achievement of independence, and now that achievement would be tested. Unless South Africa could go a different way from England, there was no independence. The answer had been unfavourable in 1932, on the currency question, but this war issue would finally decide whether anything had changed since 1914. Beyond these considerations lay the attitudes to Nazism itself. Many were inclined in its favour. Many, Briton and Boer, were steadily devoted to the democratic ideal and saw Hitler as the greatest menace in the world.

At nine o'clock in the evening the house divided. Hertzog's motion was defeated by 80 votes to 67. He played one more card; he appealed to the Governor-General for a dissolution. The latter's decision has become an interesting point in constitutional history, but at the time it was of much more than academic interest: he refused to dissolve, and called Smuts to power. War was declared on Germany,

13

WAR, APARTHEID AND THE REPUBLIC

The Smuts government was a coalition. Though the old United party was split from top to bottom, the pro-war section was strong enough to capture its machinery and retain the party name. The small Labour and Dominion parties, which had voted for war in the critical division, were given seats in the Cabinet. Hertzog's followers crossed the floor, to sit in uneasy association with those of Malan. After five years of bitter mutual recriminations their relationship could hardly be cordial. But the political circumstances forced them to co-operate, and even, after a decent interval, to merge their identities in the *Herenigde Nasionale Party*, the Reunited National Party.

Deeply divided as it was, South Africa was nevertheless more genuinely involved in the Second World War than in the first. There could be no question of conscription. But from those sections of the population that were not neutralist or pro-Nazi, from English and Afrikaners, white, black and Coloured, volunteers enlisted in greater numbers than the run-down Department of Defence could equip or organise. The Non-Europeans were used in auxiliary capacities only. All volunteers were required to take an oath to serve anywhere in Africa; on taking the oath they were distinguished by the orange tabs on their epaulettes which became the mark of the South African troops.

Starting virtually from an empty quartermaster's store Smuts was able to equip his 'boys', as he called them, in time to send the first brigade to Kenya before Mussolini entered the war. The South Africans were involved in the invasion of Abyssinia and were then moved to Egypt—160,000 of them—in the middle of 1941. They fought in all the North African campaigns, suffering the grievous loss of a division in the surrender of Tobruk. A new oath was the preliminary to sending reorganised forces to Sicily and the Italian mainland.

Inevitably, however, the main interest of South Africa's war history lies on the home front. Though there was no repetition of the 1914 rebellion, opponents of the government did what they could to frustrate the war effort by widespread sabotage, cutting telegraph and telephone wires, blowing up post offices and power lines, and passing information to the enemy. In Nationalist areas it was often dangerous for soldiers to appear in uniform. Their wives and families, if living in the wrong political environment, were boycotted and persecuted. But Smuts handled this explosive material with the restraint which a long memory and experience had taught him. Men convicted of treason or sabotage were punished only by imprisonment; no death sentence was carried out. Only the most dangerous potential traitors were interned.

The domestic history of the opposition during the war is complicated and at times bewildering. The parties of Malan and of Hertzog had merged, but the basis of their unity had still to be established. Hertzog, with a minority of his followers, held fast to the absolute equality of Boer and Briton; it was a point of honour with him, and he was an honourable man. But the course of events had unleashed forces of hatred and vengeance that could not be appeased by such old-fashioned remedies. Nothing would now satisfy them but avowed Afrikaner domination. As the war appeared to be leading to an Axis victory, Nationalists exulted in the consequences of this for themselves. Late in 1940 the provincial congresses of the H.N.P. met to decide on their principles. At the council meeting in Hertzog's own province, where he put forward his programme, the congress refused to discuss it. Hertzog and his few loyal friends walked out. He resigned his seat and retired to his farm, to die two years later an abandoned and almost forgotten man.

Hertzog's followers did not give up the struggle so easily. Under the leadership of Havenga they formed the Afrikaner party, a last relic of moderation in the world of Nationalism. If this could be regarded as a splinter party on the moderate wing, Malan's rivals on the extreme wing gave him much greater anxiety. The New Order Group of Oswald Pirow, now an avowed Nazi, was small enough and could give little trouble at elections, but the *Ossewabrandwag* had grown into something like an army of rather civilian storm-troopers. In relation to the H.N.P. it was a rival centre of power and leadership, led by Dr J. F. van Rensburg, ex-Administrator of the

Free State. Between O.B. and H.N.P. there appeared to be differences of principle, one avowedly totalitarian and the other satisfied with a parliamentary system, suitably modified. These differences were probably less important than the fact of divided leadership and allegiance. The memberships overlapped, and for a time the two bodies co-operated under an agreement of October, 1940, by which the party was to be the organ of the Afrikaner people in the political sphere and the O.B. outside that sphere.

In June, 1941, a committee on which both organisations were represented adopted a draft constitution for the future republic, a constitution whose authoritarian character was partly a reflection of the German victories. Following a misunderstanding of what had been said at the committee meeting, the O.B. disseminated 100,000 copies of this constitution and worked publicly for its acceptance. Thus it was poaching on ground reserved for the party. From this beginning the rift between the H.N.P. and the O.B. steadily widened, until at last Malan forbade members of the former to belong to the latter.

Thus it was a thoroughly disunited opposition that had to fight the election of 1943, the first at which the post-1938 party alignments could be tested. The tide of war had now turned against the Axis, and Smuts took care to arrange for his boys 'up North' to vote. He had reason to be satisfied with the result. The government parties won 105 seats, and could count on the support of a few independents, while the opposition strength fell from 63 to 43. Yet Malan had grounds for satisfaction too. The Afrikaner party and the New Order had been eliminated. The O.B. had not, as such, taken part in the election. The H.N.P. itself actually gained two seats.

This was not quite the end of the schism. The Afrikaner party, supposedly the party of the moderates, subsequently offered a political home to the equally disgruntled but certainly not moderate O.B. They drew together out of common hostility to the H.N.P., though the apparently profound differences of principle between them made the association puzzling, if not unintelligible, to outsiders. The most important common denominator was probably reverence for the memory of Hertzog. Thus the Afrikaner party, with a great accession of numbers, could no longer be disregarded. Before the election of 1948 Malan found it prudent to come to an electoral agreement with Havenga; though he was offered very few promising constituencies, Havenga thought it prudent to accept.

In the meantime the war had ended, and with it the war-time coalition. The Dominion party and Labour resumed their freedom of action. The United party could bask in the sun of victory, but in South African conditions this record was no guarantee of popular support. On the debit side, the government drew the resentment of everyone who had suffered from shortages, inconvenience or administrative confusion. Even returning ex-servicemen, treated with unprecedented generosity, often allowed themselves the luxury of 'blaming the government'.

The return of peace meant the return of the old intractable problems. A measure that combined residential segregation for Indians with some small parliamentary representation for them divided opinion in every quarter; some accepted the segregation but denounced the representation; some the reverse; others rejected both, as even the representation was to be on a segregated basis.

The Dominion party took the reactionary side on this issue, and belatedly changed its name to the South African party. The Labour party split, but the party machinery and name were retained by the liberal wing. The party prolonged its life by making an electoral agreement with the U.P.

No one expected a change of government in 1948. The opposition had a long way to go to achieve a majority in Parliament, and an atmosphere unfavourable to republicans had been invoked by the visit in 1947 of the King and Queen and of the two Princesses. How could republicans ride in on the wave of loyalty that the royal tour produced?

The pundits misjudged. Nationalist Afrikanerdom drew together by an instinct of self-preservation. British immigrants were pouring in; industrial development was subjecting simple Afrikaners from the country to alien influences; black Africa and brown Asia were stirring. These tides had to be turned back. 'Next time may be too late' seemed to be the conscious or subconscious conviction of many who had voted for Smuts in 1943. The votes of the disgruntled thrown into the scale, the votes for white bread, more meat, or barbed wire for the farmers, helped to bring it down gently on the Nationalist side. The H.N.P. won 70 seats, the A.P. 9; the U.P. 65 and Labour 6. As the three native representatives would normally vote against the Nationalists, Malan's coalition had a majority of five. As that side would provide the Speaker, the majority would in fact be four in the House and three in Committee. It was hardly a decisive expression of the people's will; the victors were well short of a majority of the votes. But it was enough. South Africa had pushed herself over the brow of the hill, and there would be no turning back. But at the moment the shock which most people felt was merely a shock of surprise. A contemporary cartoon showed Malan saying 'Who—me?'

The chief plank in the Nationalist election platform had been *apartheid*, separateness, a word newly coined to take the place of the old *segregation*. It was widely understood to mean, at least ultimately, the complete separation of the races into different territories, each racially homogeneous. This prospect would appeal to white voters whose traditions had been moulded by all the social conflicts from the frontier wars to the legislative battles of Hertzog's day, and whose prejudices had been hardened and expressed by the steadily evolving pattern of segregation. But the same voters had other traditions and interests, going back to slavery, the five African families on every farm, and the recent industrial development on the basis of black labour. The new government was careful therefore not to define *apartheid*. Nevertheless, it was to be the central theme of the era that began in 1948, and the word was destined to world-wide notoriety.

So were South Africa, its government, and that government's policy. The events of the succeeding decades, as the new policies unfolded, fall into a pattern. The Nationalist party, regarding itself less as a party than as the embodiment of a nation fighting for its life, was resolved that it should never be turned out of office. Many of its measures were designed frankly to avert that disaster. Secondly, 'saving the nation' meant saving the white race, biologically, from dissolution in the sea of colour, and Afrikanerdom, culturally, from dilution and finally extinction by the all-pervading influence of the English. *Apartheid*, the policy of separating group from group and raising the dividing walls ever higher, was constantly elaborated and extended.

These policies provoked reactions among those who suffered from them: beginning with murmurs of protest, rising in a crescendo to processions, demonstrations, boycotts, defiance and riot, the reaction expressed itself also in the rise and fall of new parties and organisations. These phenomena added fuel to the fires of Afrikaner Nationalism, which constantly gained strength in successive elections. But the active opposition, though electorally weak, gave the government the excuse to increase its powers and to curb or abolish one traditional liberty after another.

The period in which Afrikaner exclusiveness, white supremacy and authoritarian government were being applied was the very period in which the colonial empires were crumbling and the nations of Asia and Africa rising to independence. The tension within South

Africa was thus projected on to the international plane; South Africa was out of step with the world.

The theme of increasing tension and rising temperature was reflected also in the changing composition of the government itself. The bare majority of 1948 had been obtained only by alliance with Havenga's Afrikaner party. For some years Havenga exerted a slightly restraining influence, notably in the matter of disfranchising the Coloured voters. In 1950 the new members from South-West Africa gave the Nationalists an absolute majority in the House of Assembly. The Afrikaner party had then to submit to Malan's terms, and was swallowed by its ally.

Towards the end of 1954 Malan resigned office to make way for a younger man. The party caucus, which some had expected to give Havenga the premiership if only *ad interim*, passed him over for J. G. Strydom, the fiery Transvaal republican who was noted for his inflexible hostility to Non-Europeans, English, Crown and Commonwealth. Havenga retired from politics. Strydom, in the event, proved to be fiery in word rather than in deed. A simple, sincere man, he had little knowledge of the substantial part of politics. He could infuse the government with his spirit, but the measures were conceived by others. Strydom, however, after bravely bearing a long illness, died in August, 1958, and the succession had again to be decided by the Nationalist caucus. There were three candidates, none of whom was successful on the first count. On the second count, the choice fell on Dr H. F. Verwoerd, Minister of Native Affairs. Intellectually the ablest of the ministerial team, and a man of personal charm, he was also the most ruthless and un-compromising of the Nationalist leaders, and more than any other man was the brain behind the whole *apartheid* system. In retrospect, Malan now seemed a mild and benign old gentleman.

Before 1948, the old government had encouraged white immigra-tion; the new immediately reversed this policy. The flood became a trickle, and by 1960 the migration figures were showing a net loss of Europeans. As race relations became more tense, the need to strengthen the white forces by immigration was widely voiced by Nationalists, and some steps were taken to encourage it again. But immigrants seldom became Nationalists, and the white population could not be increased at the expense of Nationalist domination. It was to secure this that the flood had been stopped in the first instance. In 1949 the Citizenship Act, one of a series of such acts adopted by all Commonwealth countries, substituted a national citizenship for the old common status of British subject. One of its provisions was that British immigrants would take five years, instead of two, to get citizenship and the vote. Many of the recent arrivals would thus not vote at the next election: the wraith of Kruger was once more defending his old burghers against the Uitlanders.

He defended them also—or their children—in the schools. Afrikaans-medium schools had long been nurseries of young Nationalists. In parallel-medium schools, where the children of both groups mixed in the playgrounds, there was danger of con- tamination or at least of deviation; and in the dual-medium schools fostered by the United party in the Transvaal (where both languages were used as media of instruction for both groups, fused in the same classroom) the danger was extreme. When the Nationalists won control of the Transvaal in 1949 they abolished these systems in favour of strict mother-tongue instruction in separate schools, and they closed the remaining loophole by giving to the Director of Education, not to the parents, the power of deciding what a child's mother tongue was.

Thus a possible leak from the *Volk* was stopped, and demographic factors were called to the aid of the governing party, not only in the Transvaal but in all the provinces but Natal, which the United party continued to rule. The effectiveness of this policy was the real and hardly concealed reason for the lowering of the voting age to eighteen in 1958. Another windfall had come from South-West Africa. Smuts had proposed to give the mandated territory representatives in the Union Parliament. The proposal was taken up by his successors, who in 1949 enacted it; South-West Africa was to have six members in the House of Assembly and four in the Senate—more than twice the numbers justified by the voting population. Parliament received the new members, all Nationalists, in 1950.

Each of these measures had improved the electoral position of the governing party. But the next step in the same direction, the Separate Representation of Voters Bill, had graver and more far-reaching effects. In 1936 Hertzog had removed the Cape African voters from the common roll, but he had waited ten years to do this by the proper constitutional procedure. Malan was now determined to remove the Coloured voters also, but he had no hope of a two-thirds majority in a joint sitting. There was doubt among experts whether the entrenchments in the South Africa Act were still in force, since the Statute of Westminster had given the Union sovereign independence. There could be no doubt of the moral obligation, which members of this very cabinet had at various times solemnly proclaimed, to observe the entrenchments. But the government's first step, in 1951, was to introduce its bill and push it through each house separately by simple majorities.

The bill removed the Coloured voters of the Cape Province from the common roll, gave them four communal representatives (Europeans) in the House of Assembly and two in the Cape Provincial Council. Parliament passed it in disregard of the entrenching clause. Four of the voters affected challenged the Act in the Cape Provincial Division of the Supreme Court. When that Division, bound by an apparently relevant judgment of the Appellate Division in 1937, ruled the Act valid, the case was carried to the Appellate Division itself. In March, 1952, the highest court in the land proclaimed the Act 'invalid, void and of no effect'.

For a much smaller matter than this, Kruger had dismissed his Chief Justice, and his political heirs would not suffer the 'people's will' to be thus flouted. Their immediate response was the High Court of Parliament Act, which made a joint sitting of the two houses, deciding by simple majority, the final court of appeal in constitutional cases. The government duly lodged an appeal against the Appellate Division's judgment, and the High Court—virtually the Nationalist caucus, since Opposition members absented themselves—upheld the appeal. But the new Act was in its turn challenged in the regular courts. The Cape Division, and on appeal the Appellate Division, ruled the High Court Act also null and of no effect.

There the matter rested until the elections of 1953 had increased the Nationalists' strength in Parliament. Hoping to detach some Opposition votes, they brought in a new Separate Representation Bill, put it before a joint session, but still failed to get the two-thirds majority. In June, 1954, another version of the bill was defeated in the same way, though by only nine votes.

Undeterred, the government substituted a flank for a frontal attack. On May 10, 1955, the Appellate Division Quorum Act was signed by the Governor-General. The number of judges was raised from six to eleven, and the Act provided that in constitutional cases the full bench should sit. On the following days the Senate Bill was introduced in the lower house, and in six weeks had received the Governor-General's assent. This Act enlarged the Senate from 48 to 89 members; abolished the provincial equality in the numbers of elected Senators; substituted simple majorities for proportional representation in the electoral colleges; and increased the number of nominated Senators. A party possessing a majority in a provincial electoral college—the Nationalists, in all except Natal—would thus return all the Senators from the province. It could be foreseen that there would be 77 Nationalist Senators, and that the government would then command a two-thirds majority in a joint sitting.

The ground having been prepared, a bill was introduced in the session of 1956 to amend the South Africa Act by removing the entrenchment of the Cape franchise and, at the same time, validating the Separate Representation of Voters Act. The new bill, having the benefit of the new Senate, safely passed the hurdle of the joint sitting. It passed also the scrutiny of the new Appellate Division. The Coloured voters were duly transferred to their separate roll, and the Nationalists made sure of some additional seats in the Cape Province.

The political turmoil of those years was not due only to the great struggle over the constitution; nor was the separation of voters merely a scheme to capture a few constituencies. *Apartheid* had become, for many, a dogma. Wherever different races were inter-mixed in the same places or the same institutions they were to be separated. The white race, like a party of Voortrekkers, was to be surrounded by a wall of wagons and thorn-bushes, protecting it from attack and from contamination.

The Nationalists lost no time in striking at the heart of the problem. The Prohibition of Mixed Marriages Act, 1949, forbade marriage between white and non-white. The Immorality Amend-ment Act of 1950 prohibited extra-marital relations between whites and all non-whites—not only Africans, as the Act of 1927 had provided. Thus miscegenation was forbidden at the point where it was most likely to occur, on the borderline of colour.

The borderline was notoriously vague. The purpose of the Population Registration Act of 1950 was to define it. A Population Register and Identity Cards would record the racial classification of every individual, so that the separation of white from Coloured in marriage, the polling booth, and other spheres still to come, could be effected with precision and certainty. As there had never been any such separation in the Cape Province, where it was most relevant, the new policy would require in many cases a searching inquiry into the antecedents of individuals and families. A pall of fear, delation and personal tragedy descended upon obscure corners of the old easy-going Western Province.

After marriage came the home. Residential segregation of Africans from Europeans was an old policy, and the few exceptions to it could easily be eliminated by those who had the power and the determination. But the other Non-Europeans had never been compulsorily segregated. In the Cape peninsula and elsewhere in the Cape Province there were many areas where white and Coloured were to be found intermixed along the same street. In Natal, especially in Durban, and in many Transvaal towns, whites complained of Indian 'penetration'. In both these provinces Indian shops, in central positions in the towns, competed with rival white traders. As far back as 1941 a Pegging Act had subjected land transfers between Europeans and Indians in Natal to control, and in 1946 the Smuts government had tried to prevent such transfers everywhere but in exempted areas which might be expected to become wholly Indian.

Such tinkering could not satisfy the Nationalists, nor, it must be admitted, the English-speaking whites of Durban. The new government made a comprehensive attack on the problem with its Group Areas Act of 1950, which in subsequent years was often amended and gradually applied. Now the whole country, but notably the towns, where the problem was most acute, was to be divided into separate areas for different races. Evidence would be heard and plans made for every locality. When a Group Area was proclaimed for any race, people of other races would no longer be able either to own or to occupy property in it. Thus the Act was retrospective in its operation; it implied the forcible removal of unknown numbers of people.

When the Act began to be implemented the pretence of impartiality was quickly dropped. Where any number of Europeans was adversely affected the authorities were sensitive to their complaints; there was no squeamishness about moving thousands of Indians to the remote outskirts, and destroying their trade in the process. Under the Act there was no obligation to find alternative accommodation for people ejected from their homes. Areas allotted to Indians were inevitably small and there would be sharp competition for property in them. But areas proclaimed white, from which Indians were ejected, held little attraction for white purchasers. The move would usually compel Indians, and similarly Coloured people to sell cheap and buy dear, and many Indians would at the same time have to move their shops to places inaccessible to their customers.

Though Africans were little affected by this Act, they suffered in the same way from other legislation. There were a few anomalous townships, such as Sophiatown and Alexandra in Johannesburg, where they could still hold property in freehold, and which moreover were regarded as being in unpleasant proximity to their white neighbours. Under an Act of 1954 the government took the power to restrict residence in Alexandra and to remove the inhabitants from the 'Western Areas' altogether. This purported to be a slum clearance scheme, which in one aspect it was, but that was not its chief significance. In February, 1955, the forcible removals from Sophiatown began, under massive police supervision, and as the occupants left bulldozers moved in to reduce their homes to rubble. The background of the story was given to the world in the following year by the great Anglican missionary, Father Trevor Huddleston, in *Naught for Your Comfort*.

There were many other laws under which an African might be ordered to move from one area to another. An Act of 1956 gave the power of removal, hitherto exercised by a minister, to municipal authorities also. As orders for removal were sometimes issued illegally, and redress could then be obtained from the courts, the people affected could obtain a reprieve by getting an interdict against the minister pending the court's judgment in the case. Another Act of 1956 closed this loophole by forbidding the courts to grant interdicts in such cases.

A third field in which walls of partition were built was education. There was, indeed, no mixing of races in the schools, but here the government was concerned with more than physical separation. The Bantu Education Act of 1953, amended and elaborated in the following year, brought all schools for Africans under the control, and ultimately under the direct or indirect administration, of a central government department. Hitherto the control, as for other schools, had been provincial, but almost all the teaching had been in the hands of missionary bodies. Yet they had become increasingly dependent on government grants. Now they were given the alternatives of transferring the schools to the new department, retaining them on a subsidy that would be progressively reduced and finally abolished, or closing them. Even those that were maintained by the churches, or by private individuals, had to be registered, and the minister could at any time cancel the registration. Penalties were prescribed for running an unregistered school or permitting children to attend it.

It was made clear by Dr Verwoerd, the minister responsible for the Act, that its fundamental purpose was to adapt Bantu education to the rôle which the Bantu could expect to play in a white community. They were not to be given false notions of their position in that community, nor indeed to have access to dangerous ideas of any kind. Another purpose was to prevent Africans from becoming 'black Englishmen'; there would be less English, and more Afrikaans, in the syllabus; social studies would be adapted accordingly, and there would be more emphasis on practical subjects. The teachers would be under effective discipline, would be forbidden to comment adversely on government policy, and if dismissed would find no other employment, as there would be only one employer in their profession.

The churches, other than the Dutch Reformed, reacted with anger and dismay, which was shared by all of liberal opinions. The Roman Catholics raised enough money to preserve their mission schools in precarious independence, and the Seventh Day Adventists did the same. Some churches, including the American Board of Foreign Missions and the Anglican Diocese of Johannesburg, closed their schools rather than aid the government in its policy. The rest reluctantly submitted.

Teachers' training institutions were included in the scope of the Act, but university education was a separate problem. Non-European students attended the Universities of Cape Town and the Witwatersrand, where there was a little social but no academic segregation. This in itself was an offence against *apartheid*. In the University of Natal, however, the races were segregated, and the University College of Fort Hare (affiliated to Rhodes University) was a purely Non-European institution. Yet these too were regarded unfavourably by the government because they dispensed the same education, the same ideas and influences, to black as to white. The principle of the Bantu Education Act, that the government should control the thoughts of Non-Europeans, would not be fully realised until it was applied to higher education also.

After some years of planning and foreshadowing, countered by numerous protests from the universities, the Extension of University Education Act was passed in the session of 1959. Henceforth no non-white student, except those already embarked on their courses, could be admitted to a 'white' university without the permission of the minister. New university colleges were to be established for the various Bantu tribal groups, the Coloured and the Asiatics respectively. These would be under the all-pervasive control of the Minister of Bantu Education (for the Coloured and Asiatics, the Minister of Education, Arts and Science), who directly or indirectly could at his discretion appoint and dismiss staff, admit, refuse to admit, or expel students. Professors and lecturers were to be subject to civil service regulations, which among many other restrictions forbade them to criticise government policy.

By a separate Act of the same session the government assumed control of the University College of Fort Hare, which was destined to be the tribal college for the Xhosa group. Eight members of the staff were at once dismissed, with compensation, on political grounds. Most of the other colleges opened their doors in 1960.

The catalogue of laws and administrative acts to segregate the races was too long to be more than briefly illustrated in the space available here. It extended to trade unions, job reservation (the power of the Minister of Labour to reserve occupations or tasks for members of a specified race), the nursing profession, the amenities of post offices and railway stations, beaches (with an extension, in 1960, to the three-mile limit), and, in general, most of the spheres not fully covered by older legislation of the same kind. One such sphere was the Church, of which more will be said in another context.

Yet, to some minds, none of this was real *apartheid*; it brought no nearer the day when the races would be disentangled and concentrated in their separate homogeneous states. The South African Bureau of Racial Affairs—S.A.B.R.A., the Nationalist counterpart of the South African Institute of Race Relations—the organ of the Nationalist intelligentsia, was insistent that this total separation was the only just alternative to the complete integration advocated by the liberals. If total separation were possible, not only the Nationalists but most white South Africans would have regarded it as an ideal solution. If the Africans were given their proportional share of the country, they would no doubt have settled for this policy without more ado.

But no candid observer could believe that this solution was possible. The now highly industrialised economy was based on the joint labours of black and white. The South African 'way of life' demanded black servants. The surrender of any significant amount of land by white owners to black was politically inconceivable. Yet the ultimate total separation of the races was the only respectable covering with which the government could clothe its otherwise indecent policy.

The Tomlinson Commission was appointed to discover how to square this circle. The government had been in possession of its report for more than a year when it was published in March, 1956. The Commission planned the development of the existing reserves at a cost of £104 million for the first ten years, and worked on the assumption that the High Commission territories would be incorporated in the Union. On that basis it was hoped that, after fifty years, the reserves would have absorbed so many Africans that a rough parity of black and white populations would have been reached in the 'white' areas. As these areas would include also the Coloured and Asiatic populations, the plan was far from securing total segregation. It represented the greatest achievement in that direction that the commissioners could foresee, even on an optimistic basis of expenditure and annexation. Yet the government, while joyfully welcoming the plan, refused to countenance the expenditure.

Nevertheless it could not be deflected from what it regarded as the only acceptable long-term objective. It strove unceasingly, on one hand to make the reserves the national homes of all the black South Africans, on the other to reverse the flow of black humanity into the 'white areas'. As this two-pronged drive was the Nationalists' basic policy, from which most of its other policies were in some way derived, it is worth looking at in some detail.

In its essence it was not a new policy. As long ago as 1905, Milner's Intercolonial Native Affairs Commission had recommended much the same thing. Hertzog's Acts of 1936 had some of the same implications. But whereas in 1905 South Africa was mainly a country of farms and mines, and African labour in towns was mostly migrant labour, by the middle of the century the country was highly industrialised and some millions of Africans had struck roots in the cities. This was the change that had destroyed the foundations of the segregation system; therefore the primary aim of the advocates of segregation was to reverse it. The aim was expressed simply by the Deputy Minister of Bantu Administration in 1966: 'The Government cannot allow an unlimited flow of Bantu labour to the Witwatersrand. This flow must be reduced, then it must be stopped, then it must be turned back.'

In the agrarian days governments had tried to strike a balance by allowing five African families, and no more, to a white farm. On a farm all members of a family had their rôles; in a town, with its purely cash economy, all except the one working directly for a white employer were 'redundant'. Thus, in the new circumstances, men and women who had not found jobs or had lost them, the aged and the handicapped, widows, and in many cases the wives and children of employed men were to be removed from the towns. All were to be taught that their homes were in the reserves, and that residence in the white man's town was not the right of an African. It was a temporary concession arising from a temporary economic situation.

The Smuts government in 1945 had fathered an important act which among other things gave some Africans a right to live in a town. To qualify, the African had to have been born in a town and to have lived in it continuously since birth, or else to have worked continuously for one employer there for ten years, or for more than one employer for fifteen years. A man's right included that of his wife and younger children.

Year by year, after 1948, new laws were passed which modified or whittled away these rights and improved the machinery of 'influx control' and 'endorsing out'. The right of a wife to live with her husband in an urban area came to depend on her own right to live in that or another urban area; if a man married a rural woman he could not bring her to town. When this rule was relaxed in 1972, the permission was made to depend on there being available accommodation in the African townships of the city—the 'black ghettos'. At that time, in the great Johannesburg 'dormitory' of Soweto, there were 13,600 families on the waiting list for houses; thus the concession was inoperative.

Some African workers—domestic servants were an obvious example—lived on the premises of their employers in the white area. In their case the prohibition against having wife, husband or children in the accommodation became absolute. Sympathetic white employers who tried to circumvent this rule were prosecuted. The government assumed powers to forbid a white employer to have more than one black servant living on his premises; this power was used in one area after another. In some places no Africans were allowed to live on white premises, so that various towns and parts of towns became 'white by night'.

The compulsory use of labour bureaux made it difficult for a white employer and a black worker to seek each other out directly. The employer had to register his requirements, the worker his availability, and officials matched the man to the job. If the worker was in a reserve when he registered, he was compelled to return there at the end of his one-year contract, and apply again—even if he intended returning to the same job. Thus his domicile was established in the reserve and could never be transferred to the city. As the drive to 'endorse out' was intensified, an increasing number of Africans found themsevles in that position. The Johannesburg City Council commented that there was probably 'no more coveted and sought-after right anywhere in the world, including the vote, than the right to qualify to be in an urban area, especially Johannesburg.'

As this right, for more and more people, was turned into a privilege, the South African Institute of Race Relations concluded that 'the vast majority of Union Africans have no *right* to be anywhere where they can earn a living'.

The Western Province of the Cape, which for centuries Europeans had shared with the Coloured, was the extreme case. Black Africans were not indigenous there, and as late as the First World War there had been very few of them in the area. Since then the demands of the labour market had drawn them in. This obvious disturbance of the old racial pattern cried out to be undone. Early in 1955 the government announced its intention to remove *all* Africans from an area west of a line drawn, roughly, from Colesberg to Humansdorp. The policies of influx control and removal were therefore applied more strictly in the Western Province than elsewhere.

If the partition of the country on a racial basis were ever to be achieved, these policies were necessary; the question that arose in some minds was whether the end justified such means. In 1970 the General Synod of the Dutch Reformed Church itself expressed its deep concern about the family disintegration and moral decay resulting from this system. At one end of the process were the 'bachelors' in their single quarters; at the other the wives, children and other superfluous elements deposited in the reserves.

In many cases the people so transported had lost all connection, or had never had any connection, with their so-called 'homeland'. They were often unwelcome to the local chiefs and people, already overcrowded on their constricted lands. Townships and villages of various categories were designed for the newcomers. In most cases the land assigned was equivalent to an urban plot, with no agricultural possibilities. This was a hardship especially to those who were removed not from a town but from a white farm (if they were 'surplus' to its labour needs) or from African-owned farms in mainly white areas—'black spots' which were being eliminated. The new settlements in the reserves were not meant to be agricultural. They were labour reservoirs from which migrant workers could be drawn and to which they could be returned, while their families were kept conveniently out of the way. Most of these places, though not all, were for a long time stagnant pools of poverty, disease and hopelessness.

The drawing of labour from these places to the white cities was, from the planners' point of view, an undesirable necessity. To reduce that flow the policy of the 'border industries' was launched in 1960.

Entrepreneurs were encouraged to build their factories in places close to the borders of reserves, so that African employees could live in their own areas and commute daily to work. Encouragement took the form of public investment of capital; of public expenditure or loans for the building of factories and dwellings, for the provision of electric power, water, roads and railway sidings; of tax remissions, and generally of lower wage rates than in other areas; of rebates on railway rates and harbour charges; of favours in respect of government contracts. Moreover, in these areas African labour was easy to obtain.

The border areas used in this way were not, for the most part, remote and inaccessible. The distribution of the reserves was such that a border industry might be set up on the outskirts of Pretoria, Pietermaritzburg or East London. Many factories went up in such places, and the government had power to forbid their erection in oher places where the flow of African labour was to be stopped. The net result was that, by 1973, the border industries had provided jobs for 85,554 Africans—a very small percentage of the whole labour force. There were then between four and five million Africans in the towns.

The success of the policy, in its own terms, is not easy to measure. According to official figures, the percentage of the African population, including migrant workers, that was in 'white areas' (towns and farms) in 1960 was 62·5; in 1970 it was 53·5. The decline was partly a result of the 'endorsements out', but partly also of mere paper work: some places, especially dormitory suburbs of towns, which in 1960 had been in the white area had since been included in reserves. The total African population of almost all the cities certainly increased during the decade, though about a million (from towns, farms and 'black spots') had been 'resettled'.

The whole vast operation was of course dependent on the pass laws. Without them—the conversion of 'passes' into 'reference books' made no practical difference—it would have been impossible. We shall see in the next chapter how this fact impressed the people directly affected.

In the long run the success of removal and resettlement depended on what happened to the places—the reserves—where the displaced persons were sent. This leads us to the other half of the Nationalists' basic policy.

The Bantu Authorities Act of 1951 provided for tribal authorities in the reserves. Though the tribal authority was a chief-in-council, the chief nominating the councillors, the system bore no resemblance except in outward form to the ancient Bantu polity. The chief was now appointed, and could be removed, by the government, which could also veto his nominations. On this basis was built a hierarchy of regional authorities. Though the financial recommendations of the Tomlinson Report had been rejected, its other proposals helped to inspire the culminating measure, the Promotion of Bantu Self-Government Act of 1959.

This Act was curiously named. Though the scattered reserves were grouped by it into eight 'national' territories, each supervised by a Commissioner-General, and though there was much talk of freedom and self-realisation, the reins were held as tightly as ever by the central government. The nominated chiefs were made the basis of the structure. With a limited and insignificant exception in the Transkei, the elective element was entirely eliminated from 'Bantu self-government'. And the same Act abolished the African representation in both houses of Parliament that Hertzog had given in 1936. Critics averred that this last provision was the sole reason for the Act, the rest being an elaborate pretence to distract attention from the real purpose.

It is impossible to say whether that was so, and how this measure would have worked if the peace of South Africa had not soon been disturbed. But the violence that began at Sharpeville in March 1960 (and that will be a topic of the next chapter) in fact caused Bantu self-government to be modified in a way that was not contemplated in 1959.

World hostility to South Africa alarmed the government more than it would admit in public. In what seems like an atmosphere of panic various concessions, as sops to the international Cerberus, were discussed: a roving black ambassador from the African states; Coloured members of Parliament; a third house of Parliament to represent the Coloured and the Indians. All these were rejected, but Dr Verwoerd himself, supposedly the inflexible man of granite, decided on the 'dramatic' gesture that was to silence the foreign critics. The Transkei, as the most viable of the reserves, was to be advanced as quickly as possible to self-government, and in due course, if it were able, to sovereign independence.

It is important to note that this decision, unlike most Nationalist decisions, was not carefully thought out. It did not fit neatly into an overall plan. It was a spur-of-the-moment decision provoked by foreign danger. It started a train of developments that led far from the familiar path that the Nationalists, and all South Africa, had safely trodden till then.

In 1963 the new constitution for the Transkei came into force. As the Legislative Assembly would include sixty-four appointed chiefs as well as forty-five elected members, there seemed to be no danger to the central government from that quarter. An opposition party which rejected *apartheid* and all its works won most of the elective seats, but the chiefs ensured a majority for the party that wished to work within the system. Chief Kaizer Matanzima became Chief Minister. The powers of his government and legislature were increased in the following years, the immediate intention being to reserve for the central government only such spheres as defence, security, foreign relations, communications and currency.

The Transkei was the only one of the 'national territories' that was more or less compact. It was also far ahead of the others in previous, though limited, experience of local self-government. But once the first step had been taken, an inescapable logic led to the next. An enabling Act of 1971 opened the way, and six more Legislative Assemblies were set up in that year. The last of the important 'homelands' to fall into line (the word 'reserves' was no longer used, but in opposition circles the 'homelands' were popularly called Bantustans) was Kwa-Zulu. The Zulus had a monarchy, and their Chief Minister, Chief Gatsha Buthelezi, had by tradition an hereditary claim to such an office. Though not enthusiastic about the new system, he used his strong position to make certain demands on behalf of his people.

By 1972 the government was busy with the 'consolidation' of the scattered homelands, by exchanges of black for white lands in order to make each homeland as nearly as possible a continuous bloc. Very little could be achieved, but the Chief Ministers used the occasion to demand much more territory for their states. Without much more area and more consolidation, they pointed out, their states would not be viable. To be viable they would need, in fact, more than a few more square miles of farmland. The reserves were the back-waters of South Africa, with no sizable towns, no industries, no mineral resources and poor communications. They can often be recognised on a railway map because they are shown up by gaps in the railway network.

The 'homeland' ministers, being the products of the government's own system, could not be deposed, prosecuted or silenced without making nonsense of the system. Increasingly, as they tested their strength, they used it to make themselves the spokesmen for their fellow-Africans generally, including the townsmen and the migrant workers. As a result, Chief Kaizer Matanzima, who had been put into office by the nominees, won most of the elective seats in the Transkei in 1968. Chief Gatsha Buthelezi went abroad, to various African countries and to the United States, to speak for his people. In 1974 negotiations between the central government and the Transkei on the subject of independence were begun.

Only the cohesion and the electoral strength of the National Party made this step possible. The Africans of the 'homelands' expressed grave doubts about independence, or even total opposition to it, because of the extreme economic weakness of their territories. Independence would be a sham for a country dependent on South Africa for jobs and subsidies. White South Africans were alarmed at the prospect of Chinese agents in Umtata, Communist aid, and all the other possible consequences of this radical policy. Further, it was pointed out by the government's opponents, and realised by many of its supporters, that casting off the homelands would not even solve the problem. The real problem—race relations in the 'white area'—would be as intractable as ever. For this the Nationalists could offer no solution.

There was another problem with which they were better equipped to deal—the English. Hertzog's break with Botha in 1912 and his launching of the original National Party had been provoked by fear not of the Africans but of the English. Malan's refusal to follow Hertzog into fusion in 1934 was likewise due to a concern with the English danger, not the black peril. Verwoerd, as editor of the leading Nationalist paper of the Transvaal, had used his position to promote the Nazi cause; the Supreme Court had convicted him of this. It was his proud boast that during the whole of the Royal visit in 1947 his paper never once mentioned the presence of the unwanted guests.

The Broederbond can be accounted for in the same way. A quasi-masonic society, it was a subject of speculation, especially in the light of certain features of post-1948 politics. The unity of purpose in the Nationalist ranks, the march direct towards a goal, the crusading spirit, the contemptuous impatience of criticism, the speed with which a project, once announced, was realised in all its details and ramifications, gave rise to the question whether there was one directing brain or guiding hand behind the actors on the stage. There is evidence, though in the nature of the case it is inconclusive, that the Broederbond was indeed the spider at the centre of the web. It was a secret brotherhood to which the most influential Nationalists both at the centre and on the periphery belonged. Significantly, it became important about 1933, when the Coalition threatened to subject Afrikanerdom to more English influences. During the war Smuts succeeded in planting a spy in it; the information thus secured was circulated in a confidential document, but the brothers traced the leak and stopped it. There the intriguing subject must be left until some accident of the future brings to light documents that were not intended for the public.

The Broederbond was dedicated certainly to white, but primarily to Afrikaner domination, and this sometimes neglected aspect of Nationalist policy must once again be emphasised. Though the English-speaking whites did not suffer in any way comparable to the experience of the non-whites, they were left in no doubt about who was now on top. In the civil service, the army, the railways, indeed wherever the arm of the government could reach, Afrikaners were promoted over the heads of their English seniors. The remaining symbols of the British connection, including the Union Jack and *God Save the Queen*, which had retained an official status, were removed.

There was a close relation between this side and the white supremacy side of Nationalist policy. The destruction of the political rights of Africans and Coloured people and the drive towards a purely white community were not mere racism or nastiness. In a purely white community, or a purely white electorate, the Afrikaners had a secure and increasing numerical majority. But if the electorate were diluted ever so little with non-white voters that security would be undermined. Any reasonable non-racial but qualified franchise would make the Afrikaners a political minority. Their nation, which history had condemned to share its territory with others, would then be 'ploughed under' culturally, as a first step to being dissolved biologically.

Conversely, a greater influence of the English in politics, with their usual pragmatism and easy-going adaptability, would weaken the rigid Afrikaner attitudes to race and colour, and so lead by a different route to the same catastrophe. Afrikaner Nationalism had always to fight a war on two fronts.

It seemed at the middle of the century that some were still fighting the war that was supposed to have ended in 1902. The wound inflicted then had never healed; it had even been reopened in 1934 and 1939. Nothing would heal it but the overt defeat of monarchy and empire. Some had hoped that the Malan government in 1948 would lose no time in declaring a republic, but Malan did not have an absolute majority in Parliament, still less in the electorate. In both respects the ruling party did better in 1953 and still better in 1958, and its position had by then been improved by bringing in members

G

from South-West Africa, separating the Coloured voters and lowering the voting age of the whites.

The ground having been thus prepared, the government announced plans for a referendum on the republican issue. The announcement, early in 1960, was followed by a period of violence and disturbance precipitated by the shooting at Sharpeville. It was not an appropriate moment to celebrate the Golden Jubilee of the Union, but the calendar dictated that this should be done on 31 May 1960. The non-whites had no part in it, and there were few English-speaking people among the 100,000 who gathered in Bloemfontein. The bulk of the English individually, and the provincial and local authorities in Natal officially, boycotted the Jubilee. The Prime Minister at the end of his speech to the great crowd released a dove of peace, which—*absit omen*—refused to fly.

The referendum was held on 5 October. The republican issue, a source of hopes and fears and bitter argument for as long as anyone could remember, was now at last to be settled. Or was it? Dr Verwoerd announced that even the barest favourable majority would be decisive. But he permitted himself to say that if the majority voted the other way the matter would not be allowed to rest there; the struggle would only become 'more bitter'. The Nationalists, who organised the campaign for the republic, insisted that the issue be regarded as a constitutional question isolated from everything else. The opposition parties, opposing the republic, maintained that to support it implied support of the régime which sponsored it. Only Europeans (to the exclusion of the Coloured voters on the separate roll) would vote.

The republicans won 52 per cent of the voters on a 90 per cent poll. The provincial distribution of the votes was significant. In the Transvaal, Orange Free State and South-West Africa the republican majorities were 56, 77 and 62 per cent. The Cape Province split almost evenly with a republican majority of 50·15 per cent, and Natal was anti-republican by 76 per cent. The predominantly English-speaking areas of the Eastern Cape Province had two-to-one anti-republican majorities. The figures could almost have been predicted from a knowledge of the varied history and mutual and internal tensions of the provinces.

A demand for the secession of Natal, or of Natal and the Eastern Province, was made as a matter of course, but treated with official contempt. Again, there was a kind of spiritual contracting out of the republic by Natal, which would regard itself as a conquered and subjected people. But for the most part the defeated side accepted the decision. The government had given the assurance that the republic was to remain in the Commonwealth. Without this assurance there might have been no republican majority.

But the assurance was easier to give than to honour. The precedent of India had decided that a Dominion becoming a republic would have to apply for readmission to the Commonwealth. Apparently this could be granted only with the unanimous agreement of the other governments. South Africa had tried to get this agreement in advance at the Commonwealth Conference in 1960, but was put off on the ground that the question was still hypothetical. The Conference of March, 1961, would have to decide.

The constitutional change would not in itself have caused any difficulty. But there were Commonwealth countries, especially the non-white ones, that found association with South Africa a grievous embarrassment. Mr Julius Nyerere of Tanganyika announced that when independence came, his country would not want to belong to a Commonwealth that included South Africa. South African political exiles toured the capitals to advocate a policy of ejection. Mr Macmillan used his diplomatic skill to win the governments to a policy of patience and forbearance.

It was understood that a division of the Prime Ministers' Conference on racial lines might, at the least, make a disastrous impression. That division was averted by the initiative of Mr Diefenbaker of Canada, who substituted a positive for a negative approach. He proposed that all the member states should join in a declaration repudiating racial discrimination. South Africa was thus potentially readmitted, but on conditions which she could not accept. Dr Verwoerd withdrew his application for Commonwealth membership.

He returned to a country more deeply divided than ever before. The bitter-end republicans hoped that material losses could be avoided, and emotionally they were well satisfied with the outcome. Their opponents were stunned. Parliament proceeded with the technical details of the constitutional change. The two houses, sitting as an electoral college, chose the President who was to step into the shoes of the Governor-General; they chose Mr C. R. Swart, to succeed himself.

On 31 May 1961, the Republic of South Africa was launched and the last tenuous links with Britain severed. But not even this magic could conjure away the nightmare of white insecurity in the midst of an exasperated black majority at the end of a black continent.

14

OPPOSITION AND REPRESSION

The policy of forcing an unwilling population into a procrustean bed of 'homelands', and depriving it of most of the rights and opportunities that it believed to be its due, could not be enforced without provoking resistance. As the government was determined to achieve its ends at all costs, it overcame the resistance, assuming more and more powers of repression as they became necessary. Repression was an old practice, but it was intensified after the Nationalists assumed office and was hardly ever relaxed. Yet even this severity had its degrees. It became harsher in and after 1960 than it had been before.

The political tradition of Afrikaner nationalism, derived essentially from the old South African Republic, was not primarily authoritarian. Indeed, in Afrikaner eyes it was conspicuously democratic. But, as the reader of Transvaal history will remember, it was democratic within limits of a special kind. An almost anarchical liberty within the circle of the *Volk* was combined with a dictatorship of the *Volk* over the lesser tribes without the law.

The two principles could not be reconciled for long. As Afrikanerdom felt itself being slowly hedged into its little world by a host of enemies, it instinctively drew together in disciplined unity, the more easily to impose its will on the foe. Nationalism after 1948 had the appearance of an army. Things were made awkward for a soldier who marched out of step; talking back to a superior officer became an unthinkable offence. If this was the discipline within, little mercy could be expected by the enemy without.

A series of Acts gave the minister power to suppress various kinds of opposition. The Suppression of Communism Act, 1950, was more far-reaching than its name implied. While it enabled the government to ban any organisation and suppress any newspaper suspected of Communism, to 'name' any person a Communist and so prevent him from sitting in Parliament, belonging to any organisation, attending any meeting, speaking in public, or even moving out of a designated area, it did not define Communist. If anyone were 'named' by the minister he was a Communist for the purposes of the Act. The power was widely used, and where it was inappropriate in this form recourse could always be had to the older Riotous Assembly Acts, under which anyone could be banned from any specified area.

From the government's point of view, its new powers were acquired none too soon. There had indeed been ominous disturbances even before 1948. After that date they broke out intermittently, and became more serious and frequent, until the spirit of rebellion became endemic among Africans and required massive forces to curb it. The rioting in Durban in January, 1949, appeared not to concern the Europeans. It was a fight between Zulus and Indians, the former exasperated by the treatment they received from Indian landlords, employers and creditors. Though these antipathies could not be easily overcome, the leaders of both communities felt that they could not afford such quarrels in the face of a régime which oppressed them both. The African National Congress and the South African Indian Congress drew together to plan a campaign of Indian inspiration, Passive Resistance, in which a son of Mahatma Gandhi played a prominent part.

The Passive Resistance (or Defiance) campaign was timed to coincide with the white men's celebration in 1952 of the tercentenary of Van Riebeeck's landing. It took the form of defying the segregation laws and submitting to imprisonment. Parties of non-Europeans entered European waiting-rooms and other such accommodation and courted arrest. At a later stage a small number of European sympathisers, led by Patrick Duncan, son of the former Governor-General, took part in the campaign by entering African locations without permits. In a few months the resistance seemed to be petering out. Some thousands had been imprisoned, but the régime was not shaken, and the supply of volunteers was exhausted. Yet the campaign did have long-term effects. It established, as a programme for people who had no hope of achieving anything by armed force, the policy of trying to paralyse the administration by non-cooperation and by over-burdening its machinery. It was also an exercise in discipline.

But undisciplined action followed in its wake. A trivial incident in the Port Elizabeth township of New Brighton led to an explosion of arson and murder. Similar explosions followed in East London and Kimberley. They served the government well in the next elections.

Among other examples of resistance one of the most significant arose from an increase in fares on the bus route from Johannesburg to Alexandra township, in December, 1956. The people of the township decided that they could not pay the higher fare, and organised a boycott of the buses. They walked the distance of about ten miles. While the Minister of Transport insisted that the boycott was political and must be broken, white motorists showed their sympathy by offering lifts to the walkers. The police harassed the motorists and arrested the Africans for various offences, but the boycott succeeded. Johannesburg employers devised a scheme for subsidising the bus company, and the passengers paid the old fares.

This was not the first boycott of its kind; the method was becoming one of the standard forms of passive resistance. At the same time active resistance was developing in another context. One of its stimuli was the imposition of the new system of tribal authorities. This was resisted in Sekhukhuneland, the Eastern Transvaal reserve which had figured prominently in history before and after 1877. During the first half of 1957 the substitution (by the government) of a new chief for the old led to unrest and a refusal to cooperate, to the deportation of several leaders, to rioting by the tribesmen and shooting by the police. At that moment trouble was brewing in the reserves of the Marico district in the Western Transvaal. In this case the provocation was given by the attempt to impose the pass system, hitherto confined to men, on women. The women, supported by their men, resisted. Complicated by the deposition of an uncooperative chief, the dispute culminated in large-scale arrests, arson, murder, vigorous retaliation by the police, and the exclusion from the area of unauthorised Europeans, including the local Anglican priest.

By 1959 the disturbance had in some parts of the country, notably Natal, become almost continuous. The underlying causes were the general conditions of poverty, frustration and resentment. The immediate causes were various—the suppression of illicit brewing in Cato Manor, Durban's festering slum; the culling of cattle on eroded reserves; interference with tribal agriculture for purposes of soil conservation; the imposition of unwanted 'tribal authorities'. Resistance took the form of throwing stones and other missiles at police, officials and vehicles, of burning huts, beer-halls, schools and other buildings. Everywhere, the police moved in and in many cases used their firearms.

As far as it went this resistance, whether wise or misguided, was no more than a negative reaction. But it was given a positive content and object by the political leaders in their Congresses—the African National Congress, the South African Indian Congress, the South African Coloured People's Organisation, the non-racial South African Congress of Trade Unions, and the Congress of Democrats, a white leftist body formed in 1952. All these organised, and constituted, a Congress of the People, which met a Kliptown near Johannesburg in June 1955. There they drew up at Freedom Charter, demanding a non-racial and more or less socialist democracy based on universal suffrage. The day this was done, 26 June, was the anniversary of the launching of the Defiance Campaign in 1952, and became the 'Freedom Day' of future years.

The police were, of course, in attendance at the meeting, taking names and searching for documents. The result of their search, and of many subsequent raids on suspected premises, was not apparent until the early hours of 5 December 1956, when in a nation-wide round-up the police arrested most of the 156 people of all races who were to be accused of high treason. The Treason Trial began. It ended—in the acquittal of the accused—only when the accusers themselves were abolishing the sovereignty of the Queen against whom, technically, the treason must have been committed. But over the years it had the effect of silencing discussion of various controversial matters because they were *sub judice*.

This brief outline of events under the Nationalist government suggests the criticisms which its enfranchised white opponents might use to attack it: injustice, breach of faith, destruction of the constitution, uniting the non-Europeans in hatred of the white man while dividing the Europeans with other hatreds, undermining democracy and the rule of law—and failing to bring real *apartheid* one step nearer. In many countries an opposition party could hardly hope for a more formidable armoury than this. Yet the Nationalists improved their postion at every election. The essential reason was that the attack on the government was both negative and equivocal, not to say opportunist. The leader of liberal opinion in the United party in 1948 was the younger (a near kinsman of the elder) J. H. Hofmeyr. His liberalism made him a heavy liability. In the campaign of that year the Nationalists made an ogre of him. Many in his party believed, rightly or wrongly, that he had lost them the election, and at the end of the year he died.

Smuts had never included in the grand sweep of his vision a constructive solution of the 'native problem'. He dodged or postponed this by devoting his thought and energy to other great but less intractable questions. But it could not be dodged. Its challenge was repeated more frequently and seriously as time passed, and never provoked a successful response—a failure which, a few South Africans noted, Arnold Toynbee had recently indicated as the signal of breakdown in a society.

It certainly indicated the breakdown of the United Party. The strongest bond of union in the party was Smuts himself; and in September, 1950, Smuts followed Hofmeyr to the grave. The leadership fell to J. G. N. Strauss, whose fitness for the post was increasingly criticised until, in November 1956, the party congress in his absence deposed him in favour of Sir de Villiers Graaff. The change had no effect on the electoral trend. It may be doubted whether in the circumstances any leader could measure up to the impossible expectations of the deeply disunited party. As an opposition which had recently been the government, it naturally hungered for a return to power. But to win an election it had to win the marginal constituencies and convert the floating voters who had put the Nationalists in. This necessity created a standing temptation to dress the party in Nationalist colours; it played into the hands of what was called the conservative wing.

The assumption that the liberal wing would have perforce to accept this strategy, because it had no alternative political home, proved correct at least up to the 1953 election. People who saw little to approve in the United Party platform swallowed their scruples, kept their ideas to themselves and supported the party, as it was the only conceivable means of defeating the government.

Early in 1953 that government used a tactic which was so successful in dividing and confusing its opponents that it became a model for the future. Two drastic measures were introduced, and passed, to enlarge the government's powers. The Criminal Law Amendment Act provided severe punishment, including lashes, for inciting anyone to break a law by way of protest against that law. The Public Safety Act empowered the Governor-General to proclaim a state of emergency in the whole or any part of the Union when its security was endangered. During the state of emergency almost all laws, other than those relating to the election and functioning of Parliament, would be suspended and the government would legislate by decree.

If the United Party opposed these measures it could be presented to the electorate as aiding and abetting subversion. Afraid of being caught in this trap, it voted for the bills, to the disgust of its more liberal supporters.

Up to this point the government's opponents had all supported the U.P., together with the small Labour Party which continued to exist only by the grace of its big ally. But a new form of protest had appeared outside the party-political field. The attack on the Cape franchise in 1951 provoked ex-servicemen, who had helped to win the war but now feared that they were losing the peace, to organise the War Veterans' Torch Commando. By torchlight processions, mass meetings and various ingenious devices the Torch Commando dramatised the situation and put new heart into the opposition. It could soon claim 200,000 members. It joined the United and Labour Parties in a United Democratic Front to fight the elections of 1953. But before the elections the Front had almost disintegrated in recriminations over the pusillanimity of the U.P., and the Torch Commando itself, vigorous in its opposition to obvious abuses, faced certain dissolution if it committed itself to any positive and liberal alternative to *apartheid*.

In the 1953 elections the Nationalists increased their strength in the House of Assembly from 85 seats to 94, the United Party dropped from 64 to 57 and Labour from 6 to 5. Opportunism had failed. The discontents that had barely been held in check could no longer be contained. If elections were to be lost anyway, earnest people felt that at least they should go down flying an honourable flag. Thus, one week-end, the formation of two new parties was announced. The Union Federal Party was, as the event proved, the last despairing rally of English-speaking people, mainly in Natal, to save their heritage and preserve their allegiance. It was promoted largely by the Natal section of the Torch Commando, and sought salvation in a federal constitution which might at least save Natal from some of the impact of Nationalism. It was clear to many people at once, and to most thereafter, that however desirable such a solution might be it could never be attained by a small party appealing to a minority group and almost confined to one province. On what to do with Africans and Indians the Federalists were almost as reticent as the U.P. The electoral record of the party was therefore one of continuous failure, until it ceased to count.

The other newcomer to the scene was the Liberal Party, at first even weaker in support than the Federalists, but with much better long-term prospects. For the first time a party entered the lists with a programme of non-racialism, of a wide non-racial franchise and the abolition of all racial discrimination. Its supporters, though few, were spread over the whole country, and it opened its membership to non-Europeans. The Liberals, naturally, had no illusions about winning general elections. Their immediate function was educative. It would be true to say that their strength, and especially their impact on politics, increased during the following years; but the strength and the impact were not of the kind to be measured by the winning of seats. It was a rare achievement for a Liberal candidate to save his deposit.

The United Party welcomed the new developments, as providing a demonstration that neither liberals nor 'jingoes' now found a home in the U.P. Yet this was not strictly true. Many who might be thus described by their opponents clung to the big party because it was the only means, if any means remained, of defeating the government constitutionally. But the frustration of the helpless opposition was not resolved. The Senate Bill of 1955 therefore produced a successor to the Torch Commando, similarly inspired but different in its methods and in its sex—the Black Sash. This was a women's organisation. As the ministers refused to receive a deputation of women or the petition they brought, the women, wearing black sashes, began silent vigils outside the Union Buildings in Pretoria, outside the Houses of Parliament, and wherever a cabinet minister was due to appear. The Nationalists were not ashamed or deterred by the 'Weeping Winnies', as they called them, but as the vigils continued something was done to strengthen opposition morale.

Particular government policies, too, inspired particular types of protest and resistance. In 1957 a clause of one of the *apartheid* bills gave the minister power to exclude Africans from any church in a 'white' area. Though the races were, in practice, very generally segregated in worship, no church other than the Dutch Reformed accepted segregation in principle. This new threat provoked the clergy (other than the Dutch Reformed) and the devout laity not only to protest, but to an explicit refusal to obey this rule if it were applied. The Anglican bishops, in pastoral letters read at every service one Sunday in July, 1957, called on their flocks to obey God rather than man; having weighed the consequences, they were resolved to disobey, and to advise their people to disobey, the law. The minister refrained from using his new power, but it continued to hang in suspense over the resolute Christians.

University *apartheid* stirred up in the English-speaking universities an almost unanimous opposition, solemn and dignified among the Chancellors, Senates and staffs, less restrained in the case of students. Similarly, the laws applied to them brought forth protests from trade unionists, from nurses, from municipalities. But these bodies were divided, and even had they been united their protests would have been as fruitless as those of the universities. Continuous criticism and exposure flowed from such *ad hoc* societies as the Civil Rights League and the Education League. The Senate Bill called thousands out to large and excited mass meetings in squares and before City Halls; but to no effect.

1958 was another election year. Now the United Party abandoned its alliance with Labour, which as a result was finally wiped out. The U.P. strength fell to 53; the Nationalists pushed theirs up from 94 to 103—almost two thirds of the House, though on the most optimistic estimate they had been supported by a bare 50 per cent of the voters. The discrepancy could be explained, as always, by the delimitation, and even more by the dispersion of the Nationalist and the concentration of the opposition voters.

In 1959, with Bantustans and Commissioners-General, university *apartheid* and the interminable treason trial, more and more group areas, banning of agitators, withholding of passports, and events listed under the headings rioting, demonstrations, dispersal, disturbance and unrest, all nerves were dangerously frayed. The United Party held a congress, at which it was rumoured a determined effort would be made to eject the remaining 'liberals'. A relatively—only relatively—trivial difference about additional land for the reserves produced the showdown. Twelve members of Parliament left the party, and eleven of them shortly adopted the name Progressive and laid the foundation of a new party.

The Progressives were moderate liberals. They rejected *apartheid* and all its works. Their policy differed from that of the Liberal Party mainly in the timing of non-European advance. They had the blessing and the practical support of the greatest financial magnate in the country, Harry Oppenheimer, head of the Anglo-American Corporation, and they had eleven members in the House of Assembly. The Progressive Party quickly drew into its ranks the frustrated and cautiously liberal voters who had not been able to go all the way with the Liberal Party—Black Sash women, remnants of the Federalists and the Torch Commando, fighters on the various separated fronts: civil rights, defence of the Constitution, education. But the party had still to test its support at the polls.

1960 began ominously with nine policemen being bludgeoned to death by rioters in Durban's Cato Manor. By that time Mr Harold Macmillan, the British Prime Minister, was on his way through

Africa. He visited the Union, addressed the Houses of Parliament, and made it clear that Britain rejected the principle of racial discrimination. This was material for acrimonious discussion, which was given other matter in the promise of a referendum on the republic and in bills for censorship of publications and for the centralised control of all education, public and private.

Among Africans, mounting anger and disillusionment had resulted in a secession from the African National Congress, regarded by some as too moderate and willing to compromise. The seceders had formed the Pan-African Congress, which now launched a campaign of passive resistance to the pass laws. Gatherings of people without passes who would invite arrest were planned in various places for 21 March. The police intervened to disperse the crowds. At Sharpeville, a location outside Vereeniging, they opened fire, killing 67 and wounding 176 Africans. There was slaughter on a smaller scale also at Langa, on the outskirts of Cape Town.

The turmoil which followed included a march of 30,000 Africans into the centre of Cape Town, a work boycott which paralysed industry in some cities, violent reaction by the government, which mobilised the Defence Force and sent police into the African townships to force the inhabitants back to work, and sporadic outbreaks of rioting and arson.

On 30 March the Public Safety Act of 1953 was brought into operation and a state of emergency declared. Some 1,700 men and women, including white Liberals, were arrested for political reasons and detained without trial. The opportunity was used also to detain 17,000 'idlers'. A curtain of silence descended on this aspect of the emergency, as it was a criminal offence to identify by name any of the detainees. The rule of law was in suspense, telephones were tapped and letters opened, and the whole population passed under a pall of fear and tension. On 9 April a white man, later declared to be of unsound mind, tried to assassinate Dr Verwoerd by shooting at close range. The Prime Minister was badly wounded, but recovered.

The general state of emergency was not lifted till the end of August. Long before that, trouble had broken out in Eastern Pondoland over the imposition of tribal authorities. Unauthorised observers were excluded from the area and thousands of troops moved in. Disturbance continued in many parts of the Transkei throughout the following year, in the form of riot, murder, arson and police retaliation.

These events stiffened the resolve and hardened the heart of the government. For a brief moment after Sharpeville there were no arrests for failure to produce passes, and it seemed as if the end of the pass laws was in sight. The appearance was deceptive. As soon as the authorities had recovered their balance the shackles were put on again. The Unlawful Organisations Act gave the government power to declare the African National Congress and the Pan-African Congress unlawful, and to apply to them, their members and their ex-members the same kind of punishments and prohibitions that the Act of 1950 had applied to the Communists. The power was immediately used and the Act enabled it to be applied also to any new manifestations of the forbidden bodies under new names and guises.

The new manifestations were soon apparent. The banned African organisations went underground and each established a militant arm dedicated to violence: *Umkonto we Sizwe* (the Spear of the Nation) by the A.N.C., and *Poqo* (meaning 'only' or 'pure'—blacks only) by the P.A.C. Evidence of their existence was given in dramatic form by acts of sabotage, the blowing up of some public buildings, electric power pylons and other installations.

The government's response to this provocation was the General Law Amendment Act, commonly called the Sabotage Act, of 1962. The International Commission of Jurists thought that this Act reduced the liberty of the citizen to a degree not surpassed by the most extreme dictatorship of the Left or of the Right in any other country.

The crime of sabotage was very loosely defined. Anyone accused of one of a number of acts would be assumed to be guilty of sabotage unless he could prove the innocence of his intentions. If convicted he would be liable to the penalites for treason, which could include death, but if the sentence were imprisonment it would have to be for a minimum of five years. But the Act went far beyond the crime of sabotage to increase penalties at the disposal of the executive. The Suppression of Communism Act had enabled the minister to impose various restrictions on individuals; this power was now greatly extended. At the discretion of the minister a banned person might now be forbidden to attend any gathering whatever, including a social gathering, or to have any communication with other banned persons. (Where husband and wife were both banned, it was usual to give special permission for them to communicate with each other.)

Banning could now include house arrest, either for twenty-four hours a day or with the exception of working hours. A person under house arrest could receive no visitor except a lawyer—provided that he was not also a banned person. If anyone were forbidden to attend any gathering (this was the essence of 'banning') then nothing that he said or wrote, either before or after the banning, could be published. Not only would the banned person cease to exist as far as the rest of the South African public was aware, but his 'civil death' would be retroactive: the memory of his previous existence would be blotted out as far as the law could do it.

This ferocious measure was at once applied. The first to be subjected to house arrest was Mrs Helen Joseph. A couple of dozen others soon followed. Others, including Chief A. J. Luthuli, former President of the A.N.C. and Nobel Prize winner, were confined to their magisterial districts. The Department of Justice published a list of 102 people whose words were not to be quoted.

After 1962 there was a steady erosion of what remained of personal liberty and the rule of law. There seemed to be no escape from the vicious circle: repressive measures—more violence—more repressive measures. In 1963 the police were enabled to detain persons in solitary confinement, on the ground that they might give evidence of political offences, for up to 90 days; and after that period the detention could be renewed. In 1965 a slightly different system included detention for 180 days. There is convincing evidence that, apart from the mental torture inherent in solitary confinement, other forms of mental and physical torture were used to make the detainees 'co-operate'. The Terrorism Act of 1967—'freedom fighters' having now appeared on the border of South-West Africa—provided for indefinite detention without trial.

These were but a few of the major statutes marking South Africa's descent to the condition of a police state. There were also innumerable kinds of administrative pressures, including the refusal or withdrawal of passports, to tighten the control over persons. Progress was made, too, in the control of ideas. The Nationalist government was satisfied, for a time, with a relatively mild form of censorship. Imported books and papers were checked by a Board that looked mainly, though not only, for pornography. In 1963 a new Publications Control Board received powers of censorship over South African as well as imported literature. Most South African newspapers, which imposed a 'code' upon themselves, were exempt from the operation, but by 1970 the Board had prohibited 4,402 publications.

Some leftist periodicals had been suppressed, but the daily newspapers were still left to discipline themselves. The English language papers continued to attack the government and its policies, and to expose abuses, with little inhibition. The government bore this hostility with unconcealed impatience. At party congresses its followers regularly pleaded for curbs on the hated 'English Press'. The 'English' churches, Protestant and Catholic, were almost equally unpopular in the same circles for the courageous and increasing resistance to the tide of *apartheid* and oppression by clergy and a part of the laity. Finally there were the 'English' universities, the most conspicuous centres of ebullient opposition to the system.

The segregated colleges—which became universities—for Africans, Coloured and Indians were not at first feared, because under the legislation of 1959 they were under severe discipline and control. Nevertheless their students could not help being angry and resentful. In 1972 a student leader at the University of the North, Turfloop, made a speech attacking the segregated system and the inferior education made available to Africans. The speech triggered a chain of events, expulsions, boycotts, protests by African students, sympathetic protests by white students, drastic actions by the government culminating in an attack by the police on (white) students of the University of Cape Town outside the Anglican cathedral. As many fled into the cathedral and were followed by truncheon-wielding policemen, and as these dragged away one student leader who had been clinging to the altar, the shade of Thomas à Becket seemed to utter a warning to violators of sanctuary and of right.

The National Union of South African Students, N.U.S.A.S., was a particular *bête noire* of the authorities. It had once included Afrikaner as well as English students. The decision to admit non-white students caused the student bodies of the Afrikaans universities, though not all individuals, to withdraw and to form their own organisation. The representatives of N.U.S.A.S. were firmly excluded from the black and brown universities by the authorities that controlled them. Successive presidents of N.U.S.A.S. were banned and restricted. It was one of the tragic aspects of the situation that the black students themselves came to repudiate N.U.S.A.S. because of its white leadership and mainly white membership. They formed their own body, S.A.S.O., the South African Students' Organisation. In the aftermath of the clashes of 1972 the leaders and many members of this and of N.U.S.A.S. were either banned or charged with various offences.

When students, clergy, journalists and the miscellaneous body of supposed saboteurs and plotters were harassed, the instrument used to do it was the police force. In South Africa this was, and is, a single organisation under the control of the central government. As the enforcement of the innumerable *apartheid* laws—especially, in quantitative terms, the pass laws—was a large part of its duty, the force inevitably developed over the years something of a political appearance. The specifically political tasks, however, were the job of the special or security branch. These were the men who probed into political records before passports were granted, who were present in civilian clothes at meetings, who kept incriminating dossiers recording subversive opinions.

By 1969 they were thought to be inadequate, or not to have enough powers, for their heavy responsibilities. The change which followed can perhaps be regarded as the placing of a keystone on the arch, holding the rest in place. A Bureau of State Security was set up (the initials appropriately spelt BOSS), responsible only to the Prime Minister, paid for by a secret service vote whose details could not be disclosed, controlling the old security branch (which continued to exist) and partly superseding military intelligence. At the same time it was made a severely punishable offence to disclose any matter connected with state security (very broadly defined).

But the most important power given to B.O.S.S. was the power to forbid, at its own discretion, the production in court of any evidence which it thought prejudicial to state security. An accused person might thus be forbidden to produce evidence in his own defence. Many abuses—such as torture by the police—which the public might otherwise have known nothing about, had in the past come to light as evidence in court, and as such could be published. This leak was now closed. Information about the operations of BOSS itself was likewise taboo. As it was impossible to know which these operations were, the press had after this to tread very warily in reporting any police activity with a political dimension. It was still possible to attack the government or the Prime Minister, but from this time the police were sacred.

The suppression of radical movements did not entirely silence opposition. Two kinds of organised opposition of a parliamentary type remained: the legal and wholly or mainly white political parties, and the recognised representatives thrown up by the *apartheid* system itself. The most significant of the latter were the 'homeland' leaders and assemblies, becoming increasingly articulate and forthright.

When the Coloured voters had been removed from the common roll they had been given four separate representatives in the House of Assembly and two in the Cape Provincial Council. Though this representation was small (and white), it was in the places that mattered. No one could forget, however, that the Africans had once had the same right, and that it had eventually been abolished like the greater right that it had replaced. The same thing happened to the Coloured representatives, and in their case for political reasons that could not be disguised. They had to do with the influence of the Progressive Party.

In October 1961, following the establishment of the Republic, there was a general election in which the eleven Progressive MPs faced the electorate for the first time under their new party colours. Ten of them were defeated, their seats being recovered by the United Party, which lost three of its own to the Nationalists. For the next twelve years Mrs Helen Suzman was the sole Progressive politician representing an ordinary constituency. The party, which was multi-racial in its membership, then began to win support among the Coloured voters. By 1968 it appeared likely that Progressives would be returned at the next election of Coloured representatives; they already held the two provincial seats. There had not been, and could not be, any possibility of the choice of Nationalists by that electorate.

That year therefore saw the passage of three Acts which had for some time been casting their shadows before. One of them established a Coloured Persons Representative Council, partly elected, partly nominated. It was supposed to be more than an advisory body, in that it controlled a budget and could pass legislation; but no bill could be introduced without the prior approval of the relevant minister.

This alternative being provided, another Act abolished the Coloured representation in Parliament and the Cape Provincial Council. The expected expansion of the Progressive Party, and possibly of the Liberals, in those bodies was prevented, but there remained the danger that they would become a power in the new Council instead. This was probably the chief reason for the Prohibition of Political Interference Act, which made racially mixed parties, the assistance of a party of one race by members of another race, and the acceptance by any party of money from outside the Republic, illegal.

Rather than become a purely white organisation, the Liberal Party dissolved itself. The Progressives, following an appeal by their non-white members for the white members to carry on, continued to exist as a white party. The Coloured people had to form separate parties, of which the chief were the Federal Party, in favour of working within the system, and the Labour Party, wholly opposed to the system. At the elections for the Representative Council in 1969 the latter party won 26 seats, the former 11. The government then used its power of nomination to give the Federal Party a majority.

Nevertheless this Council gave the Coloured people, as the 'home-land' Assemblies and ministries gave the Africans, a voice that the government could not silence.

Long before these meaures, the voice of Dr Verwoerd had been silenced. The second attempt to assassinate him succeeded in dramatic circumstances: he was stabbed to death in his seat in the House of Assembly on 6 September 1966. It was the first assassina-tion of a politician—as distinct from the murder of lesser figures for political reasons—in South African history. Verwoerd's successor as Prime Minister and Nationalist leader was B. J. Vorster, who as Minister of Justice had been responsible for the punitive laws since 1961.

The old parties, National and United, were still largely based on the ethnic division of the white population; they were the Afrikaner and the English parties, though many of each group refused to conform to this pattern. The United Party still lived by the dream of Botha and Smuts, 'reconciliation' and white unity. The National Party, though paying some lip service to the same ideal, remained the defender of the Afrikaans nationality and language.

On most issues each party was divided. There had long been tensions within the National Party, but it was in 1966, the year of Verwoerd's death, that two factions or tendencies in it came to be dubbed the *verligtes* and the *verkramptes*—the enlightened and the bigoted. In each tendency there were degrees. The most 'bigoted' stood very firm against any concessions to 'Kaffirs' (they liked this word), English, Roman Catholics or any others who might threaten the identity of the security of the Afrikaners. In 1969 Mr Vorster, to prevent the party from being 'white-anted from within', took disciplinary steps which forced the more extreme *verkramptes*, led by Albert Hertzog (son of J. B. M. Hertzog) out of the party. They and the followers who rallied to them formed the *Herstigte Nasionale Party*, the re-founded National Party, whose initials might arouse nostalgic memories of the war years.

Only a minority of the bigoted adhered to this party; most thought the secession a tactical mistake. In the general election of 1970 the H.N.P. failed to win a single seat; only three of its candidates saved their deposits. What was more significant about this election was that the United Party gained nine seats from the Nationalists, reversing a trend that had continued since 1948. Analysts attributed the change to a swing of mainly English-speaking floating voters who had supported the Nationalists in several elections. The ethnic division appeared to be reasserting itself.

The United Party was at least as sharply split as its opponents. The hiving off of the Progressives had not removed all the 'enlightened' from the U.P. By 1973 they were asserting themselves more vigorously, under the leadership of Harry Schwarz, Transvaal leader of the party. Perhaps the hottest issue dividing the U.P. was its participation in a commission, the Schlebusch Commission, set up as a result of the disturbances of 1972. Its task was to probe into the affairs of the South African Institute of Race Relations, N.U.S.A.S., the Christian Institute, and another body which was then disbanded. The most important feature of the enquiry was that it was held *in camera* and that none of the evidence could be divulged, even by those who gave it. Thus, if the Commission made a hostile report on any of the organisations, every witness might be suspected of having given grounds for this hostility, but would be unable to clear himself. Many who were summoned refused to appear, thus exposing themselves to penal sanctions.

A large body of opinion was opposed to United Party participation in the Commission, but the protests were ignored. This was probably an important factor in the general election of 1974. The Progressive Party at last emerged from its isolated fortress—Mrs Suzman's constituency—to win five seats from the U.P., which at the same time lost other seats to the Nationalists.

South Africa's obsession with its insoluble racial problem colours all its politics and imposes itself on the historian. It is almost as an afterthought that one turns to the matters that in many countries are the main stuff of history.

A history of South Africa since 1948 which omitted all racial and cultural conflicts could present an impressive picture of progress and achievement. These would be most obvious in the material and technical aspects, ranging from airports and highways through atomic energy to Dr Christian Barnard's pioneering in heart surgery; but there were notable achievements also in other directions. It is impossible in space as limited as this to give a meaningful summary of the notable works of art and literature, but it is necessary to point out that Afrikaans literature was now emancipated from its once overwhelmingly bucolic and inward-turning tradition. This was due largely to the poets of the sixties—the *sestigers*—who brought Afrikaans poetry, in both form and content, into line with the contemporary world.

Yet literature can no more be insulated from the general obsession than politics or education can. Writers in English, harping on the racial theme, often found their books, or even themselves, banned.

Early in 1974 this screw was given another twist: the censors suppressed *Kennis van die Aand*, a novel by André Brink. It was the first banning of an Afrikaans book, and succeeded in getting those Afrikaans writers who had not yet done so to join in the campaign against censorship.

C. W. de Kiewiet coined the aphorism that South Africa has progressed economically by windfalls and politically by disasters. The chief windfall, gold, has the peculiar quality of becoming more valuable as all other commodities become less. South Africa therefore entered a period of boom when most of the world, in the thirties, was in the depths of depression. From 1933 onwards, before, during and after the Second World War, the boom continued with only minor interruptions. The chief of these was due to the political disturbances of 1960; but within five years the foreign capital, which had flowed out so fast as to reduce the reserves by half, was flowing in again on a large scale. From 1933 to 1965 the real gross national product (i.e. adjusted to compensate for rise in prices) increased on the average by 5 per cent per annum. From 1972 to 1973 the rate of growth was 5·5 per cent. Between 1945 and 1954 the physical volume of manufacturing output doubled.

The growth was thus not merely in gold production, though the rise in the price of gold in the late sixties and seventies was a bonus for the world's greatest gold producer. The Second World War, like the first but on a much larger scale, had promoted manufacturing development by cutting off outside sources of supply. After the war this development continued for economic reasons, but after 1950 it was given a new stimulus by the threat of boycotts and sanctions by a hostile world. South Africa began to give more attention to the manufacture of chemicals, automobiles, aircraft and ships.

The chief curb on industrial development was the shortage of skilled labour, traditionally (and to a great extent by law) the preserve of the whites. European immigrants did not suffice to meet the need. White trade unions, which from the beginning had existed largely to protect white workers from the competition of cheap black labour, began to realise that the prosperity of their members depended on continued economic growth, and that this had come to depend on the admission of non-whites to skilled jobs. By the seventies the old pattern of job reservation was breaking down at many points. By 1973 African workers, striking illegally, had succeeded not only in winning wage increases but in forcing some degree of recognition for their unions and their right to strike. The needs of the national economy protected them from the customary violent response to black impertinence.

As might have been expected under South African conditions, various elements of the population were differently affected by this national prosperity. In spite of considerable increases in African wages, the notorious white-black 'wage gap' was continuing to widen throughout the sixties and the early seventies. In Durban in 1970, 54 per cent of African families had incomes below the poverty datum line, which has been described as the minimum needed to sustain life in the short run. The more humane *minimum effective level* was still farther out of reach: 85 per cent of African families in Durban fell below it. Comparable figures were reported from other cities. According to most estimates, African wages were increasing at a higher percentage rate than white, but because the gap was so wide to begin with this difference was not enough to narrow it.

The question provoked by these and other facts was: would the Africans of South Africa benefit more from increasing national prosperity, in which they might hope to share, or from economic collapse, which might lead to the collapse of the political system? The question cannot be pursued here, but it may be noted that the black and coloured South Africans themselves continued to be divided on it. So were foreign sympathisers with the Africans in their plight; but the rôle of the outside world calls for another chapter.

15

AGAINST THE WORLD

The end of the Second World War was a turning-point in history. There are many evidences of this, but almost certainly the most important is the emergence of the so-called Third World. For more than four centuries Europeans, with their various technical and cultural advantages, had dominated the globe, gradually subduing the people of other continents and colours. For about sixty years almost all the world had been directly subjected to their rule. Now the subject peoples became independent and began to make themselves heard in the councils of the nations. For South Africa this stupendous change happened, with grim irony, at the very moment when the policies of racial discrimination and white supremacy came to their final flowering.

That is what South African foreign relations after 1945—not only after 1948—were all about.

The peoples and governments of western Europe and North America disapproved of *apartheid* and frequently denounced the system officially, but if those countries had dominated the world as of old South Africa's sins would have been a small item in international politics. They became a big item because the newly independent states of Asia, and then of Africa, became members of the United Nations and eventually commanded a numerical majority there; and because of the Cold War, which set East and West against each other, competing for the support of the uncommitted Third World. For these reasons South Africa's difficulties increased in direct proportion to the growth of what became the Afro-Asian bloc (always supported by the Communist bloc) in the U.N.

On the issue of South Africa's racial policies as such there was no great difference between one bloc and another; the Western powers would have condemned them even if there had been no reason of *Realpolitik* to make them do so. But what was originally a concern with racial discrimination became more complicated as attempts were made to express the concern in action, and the complications often led western countries (to their own embarrassment) to support South Africa for reasons of a different order.

Most governments in the world, and many private citizens and organisations, wished either to persuade or to force South Africa to abandon her racial system. At the official level the chief objects of attack were: the *apartheid* system generally; the treatment of Indians; South Africa's control of South-West Africa; her membership of international organisations; the trade of other countries with her, and specifically the sale of arms and military equipment; her communications by sea and air; and the diplomatic relations of other countries with her. At the unofficial level (though these matters were sometimes taken up by governments too) the principal issues were: the boycott of South African goods and the discouragement of investment; the exclusion of South African teams and individuals from international sport, and the discouragement of South African tours by sportsmen from other countries; similar boycotts by performing artists, and refusal of permission for the performance of plays in South Africa; and financial help to the victims of the repressive laws, and to their dependents. South Africa, through both official and unofficial channels, tried to win friends and to persuade them to call off these attacks.

When the U.N. General Assembly met for the first time in 1946, its membership was not unlike that of the old League: essentially European and North and South American, with a very small contingent from the other continents. Yet in the very first session South Africa, in the person of Smuts himself, was bitterly attacked for her treatment of her citizens of Indian origin. The attack was led by India and the Soviet Union. This subject was then brought up every year, until in 1962 it was merged in wider issues. Regular attempts to persuade South Africa to discuss the question with India and Pakistan were as regularly rebuffed. In 1954 India closed her High Commission in South Africa; Pakistan had never had one.

South Africa's refusal to discuss her Indian policy, or any other policy, with any foreign government was based on Article 2 (7) of the United Nations Charter, which forbade interference in the domestic affairs of a state. There was not a member of the U.N. that would not have insisted at all costs on the observance of this article in its own case. This was the most important reason for the considerable support of South Africa, especially by western countries, in the voting on Indians, *apartheid* and the rest. They scented danger in the precedent of interference in such matters. Those who condemned South Africa relied rather on Article 55, which dealt with human rights; they claimed that this should take precedence over 2 (7). But their legal case for this claim was as weak as their moral case was strong.

This was the difficulty faced by all governments that tried to use established international machinery as a weapon against South Africa. It was not designed for such purposes. Before 1960, however, the legal niceties were generally observed. In 1952 the General Assembly appointed a three-man commission to investigate the racial situation in South Africa. The latter, for the usual reason, refused to cooperate, so that the commission had to investigate at long range. Before it was allowed to lapse in 1955 the Commission produced three reports, which are still useful to the student but are not primary sources. For the rest, the Assembly repeatedly invited South Africa to mend its ways, and every year expressed its regret that the request had been ignored.

In 1960 a different note was struck. The shooting at Sharpeville and the emergency were on the front pages of the world's newspapers, and rebukes seemed to be called for. That was also the year in which sixteen African countries were admitted to the U.N. Between 1957 and 1963 the African contingent increased by twenty-seven. By the latter date the Afro-Asian bloc (excluding African and Asian countries that did not vote with the bloc, and not counting the Communist countries which regularly did) was not far short of a majority of the General Assembly.

The events of 1960, however, were alarming enough to be debated not merely by the Assembly, but by the Security Council. Though no action was taken, the resolution that was passed introduced an ominous note by referring to the possibility that what was happening in South Africa might, if continued, endanger international peace and security. The Council also required the Secretary-General, Dag Hammarskjöld, to consult with the South African government about the means of upholding the principles of the Charter in that country. He did visit it, with the cooperation of the government, early in 1961, but his death a few months later prevented him from following up the visit as he had intended.

When the General Assembly met in 1961 the Afro-Asians were in a position to call the tune. From this time there were no more gentle rebukes. Resolutions were now directed not to the offender but to the other members. The one passed in 1961 called on all member-states to take what action they could to bring about a change in South Africa. In 1962 all states were called on to break off diplomatic relations, close airports and seaports to South African traffic, and boycott South African goods. A special committee was appointed to watch developments. In 1963 the question was discussed again by the Security Council which decided that the situation was 'seriously disturbing' international peace and security. South Africa was called on not only to abandon her racial policy, but to liberate all political prisoners. Member states were asked to refrain from supplying arms and military equipment to South Africa.

Thus, year by year, the hostility grew more intense, but it was too ineffective for the liking of the militant Africans. The independent black states gave the highest priority in their foreign policy to the liberation of their brothers in the 'white south'. The intensity of this concern was puzzling to many outsiders, in view of the size of the domestic problems the black countries had on their hands, and of the fact that many of them had nasty skeletons in their own cup-boards. It was all the more puzzling because the real reason for it was never explained. The real reason was the humiliation burnt into the soul of the black man, like a brand on the body of a slave, by the treatment his race had received from its white masters: oppression of course, but also condescension. Just as many Afrikaners suffered from a wound which could never be healed until they were seen to be on top of the English, so the black race had an even bigger 1902 to wipe off the slate.

This said, and their position being sympathetically understood, it must be admitted that their ways of getting even with South Africa often threatened to undermine the rule of law in international relations. So bitter was the feeling of many against the whites—at least whites of the South African kind—that they came to regard their feud with this enemy as unique. Thus their proceedings could not, in their view, set precedents for any other case. The governments that voted against them were usually those with a longer experience of precedents and their consequences, and a stronger commitment to the rule of Law.

One of the methods used by the Afro-Asians, whether in the General Assembly or in subordinate agencies, was to walk out *en masse* when the South African representative rose to speak. Related to this was the challenging of the latter's credentials; this was done successfully for the first time in 1970, though South Africa was not thereby expelled from the Assembly. There were motions to expel the country from the U.N. These did not succeed, but the same tactics of walking out, refusal to recognise credentials and motions to expel were more effectual in the subordinate agencies. Generally, membership of these was conferred automatically by membership of the U.N., so that they had no power to expel. Nevertheless motions to do so were carried, in some cases meetings broke up in confusion, and from some South Africa withdrew rather than submit to insult or allow the organisation to collapse. She withdrew, for example, from U.N.E.S.C.O., the International Labour Organisation and the Food and Agricultural Organisation. There were others whose meetings she could not in practice attend.

These pressures were far from having the desired effect. In many or most of the organisations South Africa was a donor rather than a recipient. There was a demand for something with teeth in it. Among the proposals regularly put to the General Assembly after 1961 was one for sanctions. Passed by the Assembly, this could be no more than a recommendation, but it was widely obeyed. Many countries in Africa, Asia and the Caribbean enforced trade boycotts, but the countries that enforced them had little trade to boycott. More importantly, most black African countries denied their air space, as well as landing facilities, to South African aircraft, and their ports to South African ships; holders of South African passports were denied admission to these countries.

The boycott of trade by such countries meant little. To have any meaning at all, it would have had to be applied by Britain, the European Economic Community and the United States, but they showed no willingness to do so. The Afro-Asian states, however, concentrated their attack most specifically on the trade in arms, ammunition and military equipment, as well as joint military exercises and the provision of training facilities for South African personnel. The country involved in all of this was Great Britain.

In 1955 the Nationalists were able to enlarge their sovereign independence a little by an agreement to take over the historic base at Simonstown from the Royal Navy, which had continued to hold it as the South Atlantic station. The agreement provided, among other things, for the use of the station in wartime by Britain and her allies, even if South Africa were not a belligerent. It included cooperation in many ways between the two countries, notably a joint defence of the Cape sea route. The sale of certain arms and equipment by Britain to South Africa was linked to this agreement.

When the British Labour government took office late in 1964,

Mr Wilson confirmed his pre-election promise to stop the export of arms to South Africa, except for certain ships to be taken over in terms of the Simonstown agreement, and sixteen Buccaneer strike reconnaissance aircraft already contracted for. There were to be no further contracts. The United States had already forbidden the sale of arms that could be used in internal operations, but allowed those suitable only for external defence. Until 1969 the British government permitted, but then stopped, the sale of certain anti-submarine equipment needed for the implementation of the Simonstown agreement.

The Conservative government which came into power in 1970 resumed the supply of equipment that it was legally bound to provide under that agreement, and thereby strained relations with the African and Asian members of the Commonwealth. On this issue, however, the African states were unable to combine. When the supply of arms to South Africa was stopped by other countries, it was continued by France. In June 1971 it was announced that the Atlas Aircraft Corporation, near Pretoria, would manufacture Mirage III and F1 jet fighters under French licence. The peculiar relationship between France and many of her former colonies ensured that the Francophone African states would not support any motion on arms for South Africa that included France in the condemnation. Nevertheless this traffic became politically more difficult, and at the same time South Africa bent her efforts to become self-sufficient in production for war.

It is not incongruous to speak in the same breath of the battlefield and of the playing field. White—and not only white—South Africans took their sports very seriously. International rugby, Springboks against All Blacks (New Zealand) or Lions (Britain), cricket against the M.C.C. or the Australians, tennis and golf on the courts and courses of the world, were excitements dear to the South African heart. The exclusion of the Springboks from all international sport was therefore a cunning and promising move. For the most part it could not be an affair of governments, though some used what means of pressure were open to them. It was a privately organised campaign, in Britain, Australia, New Zealand, and in connection with the Olympic Games. Unlike some of the other pressures, it did not depend for success on the total collapse of the South African system. Its purpose was to remove the colour bar from sport. It would succeed if each sport under attack came to be so organised that the teams playing in South Africa, and those sent abroad, were recruited on a basis of merit without regard to race.

In many sports, including soccer, boxing and table tennis, South Africa was banned by decisions of the international controlling bodies. This was not done in rugby or cricket, which were the most important. In those cases demonstrators in Britain, Australia and New Zealand tried to disrupt the matches played against South African teams by physically interfering with them. In some cases trade unions played a part by denying services to the visitors. When the British rugby team, the Lions, visited South Africa in 1974, its own government ordered its ambassador to boycott them. In 1970 the government had persuaded the M.C.C. to withdraw an invitation to the South African cricketers. South Africa was excluded from the 1972 Olympic Games because too many other countries would have withdrawn if it were not.

The list could be greatly extended. It is the effects of these pressures that are important. White South African sports enthusiasts, both players and spectators, increasingly called for concessions to the foreign demands—any concessior that would get the teams playing again. Non-white sportsmen and sports officials generally regarded this change of heart as insincere. White controlling bodies invited the non-white—but in principle non-racial—bodies to affiliate to them, but the invitation was generally rejected. The government was placed in a dilemma. Its policy was obviously responsible for the disaster to sport, yet it could not abandon its most sacred tenets. It made subtle distinctions. South Africa might field mixed teams in some sports and in some circumstances, but not in others. Similar distinctions were drawn for visiting teams and individuals. But the government was adamant in its refusal to allow non-racial sport at the club, provincial or national level. The concessions, such as they were, were for foreign consumption only. There is some evidence that foreign pressure in a matter so important to ordinary white South Africans was beginning, in the early seventies, to change their ideas about the colour bar in this sphere at least.

After all these trumpets had blown, the walls had not fallen, but not all the possible means had yet been exhausted. From the first days of the U.N. South Africa's enemies thought that they had found her weak spot in South-West Africa. This might be a weak spot because its administration by South Africa was based on, and limited by, an international instrument, the mandate of the old League of Nations. As a C mandate, it could be administered as an integral part of the mandatory country, but could not be incorporated in it. This was not quite, as it might seem, a distinction without a difference, because the well-being of the indigenous inhabitants of a mandated territory was a 'sacred trust' of the mandatory, which had to submit annual reports about its discharge of its responsibility. It could be argued what happened in the mandated territory was not a purely domestic matter in which no other country could interfere.

It was also possible, after 1946, to argue the opposite. For about six months the League of Nations and the United Nations coexisted. The League had its mandates, the U.N. its trusteeship system. It was the clear intention of most of the powers involved that the old mandates should now become trust territories, and it might have been expected that this transformation would be provided for in a formal way. This was not done either by the dying League or by the U.N. What is more, proposals to this effect were made in both bodies, and were specifically rejected or abandoned. The only way by which a mandate could become a trust territory was by the voluntary decision of the mandatory power. All of them accordingly made the decision—except South Africa.

Mandate and trusteeship were different things. Under the old system the mandatory had to submit annual reports to the Council of the League. The Council was advised by the Permanent Mandates Commission, which consisted of 'experts' appointed in their individual capacities, not representatives of states. Although the Commission was regularly critical of South Africa, it had no power to act. Nor, in this matter, had the other League organs. Decisions had to be unanimous, so that the mandatory power had a veto on any decision that could apply to it. The League was dominated by countries that were European or American, and white. The United Nations Trusteeship Council consisted of representatives of states, equally divided between those holding and those not holding trust territories. It was flanked by the Trusteeship or Fourth Committee of the General Assembly; all member states were represented on this. The General Assembly could decide by a two-thirds majority. All these bodies could and did make political decisions. The U.N. very quickly became predominantly black, brown and anti-colonialist. For all these reasons South African governments intensely distrusted the new organisation, and were determined to keep it at arm's length.

South Africa had refused to place her dependency under trusteeship. For two years she submitted reports to the U.N., as formerly to the League; but then, the U.N. having shown too active an interest, and Malan having come into power, the reports ceased to be sent. It was a confused situation. The mandate had never been terminated, but the League had. The General Assembly asked the International Court of Justice for an Advisory Opinion on a number of points.

The opinion, given in 1950, was to the effect that the mandate was still in force: that the League's supervisory functions had passed to the United Nations, though the supervision could not exceed in degree or kind that which had been exercised by the League, that South Africa was not legally bound to place the mandate under trusteeship, but could not herself alter the status of the territory except by agreement with the United Nations.

The General Assembly accepted the opinion; South Africa did not, because she maintained that as there was now no League, there was no longer a mandate or supervision. From that time the United Nations continued to try by every possible means to persuade or compel South Africa to submit to the trusteeship system. This object was not achieved, but the effort was not entirely fruitless.

One of the methods was to seek a ruling from the International Court. A judgment of that court, as distinct from an advisory opinion, would be binding on all parties, including South Africa. Only states, however, not international organisations, could be litigants before the court. It was therefore agreed among the Africans that Ethiopia and Liberia, which had been members of the League, should bring an action against South Africa, essentially on the same questions that had been at issue in 1950. The proceedings began in 1960, and judgment was given in 1966.

The applicants did not confine themselves to the technical questions that had concerned the court in 1950, but went on to charge that the *apartheid* policies applied in South-West Africa were oppressive in nature, and were designed specifically to subordinate the interests of the blacks to those of the whites. If this were so, South Africa had violated the terms of the mandate.

It would be difficult for any impartial observer, after a thorough study of the *apartheid* system, to doubt that these charges were true. This conclusion, however, would be based largely on inference. Against this, the accused government could point to any number of official statements to the effect that the policy was conceived in the interests of the blacks as much as of the whites. What was still more to the point was the material condition of the indigenous inhabitants, in comparison with that not of the local whites, but of Africans in other parts of the continent. Whether South Africa succeeded in refuting the charge of oppression may still be a matter of opinion, but in terms of the court proceedings she certainly did so. The applicants withdrew those charges, and substituted another, that segregation was in itself an offence against an 'international norm of non-discrimination and non-separation'. They claimed that article

2 of the mandate implied a prohibition on 'the allotment, by governmental policy and action, of rights and burdens on the basis of membership in a group'.

South Africa retorted with evidence that this prohibition was not observed in forty member states of the U.N., including both the applicant states. She invited the judges of the court to visit South-West Africa, as well as Ethiopia and Liberia, to make comparisons for themselves. The invitation was declined. Nevertheless the court, in its judgment of July, 1966, rejected the applicants' claims. The basis of the decision was that the applicants had no direct interest in the case. The mandate provided for jurisdiction by the court in a 'dispute' between the mandatory and another member of the League. As neither Ethiopia nor Liberia had any material interest in this case, there was no dispute.

The anger among the African states and the jubilation in South Africa were both moderated by the knowledge of how the judgment had been arrived at. The court had divided equally, seven to seven, and the decision had rested with the President, Sir Percy Spender of Australia. It has been contended that the judgment would have gone the other way if an Egyptian judge had not died during the proceedings. This and some other elements in the case, and in the next case where an opposite opinion prevailed, gave rise to the disturbing impression that political factors might have too much influence with the court.

However this might be, the General Assembly of the U.N. decided that, in the absence of a satisfactory judicial decision, there would have to be a political one. On October 27, 1966, the Assembly passed a resolution which became the basis of all its subsequent policies in this regard: South Africa had failed to fulfil its obligations under the mandate; the mandate was therefore terminated; a committee of fourteen was appointed to recommend steps to be taken to place South-West Africa under U.N. administration. Doubts were raised by some whether this decision was legal in terms of the Charter, and in view of the fact that the International Court had ruled otherwise, but feelings were too strong to allow these doubts to carry any weight. From this time the U.N. treated South Africa's presence in the mandated territory as illegal, and, increasingly, as a threat to international peace and security.

In 1967 an eleven-member Council was appointed to go to South-West Africa and take over the administration. The following year it tried to do so, but as South Africa offered resistance the mission got no further than Lusaka. Though the Security Council censured

South Africa for its refusal to give up 'Namibia', as South-West
Africa had been re-named by the U.N., attempts to apply mandatory
sanctions were blocked by the major Western powers.

The next step was to obtain an advisory opinion from the International Court—whose composition had changed since 1966—on the
legality of the Assembly's decisions of that year. South Africa asked
three of the judges to recuse themselves on the ground that they had
already committed themselves to a hostile opinion when they had
represented their countries at the U.N. She also asked, as a party to
the dispute, to have a South African judge appointed to the court
for the case, and that the question of the court's jurisdiction should
be settled before the other matters were considered. Further, South
Africa offered to hold a plebiscite of all races in 'Namibia', supervised
jointly by herself and the court, to ascertain the wishes of the
inhabitants. The court rejected all these requests and advised, in
1971, that the Assembly's decision terminating the mandate was
valid.

An advisory opinion was not binding, and South Africa rejected it.
From the beginning the official opinion had been that when the
League died the mandate died with it. The government had,
however, been prepared within certain limits to compromise. As far
back as 1952 it had offered to negotiate a new instrument equivalent
to the old mandate. It would be accountable to the three remaining
'Principal Allied and Associated Powers' which had conferred the
mandate in the first place—Britain, France and the United States;
that is to say, white powers.

The United Nations having rejected this proposal, South Africa
reverted to what had been her real object all along—the annexation
of the mandated territory. This was not done in so many words, no
doubt from a desire to keep on the right side of as much of the law
as possible. But the terms of a C mandate had included administration 'as an integral part' of the administering country. The Union
government had from the beginning assumed direct responsibility
for such services as defence, customs and currency in the mandated
territory, The powers delegated to the local administration were
greater, but not much greater, than those of a province of the Union.
In 1924 the Germans in the territory were naturalised, after which
there was no difference of citizenship between the Union and the
dependency.

In 1949, as mentioned in an earlier chapter, representation in the
Union Parliament was given to the territory. Many though not all
of the *apartheid* laws extended to it as well. In 1954 all Native Affairs

in South-West Africa were transferred to the Union department of that name. In 1964 the Odendaal commission, which had been appointed to make recommendations for the future of the territory, presented its report. The main feature of this was the extension to territory of the 'homeland' system of the Republic. This part of the plan was more or less suspended until after the International Court's judgment in 1966; then it began to be implemented.

This piecemeal integration was one of the kinds of defiance that raised the blood pressure of at least the Afro-Asian bloc at the U.N. It was scarcely lowered by South Africa's apparently jaunty confidence in meeting criticism. In 1962 a committee of seven, appointed by the President of the General Assembly, was under instructions to visit South-West Africa and to prepare for a U.N. take-over. Instead of a blank refusal, Verwoerd offered to admit not the whole committee, but its chairman and vice-chairman. These were given an official aircraft in which to make an unrestricted ten-day tour of the territory. South Africa, in terms of its own 'homeland' policy, did not and could not oppose the idea of self-determination. But it advocated self-determination for each of the 'nations' separately, whereas the U.N. insisted on independence for the whole country as a unit. At the end of the tour the U.N. representatives and Verwoerd issued a joint communiqué which suggested that the visitors had little fault to find. After they had left the country they submitted a hostile report.

There were further attempts to send missions to assume control of 'Namibia' (they were refused admission), and further demands that South Africa cease her illegal occupation (they were ignored). On the contrary, integration into the Republic was taken a step further by an Act of 1969. Most of the functions hitherto left to the local authorities were now assumed by the government and Parliament of the Republic. The 'homelands' came directly under their control, and what remained to the Legislative Assembly and Administrator—over the 'white' area only—was less than the power of a South African province. A beginning was made with the 'homelands' by conferring a constitution, including in 1973 elected councillors, on the important territory of Owambo. This small reserve next to the Angola border contained nearly half of the total Namibian population.

Up to about 1971 the South African government appeared to have the situation well in hand. The U.N. was defied, tribal chiefs declared their confidence in the government and in 'separate development', and that policy was being implemented. Then things

H

began to go wrong. Large numbers of the 'homeland' people, and especially of the Owambo, had like Africans elsewhere been driven by economic necessity to seek work in the 'white' area. They had to work on contracts of a particularly harsh kind (for instance, their families were not allowed even to visit them during the period of the contract) and for very low wages. In 1971 resentment against this system erupted in strikes all over the territory. There were police action, repatriation of Owambo workers to their reserve, shortage of labour in towns and on mines, and then, belatedly, a reform of the system. Wages and condition were improved and labour drifted back.

Opposition to the government and to 'separate development' then became apparent on a bigger scale than before. As the Legislative Assembly of Owambo was about to be elected, the strength of this opposition presented a grave danger to the government. Severe restrictive measures were imposed: no party, for instance, could function in Owambo without the permission of the pro-government chiefs. These refused permission to all opposition parties, which therefore decided to boycott the elections. Of an estimated 50,000 Owambo electors, about 1,300 cast their votes.

Numerous arrests had been made during the protests before the elections. Magistrates sentenced many to terms of imprisonment. Then a new way of dealing with such political offenders was found. They were handed over to the Owambo tribal courts, which in some cases did not allow the accused an opportunity to defend himself. The punishment inflicted was flogging, in public and without any of the limitations or safeguards which South African law provided. Amid the outcry and protests both in South Africa and abroad, and the refusal of the government to intervene, the Supreme Court in Windhoek granted an interdict against the floggings.

These were not conditions which the government liked to advertise to the world. Journalists and visitors in general were excluded from the troubled area in the north. The Anglican Bishop (a 'trouble-maker') was deported. But in 1972 the government had thought it expedient to allow the Secretary-General of the United Nations, Dr Waldheim, as instructed by the Security Council, to visit both South Africa and 'Namibia'. His visit was followed by that of his representative Dr Escher. Both described their visits as useful and worth repeating, but in 1973 the Organisation of African Unity asked that these consultations be ended, and the U.N. complied with the request.

There were other setbacks at about that time. It had long been obvious that the safety of South Africa would depend largely on the friendliness of neighbouring and even distant African countries. Though there were many causes of friction with Lesotho, Botswana and Swaziland, as these became independent, they were too dependent on South Africa economically and in other ways to constitute a danger. Relations with them were carried on, as a rule, politely if not always cordially. With Malawi, dependent in important ways on Portugal and Rhodesia, South Africa's relations were more than polite. Malawi was given loans and technical assistance. Mr Vorster visited the country in 1970 and was enthusiastically received. President Banda in turn made a state visit to South Africa in 1971, was given appropriate hospitality, and was warmly welcomed even in such unexpected places as the University of Stellenbosch. The Malawian Ambassador was the first black diplomat to be accredited to Pretoria. His daughter was enrolled at a white girls' school.

This was the most positive result of Mr Vorster's 'outward policy', but there were some others. Several African countries, notably the Ivory Coast and the Malagasy Republic, showed interest in a policy of influencing South Africa peaceably, in 'dialogue' rather than confrontation. A Conference of East and Central African states in 1969 issued the Lusaka Manifesto, a moderate document in which a minimum demand was made of South Africa—a commitment to the principles of human equality and self-determination. There would be no concerted African pressure on timing or details.

There was of course no favourable response to this, and by 1972 most of the African receptiveness to 'dialogue' had petered out too. Contrition had to come before absolution. The best that could be done in 1974 to show that South Africa was not without friends was to arrange a visit by President Stroessner of Paraguay.

The alternative to dialogue was force. This had begun to be used against Portugal by African nationalists in Angola in 1961, and in Mozambique in 1964. After the Rhodesian Unilateral Declaration of Independence in 1965 the exiled nationalists of that country began to use the same methods. Men trained in other African or in Communist countries in guerrilla tactics infiltrated across the border, tried to influence the local population, sabotaged various installations, attacked isolated farmhouses with machine guns or grenades, and placed mines under roadbeds.

South Africa was not directly affected by these attacks. The Portuguese territories and Rhodesia formed a buffer between her and the hostile countries to the north. She reacted cautiously to the Rhodesian U.D.I., refusing either to apply economic sanctions against that country (though the sanctions ordered by the U.N. were mandatory) or, on the other hand, to recognise the new régime *de jure*. But when Rhodesian armed forces began their operations against guerrilla infiltrators in the Zambezi valley, South African police were with them. Moreover, although the Republic itself was sheltered by the buffer states, South-West Africa was not. In 1966 trained guerrillas and saboteurs began to enter Owambo and the Caprivi Strip from Zambia.

After this South African police forces were in continuous operations against the guerrillas in the Caprivi Strip, and in Rhodesia in support of that country's army. The so-called Terrorism Act of 1967 had been passed in response to the first threat on the borders. Nevertheless the danger was still far from the Republic itself. The 'freedom fighters', who were getting increasing financial support from governments, including Western governments, and from the World Council of Churches and other international bodies, were concerned at this stage mainly with Portugal and Rhodesia. The successes of Frelimo in Mozambique enabled the Rhodesian guerrillas to enter their country from the north-east, a much easier operation than crossing the Zambezi from Zambia. By 1973 they were penetrating deep into Rhodesia from that direction, while Frelimo was attacking the track, and the trains, on the Umtali–Beira railway.

The operations against the Portuguese were on a much larger scale, had lasted longer and had achieved much more than those against Rhodesia, not to mention the hit-and-run raids in the Caprivi Strip. There was also this difference, that whereas the white Rhodesians were defending their families, their lives and their property, the troops in Mozambique were metropolitan Portuguese, who had no direct interest in the war and were desperately anxious to get out of it.

This was the main reason why the army in Portugal, led by General Spinola and by officers of middle rank, overthrew the dictatorship of that country on 25 April 1974, the day after the South African election. In its importance for the future of South Africa that election quickly took second place to the events in Lisbon. The new Portuguese government proposed to end the wars in Africa by the grant of 'self-determination' to the peoples of the overseas provinces. Though the details and the timing presented problems and aroused controversy, the issue could hardly be in doubt.

South Africa could expect to see one domino falling after another, the buffer disappearing, and armed enemies gathering along the of her landward frontier.

SELECT BIBLIOGRAPHY OF
BOOKS IN ENGLISH

SELECT BIBLIOGRAPHY OF
BOOKS IN ENGLISH

PUBLISHED DOCUMENTS

EYBERS, G. W., *Select Constitutional Documents illustrating South African History, 1795-1910.* London, 1918

HEADLAM, CECIL, *The Milner Papers, 1897-1905*, 2 vols. London, 1931-3

HANCOCK, SIR KEITH, and VAN DER POEL, J., *Selections from the Smuts Papers*, 7 vols. Cambridge, 1966-74

KRUGER, D. W., *South African Parties and Policies*, Cape Town, 1960

GENERAL

THEAL, G. M., *Ethnography and Conditions of South Africa before 1505*, London, 1922

History and Ethnography of Africa south of the Zambesi, 1505-1795, 3 vols. London, 1927

History of Africa south of the Zambesi, 1795-1872, 5 vols. London, 1926-7

History of South Africa from 1873 to 1884, 2 vols. London, 1919

CORY, SIR G., *The Rise of South Africa*, 5 vols. London, 1910-30

WALKER, ERIC A., *A History of Southern Africa*, 3rd edition. London, 1957

The Cambridge History of the British Empire, Vol. VIII, Revised edition. Cambridge, 1963

WILSON, MONICA and THOMPSON, LEONARD (Eds.), *The Oxford History of South Africa*, 2 vols. Oxford, 1969, 1971

MULLER, C. F. J., *Five Hundred Years, a History of South Africa*, Pretoria, 1969

DE KIEWIET, C. W., *A History of South Africa, Social and Economic*. Oxford, 1941

GOODFELLOW, D. M., *A Modern Economic History of South Africa*. London, 1931

BROOKES, E. H., and WEBB, C. DE B., *A History of Natal*. Pietermaritzburg, 1965

TYLDEN, G., *The Rise of the Basuto*, Cape Town, 1950

MARAIS, J. S., *The Cape Coloured People, 1652–1937*. London, 1939

PEARSE, G. E., *The Cape of Good Hope, 1652–1853*. Pretoria, 1956

SERIES

The Van Riebeeck Society. This Society republishes, with English translation where necessary, p: mary materials such as travellers' accounts, memoirs, diaries and collections of letters, long out of print or, in a few cases, hitherto unpublished.

The Archives Year Book for South Africa. These volumes, one or two a year, consist mainly of M.A. and Ph.D. theses, and are the standard channel for their publication in South Africa.

The Annual Survey of Race Relations, published by the South African Institute of Race Relations.

BIOGRAPHIES, IN APPROXIMATE CHRONOLOGICAL ORDER OF SUBJECT

LEIPOLDT, C. L., *Jan van Riebeeck*. London, 1936

MILLER, A., *A Plantagenet in South Africa, Lord Charles Somerset*, Cape Town, 1965.

SOLOMON, W. E. G., *Saul Solomon*. Cape Town, 1948

NATHAN, MANFRED, *Paul Kruger, His Life and Times*. London, 1925

LEWSEN, PHYLLIS (Ed.), *Selections form the Correspondence of John X. Merriman*, 3 vols. Van Riebeeck Society, 1960, 1963, 1966

HOFMEYR, J. H., *The Life of Jan Hendrik Hofmeyr*. Cape Town, 1913

WALKER, ERIC A., *Lord De Villiers and his Times*. London, 1925

LOCKHART, J. G. and WOODHOUSE, C. M., *Rhodes*. London, 1963

COLVIN, IAN, *The Life of Jameson*, 2 vols. London, 1922

ROSE-INNES, SIR JAMES, *Autobiography*. Cape Town, 1949

WALKER, ERIC A., *W. P. Schreiner, a South African*. London, 1937

WALLIS, J. P. R., *Fitz, the Story of Sir Percy Fitzpatrick*. London, 1955

ENGELENBURG, F. V., *General Louis Botha*. London, 1929
VAN DEN HEEVER, C. M., *General J. B. M. Hertzog*. Johannesburg, 1946
HANCOCK, SIR KEITH, *Smuts*, Vol. I: *The Sanguine Years, 1870–1919*, Cambridge, 1962. Vol. II: *The Fields of Force, 1919–1950*, Cambridge, 1968
MILLIN, S. G., *General Smuts*, 2 vols. London, 1936
SMUTS, J. C., jr., *Jan Christian Smuts*. London, 1952
PATON, ALAN, *Hofmeyr*. Cape Town, 1964
LUTHULI, ALBERT, *Let My People Go, an Autoiography*. London, 1962

SPECIAL PERIODS AND TOPICS, IN
APPROXIMATE CHRONOLOGICAL ORDER

(The dates give a general indication of the period to which
the books relate; there is overlapping in some cases.)

(a) *Before 1850*

AXELSON, ERIC A., *South-East Africa, 1488–1530*. London, 1940
BOTHA, C. GRAHAM, *The French Refugees at the Cape*. Cape Town, 1919
Social Life in the Cape Colony in the Eighteenth Century. Cape Town, 1921
BRYANT, A. T., *Bantu Origins, the People and their Language*. Cape Town, 1963
A History of the Zulus and the neighbouring Tribes. Cape Town, 1964
Olden Times in Zululand and Natal, new edition, Cape Town, 1965
MARAIS, J. S., *Maynier and the First Boer Republic*, 2nd edition. Cape Town, 1962
FAIRBRIDGE, D., *Historic Houses of South Africa*. London, 1922
Historic Farms of South Africa. London, 1931
Lady Anne Barnard at the Cape of Good Hope. Oxford, 1924
EDWARDS, I. E., *The 1820 Settlers in South Africa*. London, 1934
HOCKLY, H. E., *The Story of the British Settlers of 1820 in South Africa*, revised edition. Cape Town, 1957
MACMILLAN, W. M., *The Cape Colour Question*. London, 1927
Bantu, Boer and Briton, revised edition. Oxford 1963
Complex South Africa. London, 1930
WALKER, ERIC A., *The Great Trek*. London, 1948
RANSFORD, OLIVER, *The Great Trek*, London, 1972

AGAR-HAMILTON, J. A. I., *The Native Policy of the Voortrekkers.* Cape Town, 1928

GALBRAITH, JOHN S., *Reluctant Empire: British Policy on the South African Frontier, 1834–54.* Berkeley, 1963

HATTERSLEY, A. F. *The British Settlement of Natal.* Cambridge, 1950

(b) *1850–1884*

KILPIN, R., *The Old Cape House.* Cape Town, 1918
The Romance of a Colonial Parliament. London, 1930

MCCRACKEN, J. L., *The Cape Parliament, 1854–1910.* Oxford, 1967

DE KIEWIET, C. W. *British Colonial Policy and the South African Republics.* London, 1929
The Imperial Factor in South Africa. Cambridge, 1937

LEYDS, W. J., *The First Annexation of the Transvaal.* London, 1906
The Transvaal Surrounded. London, 1919

AGAR-HAMILTON, J. A. I., *The Road to the North.* London, 1937

GOODFELLOW, C. F., *Great Britain and South African Confederation, 1870–81.* Cape Town, 1967

WELSH, DAVID, *The Roots of Segregation.* Cape Town, 1971

MORRIS, DONALD R., *The Washing of the Spears.* New York, 1965

PRESTON, ADRIAN, (Ed.) *The South African Journal of Sir Garnet Wolseley, 1879–80.* Cape Town, 1973

PRESTON, ADRIAN (Ed.), *The South African Diaries of Sir Garnet Wolseley, 1875.* Cape Town, 1971

COUPLAND, SIR REGINALD, *Zulu Battlepiece.* London, 1948

VAN JAARSVELD, F. A., *The Awakening of Afrikaner Nationalism.* Cape Town, 1961

SCHREUDER, D. M., *Gladstone and Kruger.* London, 1969

(c) *1884–1910*

LOVELL, R. I., *The Struggle for South Africa, 1875–1899.* New York, 1934

DAVENPORT, T. R. H., *The Afrikaner Bond, 1880–1911.* Cape Town, 1966

VULLIAMY, C. E., *Outlanders.* London, 1938

CARTWRIGHT, A. P., *The Corner House.* Cape Town, 1965

VAN DER HORST, SHEILA T., *Native Labour in South Africa.* London, 1942

VAN DER POEL, L., *Railway and Customs Policies in South Africa, 1885–1910.* London, 1933
The Jameson Raid. Cape Town, 1951

PAKENHAM, ELIZABETH, *Jameson's Raid*. London, 1966

MARAIS, J. S., *The Fall of Kruger's Republic*. Oxford, 1961

WORSFOLD, W. BASIL, *Lord Milner's Work in South Africa*. London, 1906

AMERY, L. S. (Ed.), *The Times History of the War in South Africa, 1899–1902*, 7 vols. London, 1900–9

HOLT, EDGAR, *The Boer War*. London, 1958

KRUGER, RAYNE, *Good-Bye, Dolly Gray*. London, 1959

REITZ, DENEYS, *Commando*. London, 1929

CHURCHILL, WINSTON S., *London to Ladysmith via Pretoria*. London, 1900

PEMBERTON, V. B., *Battles of the Boer War*. London, 1964

RANSFORD, OLIVER, *The Battle of Spion Kop*. London, 1969

SYMONS, JULIAN, *Buller's Campaign*. London, 1963

MARTIN, A. C., *The Concentration Camps*. Cape Town, 1957

CURTIS, LIONEL, *With Milner in South Africa*. Oxford, 1951

LE MAY, G. H. L., *British Supremacy in South Africa, 1899–1907*. Oxford, 1965

PYRAH, G. B., *Imperial Policy and South Africa*. Oxford, 1955

BLEY, HELMUT (trans. Ridley, Hugh), *South-West Africa under German Rule, 1894–1914*. Evanston, 1971

THOMPSON, L. M., *The Unification of South Africa, 1902–10*. Oxford, 1960

(d) *1910–1974*

KRUGER, D. W., *The Making of a Nation*. Johannesburg, 1969

MANSERGH, NICHOLAS, *The Price of Magnanimity: South Africa, 1906–61*. London, 1962

MARKS, SHULA, *Reluctant Rebellion: the 1906–8 Disturbances in Natal*. Oxford, 1970

TATZ, COLIN, *Shadow and Substance in South Africa*. Pietermaritzburg, 1962

ROUX, E., *Time Longer than Rope*, 2nd edition. Madison, 1964

ROBERTS, M., and TROLLIP, A. E. G., *The South African Opposition, 1939–45*. London 1947

HELLMANN, E. (Ed.), *Handbook of Race Relations in South Africa*, Cape Town, 1949

MACCRONE, I. D., *Race Attitudes in South Africa*. Johannesburg, 1957

CALPIN, G. H., *There are No South Africans*. London, 1941

CALPIN, G. H. (Ed.), *The South African Way of Life*. London, 1953

MARQUARD, L., *The Peoples and Policies of South Africa*, 2nd edition. Cape Town, 1952

PATTERSON, SHEILA, *The Last Trek*. London, 1957

CARTER, GWENDOLEN M., *The Politics of Inequality*. New York, 1958

MUNGER, EDWIN S., *African Field Reports*. Cape Town, 1961

HUDDLESTON, TREVOR, *Naught for your Comfort*. Johannesburg, 1956

KUPER, LEO, *Passive Resistance in South Africa*. New Haven, 1957

FIRST, RUTH, *South West Africa*. London, 1963

LEGUM, COLIN and MARGARET, *South Africa, Crisis for the West*, London, 1964

HOOPER, CHARLES, *Brief Authority*. New York, 1961

VAN DEN BERGHE, PIERRE, *South Africa, a Study in Conflict*. Middletown, Connecticut, 1965

DRURY, ALLEN, *A Very Strange Society*. New York, 1967

HEARD, KENNETH A., *General Elections in South Africa 1943–1970*. London, 1974

INDEX

INDEX